HOLY FIRE

THE BATTLE FOR CHRIST'S TOMB

VICTORIA CLARK

HOLY FIRE

THE BATTLE FOR CHRIST'S TOMB

VICTORIA CLARK

MacAdam/Cage

MacAdam/Cage Publishing
155 Sansome Street, Suite 550
San Francisco, CA 94104
www.macadamcage.com

Library of Congress Cataloging-in-Publication Data

Clark, Victoria.
  Holy fire / by Victoria Clark.
      p. cm.
  Includes bibliographical references.
  ISBN 1-59692-156-0 (hardcover : alk. paper)
  1. Holy Light of Jerusalem. 2. Jerusalem (Orthodox
patriarchate)—History. 3. Jerusalem—Church history. I. Title.
  BX440.C58 2005
  263'.042569442--dc22

                                        2005026275

Manufactured in the United States of America.
10 9 8 7 6 5 4 3 2 1

For John C., with thanks

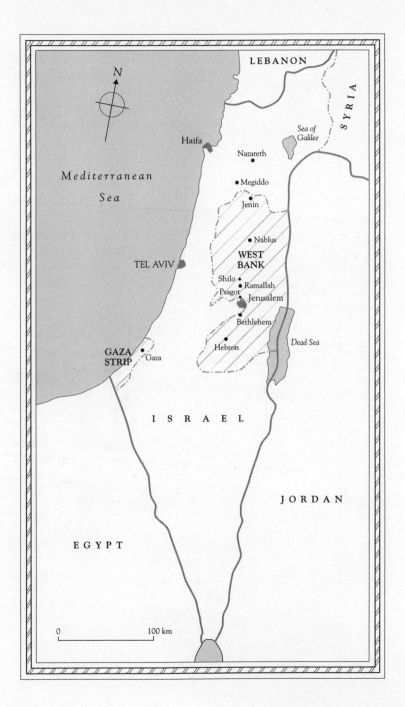

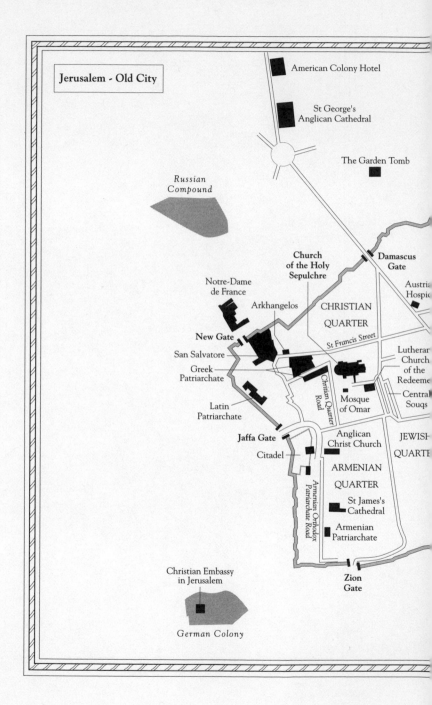

Jerusalem - Old City

American Colony Hotel

St George's
Anglican Cathedral

The Garden Tomb

*Russian
Compound*

Church
of the Holy
Sepulchre

Damascus
Gate

Notre-Dame
de France

Austria
Hospic

Arkhangelos

CHRISTIAN

QUARTER

St Francis Street

New Gate

Lutheran
Church
of the
Redeeme

San Salvatore

Greek
Patriarchate

Central
Souqs

Mosque
of Omar

Christian Quarter Road

Latin
Patriarchate

Anglican
Christ Church

JEWISH

Jaffa Gate

QUARTE

Citadel

ARMENIAN

QUARTER

St James's
Cathedral

Armenian Orthodox Patriarchate Road

Armenian
Patriarchate

Christian Embassy
in Jerusalem

Zion
Gate

German Colony

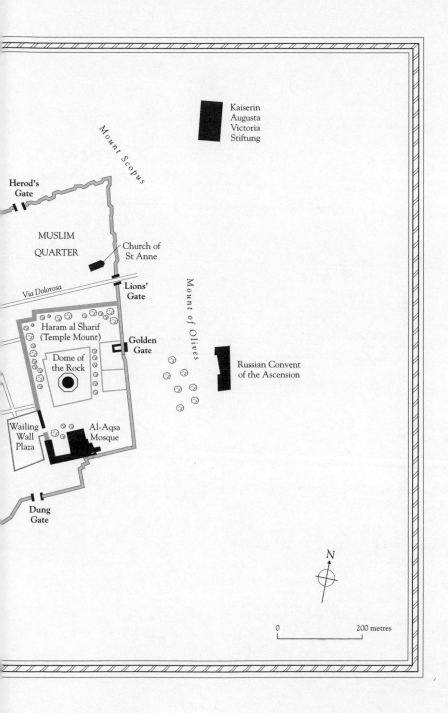

Kaiserin
Augusta
Victoria
Stiftung

Mount Scopus

Herod's
Gate

MUSLIM

QUARTER

Church of
St Anne

Via Dolorosa

Lions'
Gate

Mount of Olives

Haram al Sharif
(Temple Mount)

Golden
Gate

Dome of
the Rock

Russian Convent
of the Ascension

Wailing
Wall
Plaza

Al-Aqsa
Mosque

Dung
Gate

N

0   200 metres

PREFACE

One hot, still afternoon in West Jerusalem a police helicopter circled deafeningly above an empty main street lined with hundreds of Israeli soldiers and a few dozen curious bystanders.

It was early autumn 2001 and, because al-Qaeda had recently attacked New York and Washington and many in Europe believed that the war on terror could only be won by securing a peace between Israelis and Palestinians, I guessed we were about to witness a peace demonstration. The appearance of the first column of marchers and an accompanying din of bells, shrieking whistles and hooting shofars* forced me to guess again.

More celebration than demonstration, this was parade rather than protest. One after another, groups of folk dancers, musicians and cheerleaders passed me. No one looked angry or outraged and not one of the banners mentioned Palestine or peace. One declared OHIO LOVES JERUSALEM, the next, ALASKANS FOR ISRAEL! Men in fancy dress with happy grins on their faces were breaking ranks to shake the hands and slap the backs of any black-suited Orthodox Jews they passed. Women scattered sweets and kisses among the children who were watching all those Americans and British in red and white and blue ensembles, Austrians in dirndls and lederhosen, Brazilians in bright yellow baseball caps strolling by, smiling and laughing and shouting 'Shalom!' More banners passed, proclaiming ISRAEL YOU ARE NOT ALONE and BRITISH CHRISTIANS LOVE ISRAEL.

* Jewish ram's horn trumpets.

XI

An amplified Israeli voice thanked Indonesian, Estonian and Guatemalan Christians, and Australian and Swedish and Spanish Christians for 'coming all this way'.

Like most of the Israeli witnesses of that event I knew far less about passionate Christian love for modern Israelis than I did about passionate Christian hatred traditionally displayed towards Jews as 'Christ-killers'. Like most of them I was mistrustful, but also interested. Back in London I would uncover two salient facts about a brand of Christianity now known as Christian Zionism. First, it is a branch of Protestant fundamentalism whose roots lie deep in sixteenth-century Puritan England. Second, its modern adherents firmly oppose any resolution of the Arab–Israeli conflict that would grant the Palestinians a viable independent state.

Christian Zionists believe that to acknowledge the Palestinians' claim to this land between the Mediterranean Sea and the Jordan River, is to defy the will of God as expressed in the Bible. An extreme position and one naturally resented by Palestinians, it is also only shared by the estimated 15 to 20 per cent of Israelis who might be described as fundamentalists.* Informed by a close and literal reading of the Hebrew prophets of the Old Testament many Christian Zionists also share the Jewish fundamentalist conviction that the messiah will not appear to usher in a new and perfect age until Jews have been re-gathered into this land from the ends of the earth, until Jerusalem is their undisputed capital and the Jewish Temple has been rebuilt on the present site of the Muslims' Haram al-Sharif.† In fact, the only obvious difference between the beliefs of these Christian fundamentalists and those of their Jewish counterparts is the identity of the messiah they are waiting for. The Jews expect a stranger, the Christians their saviour, Christ.

Christian Zionism has been flourishing since the biblically prophesied creation of Israel in 1948 and the Israeli capture of East

---

* The 'national religious' grouping that emerged after victory in the Six Day War of 1967, and much of the Ashkenazi ultra-Orthodox community.

† The Noble Sanctuary, where the Dome of the Rock and al-Aqsa mosques are located.

Jerusalem in 1967, wherever love of the scriptures is strongest and wherever Christian Zionists have travelled and evangelized, in South America, the Far East and Africa. But the United States is its heartland. In America's Bible Belt, communities of Christians who, in the words of Donald Wagner, author of Anxious for Armageddon and profession of religion and Middle Eastern studies at Chicago's North Park University, 'see the modern state of Israel as the fulfilment of biblical prophecy and thus deserving of political, financial and religious support' are proud to rename their region 'Israel's safety belt'. More importantly, by stridently promoting the most extreme and uncompromising Israeli position, Christian Zionists are destroying their country's usefulness and credibility as an impartial arbiter in the dispute, to say nothing of imperilling Israel's future.

But today's American Christian Zionist is only the most recent variety of foreign Christian to taken an intense and active interest in the Holy Land. Christians of all nationalities and denominations have been involving themselves in, or taking charge of, affairs in that remote corner of the Middle East for almost two millennia. The grand total of 450 years when Christian powers have actually ruled the region turns out to be an inaccurate measure of the influence they have been exerting there since the fourth century when Emperor Constantine the Great espoused Christianity and decreed the promotion of a Roman legion garrison town on the road to nowhere the pilgrimage centre of the Christian world. The later race for wealth and empire and, still later, the greed for oil and influence only intensified a fascination rooted in a deep love for the land where Jesus Christ lived and died and rose again.

The story of that long fascination is perhaps best told from Jerusalem because the past is ever-present there, in its stones and in the minds and hearts of its inhabitants. On six separate visits to the city between the spring of 2002 and autumn 2003 I lodged with Arab Christians in a former monastery and mostly consorted with Christians, immersing myself in Jerusalem's Christian past while observing its Christian present. I have not set out to record the centre-stage struggle between the Israelis and Palestinians for the right to occupy the Holy Land and nor have I attempted a comprehensive history of Christianity in the region. Rather, my aim has been to trace the parts played by a succession of outside Christian powers – Byzantines, Crusaders, Italian princes, French and Spanish kings, Russian, German and Austrian emperors, and more recently British and American governments – in the creation and maintenance of the planet's most intractable conflict.

My argument is that fourth century Byzantine Orthodoxy and twenty-first century American Christian Zionism are two ends of a single long continuum in the eyes if many non-Christians. Three years on from nine-eleven 2001 it seems more urgent than ever that we in the traditionally Christian West begin to see ourselves as others see us.

EASTER 2002

'a fresh new Jerusalem'

– BISHOP EUSEBIUS OF CAESAREA,
FOURTH CENTURY

Holy Saturday, late March 2002, in Jerusalem's Church of the Holy Sepulchre.

Squeezed into a crowd behind a metal police barrier, a few feet from the shrine containing a fragment of Jesus Christ's empty tomb, I am attending a 'Holy Fire' ceremony.

The ancient Byzantine hymns have begun and so has the procession of churchmen but a nun's broad back is blocking my view, someone's damp armpit capping my left shoulder and a stomach rudely nudging me from behind. To my right an excited young Cypriot monk, whose beard is tickling my forehead, is asking me if his breath smells bad. I fib politely.

'I've been standing here for five hours and fasting since yesterday,' he explains, 'so I wouldn't be surprised . . .'

A miracle is about to happen. The shepherd of all the city's Orthodox Christians, Patriarch Irineos, and his retinue of chanting churchmen have already made their third circuit of the shrine.* Now he is disappearing inside, to the tomb, with a single Armenian priest for company. In silent awe and hope we must wait for the Holy Fire to appear – maybe five minutes, maybe twenty, maybe all afternoon.

In another noxious whisper my Cypriot neighbour informs me,

* Jerusalem is one of the five ancient Christian patriarchates. The others are Rome, Constantinople, Antioch and Alexandria. The patriarch of Jerusalem is always a Greek.

3

'The Holy Fire rises from a crack in the marble top of the tomb. It can be a strange colour, blue or white, and it doesn't burn anything it touches for the first half-hour. You can even put your lighted candle against your cheek.'

Less than five minutes later, inside a structure no larger than a small garden shed, on the spot where the body of Jesus once lay, the marvel has come to pass. Two round holes in the walls of the shrine are blazing with Holy Fire and the church bells tolling out the joy-ous news that God has heard the prayers of the faithful. Now Patriarch Irineos is lighting his candles and passing the precious gift out to the clamouring crowd of the faithful. Holy Fire invades the church, a fast-breeding light transfiguring faces, transforming the dark stone space. I hear gasps and cheers and sobs and tears. The emotion is overwhelming, the heat suffocating.

Now television crews are switching off lights and unplugging cables and the Russian pilgrims who camped by the tomb last night are hurriedly packing their bags and folding chairs. The church bells are still clanging like fire alarms, and people pushing and shoving towards the exit and fresh air, gasping out their Easter greetings to one another – 'Christ is Risen!' 'Indeed, he is risen!' – in a medley of Arabic, Greek and Slav languages.

The Holy Fire begins its travels. As the faithful stumble out into the prosaic white light of an early afternoon, shielding their flicker-ing flames from the breeze, passing the lines of Israeli police and dis-persing towards their homes, an Orthodox priest on special day release from Bethlehem's besieged Church of the Nativity heads back through the Israeli checkpoints, his Holy Fire safe in a flicker-ing lantern. A Greek bishop, settled in the back of a limousine with another lighted lamp on his lap, is already speeding down the motorway towards Ben Gurion Airport to catch the specially char-tered Olympic Airways flight back to Athens in time for the mid-night Easter service. From Athens, another aeroplane will ferry the fire to Istanbul, to the ancient Greek Orthodox Patriarchate of Constantinople and another to the island of Patmos.

In need of fresh air I walk the long way back, through the bus-

tle of the Muslim Quarter's twilit souk with its sacks of spices, stacks
of pans and bristling heaps of hairbrushes, up as far as Damascus
Gate, then out into brilliant sunshine again and along the Old City
walls for a few hundred yards, to New Gate.

Here in Jerusalem, where Jews, Christians and Muslims have
been noisily peddling their wares for centuries, no religion can be
viewed in isolation. Here, much more clearly than elsewhere, one
can see how each of the great monotheistic faiths has cornered its
share of the eternal salvation market. If Judaism can boast venerable antiquity and a hardy pedigree, Islam can claim to be the most
modern of the three and to offer a detailed guide to righteous living.
But what is Christianity's special attraction? Christians would probably say that it is Jesus, the Redeemer, who exalted the poor above
the rich and advocated non-violence before sacrificing himself for
all our sakes. But here and now the Holy Fire is suggesting a
different answer: the astounding claim that some 2,000 years ago
God came down to earth to live and suffer as a man, is what sets
Christianity apart from Judaism and Islam.

When viewed beside Jehovah and Allah here, the Christian
God is a perilously attractive hybrid – a man-god – and the Holy
Fire ceremony a cautionary tale of where worship of such a hybrid
can lead. Neither Judaism nor Islam has sought to shrink the distance between the deity and his creation like this, dragging God to
earth while, at the same time, hoisting man heavenward. Neither of
those two religions has ever dared lay claim to the favour of such a
rendezvous with God. Nor has any rabbi or imam claimed as St
Athanasius did in the second century that 'God was made man so
that man might become God.'[i]

The roots of this Christian boldness, this sublime confidence –
hubris the ancient Greeks would have called it – may lie in fear lest
the gulf between the Almighty and mankind be too discouragingly
great. But I think I recognize this same boldness as the spirit in
which the Christian world has been behaving in this land between
the Jordan River and the Mediterranean Sea since 300 years after
Jesus Christ died.

Plunging back into the Old City again I pass a group of Orthodox slowly climbing the alley steps with their flickering Holy Fire still lit. Down past the Franciscans' fortress headquarters of San Salvatore I go, past the Arab Catholic Scouts' headquarters and the Palestinian beggar whose dress reminds me of a cardinal's robes, until I reach the bakery selling round Easter loaves with coloured eggs baked into their centres, and finally, the low stone entrance leading into Arkhangelos.* The threshold of the former Orthodox monastery stinks of cat pee and fermenting rubbish but its flagstoned passageway is cool and freshly mopped, the little inner courtyard empty but for two pots of red geraniums and a snoozing cat occupying the sunny stone steps leading up to the grey metal door of Rahme's flat. I am home.

Rahme has not moved from her sofa in the darkened sitting room, nor has she changed out of her nightdress. With the television tuned to an Arab newscast and the radio crackling an Orthodox Easter chant, she is knitting something large and orange. On the coffee table beside her is a fancily ribboned candle, already lit with Holy Fire by one of her nephews. She calls out to me, 'I listened to the church bells when the Holy Fire came. Orthodox Christians all over the world are so happy today!'

Not for long. Between cuts to the siege of the Church of the Nativity, the television is showing President Bush, with his mouth opening and closing helplessly and Arabic subtitles bouncing off his chest like shrapnel. Rahme gasps and furiously shunts stitches down her knitting needle, as if she were loading a gun.

'He has no shame! His axis of evil! Oh, my *God*! Iraq, Iran, Afghanistan, Syria, North Korea! Axis of evil no – Bush is evil!'

Rahme does not care for Saddam Hussein, nor does she support Yasser Arafat or her fellow Palestinians' suicide bombing campaign. But she loathes what the Israelis are doing to her people, and America too for subsidizing Israel. The force of all that hatred is only exceeded by her latest terror, that the entire Middle East will

* Greek for Archangel – shortening of St Michael the Archangel.

6

erupt in apocalyptic chaos if America carries out its threat to invade Iraq.

In my room, once the cell of Orthodox monks but now hung with crookedly framed photos of Rahme's dead father, I am assaulted by cooking smells and sounds, both amplified by the enclosed court-yard: roasting meat, television news, frying potatoes, church music, the tinkling of cutlery and glass, a child laughing. The Arab Orthodox Christians living in the other flats fashioned out of this 500-year-old monastery with its narrow courtyard and tiny stone church are all celebrating the miraculous descent of the Holy Fire. Outside the window at the foot of my bed some cats are fighting, but I sleep.

Evening. The entire Christian Quarter is alive with rumours. Rahme's younger sister Nasra has heard an astonishing tale.

It appears that the Holy Fire ceremony did not, after all, go as planned. Instead, behind the closed doors of the edicule,* out of sight of the faithful, an unholy rumpus came to pass. Nasra has learned that the Armenian priest accompanying Patriarch Irineos into the edicule decided to hurry the miracle along a little. Improvising his own Holy Fire with the aid of a cigarette lighter, he moved swiftly towards one of the holes in the wall of the antecham-ber, and was on the point of passing his lit candles out to a waiting fellow Armenian when the patriarch intervened. Enraged, Irineos had put a stop to his companion's crime by blowing out his candles. In that confined and cluttered space, the holiest spot in the Christian world, an ugly tussle had ensued. The Armenian had sus-tained a painful injury. The patriarch had lost a shoe.

Squeezed behind that police barrier, the Russian nun in front of me, the Cypriot monk beside me, I had missed the sequel – two burly Orthodox monks bursting through the doors of the edicule to go to their patriarch's aid, and the storming of the shrine by Israeli police.

~

* Shrine containing the remains of Christ's empty tomb, from the Latin *aedicula* for little house.

Passing again the monastery of San Salvatore, I chance to meet an acquaintance from a previous visit, a solemn young Catholic friar from Texas with four years residence in the city to his credit. While couples stroll by enjoying the cool of the evening and playing children richochet back and forth across the narrow alley, Father Athanasius gives my account of the Holy Fire rumours his fullest attention.

'Perhaps not every last detail,' he says, unable to restrain a smile, 'I've heard there was some trouble. But this was right inside the edicule you say? With a lighter?'

We are interrupted by an electronic buzzing. Out of a deep pocket in his tobacco-brown habit comes his mobile phone. The call, conducted in Italian, the lingua franca of the Franciscans here, concerns the progress of the siege of the Church of the Nativity in Bethlehem.

It is not good news.

If much of the world has forgotten or never known that there are Christians as well as Muslims and Jews in the Holy Land, the siege of the Church of the Nativity, the climax of this almost two-year-old intifada, has acted as a startling reminder of that fact. The Christian guardians of Jesus' birthplace in Bethlehem – thirty-one mostly southern European Catholic friars, four Catholic nuns, nine Greek Orthodox and five Armenian clergy – never offered the place to some 200 Palestinian civilians and armed militants, Christians as well as Muslims, for use as a sanctuary from Israeli mass arrests. Nor did they invite Israeli troops with tanks, guns, infrared sights and megaphones to besiege the holy place. There is not one iota of Christian hubris about this particular situation; under a rooftop statue of Christ's mother Mary that has lost an arm in the fighting, inside sturdy stone walls pitted by sniper bullets, without electricity, sufficient food or medical supplies, they are helplessly suffering too.

'You know, normally this Holy Fire ruckus would be a very serious matter for all the Christian communities, but right now – with the siege in Bethlehem going on – we can't be worrying about candles and cigarette lighters,' says Father Athanasius, snapping his phone shut. We go our separate ways, he through San Salvatore's great doors to evening prayers and me a few steps down the alley to Arkhangelos.

Rahme is holding court from her sofa tonight. The flat is filled with smoke and smells sweetly of rotting apples; two of her burly nephews, one of them at Bethlehem University, the other studying Hebrew and computing, are bubbling gently into the narghile.

Like most of those renting the Arkhangelos flats from the Greek patriarchate, Rahme and her family belong to the tiny Palestinian Orthodox community still residing in the old city's Christian Quarter. After weathering centuries of eroding conversion to either Roman Catholicism or Protestantism, followed by decades of accelerated emigration since the birth of Israel in 1948, it is only about 2,500 souls strong.* But its members still boldly advertise their religious allegiance by wearing gold crosses on chains about their necks, by hanging icons on the walls of their homes and displaying photographs of Patriarch Irineos in their shops and offices.

More pious than most, Rahme is in the habit of gazing lovingly up at the plastic crucifix plugged into an electric socket in her kitchen and pleading, 'When will he come again?' Her passionate reverence for the broken man-god on his cross also extends to the small army of Greek churchmen who inhabit the sprawling maze of the patriarchate which backs onto this same alley; they are all 'angels', she tells me, some of whom she has known since she was a child. Rahme counts herself as direct an heir to the Greek Orthodox Christianity of the late Roman or early Byzantine empire – 'the original, the true Christianity of the Holy Land,' she calls it – as any of them. Rahme would have me know that the first period of Christian rule over Jerusalem began some two centuries before the collapse of the Roman empire, about 250 years after the Romans' destruction of the second Jewish Temple in the city and 300 years after Christ's death and resurrection.

* When Israel was created in 1948, 25,000 Christians – Orthodox, Catholic, Armenian, Copt and Ethiopian – lived in the Old City. Today, there are an estimated 8,000.

9

In 312 the Roman Emperor Constantine the Great had been marching towards Rome to do battle with his rival Maxentius for sole control of the western Roman empire when he had a vision of a dazzling cross and heard a voice commanding him to 'Go forth and conquer in this sign!' His subsequent victory at Milvian Bridge can only have confirmed his feeling that the Christian god was all-powerful and his hitherto illicit cult ideally suited to the task of reviving and uniting the Roman empire.

Three hundred years of persecution had fostered some admirable attributes among the empire's Christians: they were disciplined, organized and possessed of a communications network extending to every corner of the Roman world. Constantine believed that, armoured in this faith and buttressed by a new Christian capital in the east, at Byzantium* on the Bosporus, the empire could not fail to prosper. He was mistaken. Freed at last to practise and proclaim their faith, Christians were also free to air their disagreements about it. By 325 the Byzantine Church was violently divided by a dispute over whether Jesus of Nazareth was both man and God. Neither side doubted that he was the messiah, but Bishop Arius of Alexandria and his followers declared him to have been man, rather than man-god.

The Arian schism caused strife among the ranks of the very organization Constantine was relying on for unity and mightily displeased him. Opting for what would become Orthodoxy† – the belief that Jesus was equally man and God – over Arianism, Constan-tine swiftly summoned a Church council at Nicaea‡ to impose the ruling. The most senior bishop in Palestine, the elderly Eusebius of Caesarea, relates how on receiving the emperor's order churchmen dashed to Nicaea 'like sprinters from the starting line'.[ii] One of those sprinting prelates was Bishop Eusebius' neighbour and arch-rival, the ambitious and fervently Orthodox Makarios of Jerusalem,§ who had

* Renamed Constantinople in 330.
† The Greek-derived word literally means right worship.
‡ Today Iznik, in western Turkey.
§ The Romans had renamed it Aelia Capitolina.

something quite other than theological disputes on his mind. Why should he not upstage Eusebius and Caesarea by turning his own depopulated and half-ruined Jerusalem into the wealthiest, most frequented and loyally Orthodox city in Palestine?

Makarios seized the occasion of the Council of Nicaea to inform Emperor Constantine that Jerusalem's Christians were convinced – admittedly on the basis of only hearsay and tradition – that the miraculously vacated tomb of Jesus Christ lay intact and untouched under the foundations of the city's pagan temple to Aphrodite. Would it not be the greatest gain for Christianity over paganism if this holy of holies were excavated, adorned and honoured? Constantine, just then casting around for a way to lend the new state religion some marks of a past august enough to impress reluctant converts, was enthralled by the idea. He ordered an immediate start to excavations.

Back in Jerusalem, Makarios set to work on two tasks. As well as demolishing the temple to Aphrodite in order to excavate the tomb, he had undertaken to build the grandest basilica church in the whole of the Roman empire. But it was locating a cave tomb answering to the New Testament's laconic description of Christ's temporary resting place, 'a tomb which had been hewn out of the rock', that proved the most arduous aspect of the project. Two anxious years were to pass before teams of slaving workmen uncovered such a cave.* Relieved and delighted, Constantine wrote to tell Bishop Makarios that 'no power of language seems adequate to describe the wondrous circumstances'.[iii] Even Eusebius, who could not have relished Makarios' success and whose abstract Greek mind distrusted the populist literalism of the scheme, was moved to liken the reappearance of the tomb to the resurrection of Christ and concede its usefulness to the faithful: 'after [the tomb's] descent into darkness it came forth again to the light, and it enabled those who

---

* A leading authority on Holy Land archaeology, Otto Meinardus, has written: 'we may not be absolutely certain that the site of the Holy Sepulchre Church is the site of Jesus' burial, but we certainly have no other site that can lay a claim nearly as weighty'. (Quoted by Biddle, M., *The Tomb of Christ*, 1999, p. 69)

came as visitors to see plainly the story of the wonders wrought there'.[iv]

Constantine ordered a large amount of rock around the precious tomb to be hacked out of the hillside. An area forty metres in diameter around that, including a large rounded stone that had been happily identified as Calvary, the remains of the hill on which Christ had been crucified, was set aside for the basilica. A rotunda of twelve sturdy columns, one for each of the apostles, would ring the precious tomb, each of them crowned with a great silver bowl donated by the emperor. Bishop Eusebius tells us that the place was further adorned 'with untold beauties in innumerable dedications of gold and silver and precious stones set in various materials'.[v] Pilgrims would pass from the glorious grandeur of the basilica, through a magnificent garden, to the still greater splendour of the rotunda and the tomb.

Between them, Constantine and Bishop Makarios masterminded the creation of a holy place so gorgeously glittering that Eusebius hailed it as 'a fresh new Jerusalem'.[vi] All around the central site the Old City was vanishing. The Jewish capital might never have existed; the ruins of the Jews' second Temple were merely a permanent and pleasing reminder to Byzantine Christians of how God had punished his chosen people. What further proof was needed that, as Eusebius put it, 'the historic world mission of the people of Israel has been taken from them and has been given to the Christian churches'?[vii]

A state visit cum pilgrimage by Constantine's octogenarian mother in 326 set the seal on Christian Jerusalem's fortunes. The dowager Empress Helena came 'with the eagerness of youth to apply her outstanding intellect to enquiring about the wondrous land', Eusebius wrote. But she was also there 'to inspect with imperial concern the eastern provinces'.[viii] The eastern half of the empire was more Christian than the western half at the time, but Constantine's cohorts were nevertheless hard at work, breaking into pagan shrines, stripping idols of their precious adornments and melting down gold for reuse in Christian ornaments.

The emperor, meanwhile, was supplying his peoples with

wonderful new aids to worship. Christ's empty cave tomb was only the start. After some more exploratory excavation around the Anastasis* his mother unearthed not just the cross on which Jesus was crucified, but the very nails that had pierced his hands and feet while he hung on it. Constantine set one of them in his helmet and another on his horse's bridle. A good portion of the True Cross was shipped to his new capital while the remainder stayed in Jerusalem, an irresistible attraction for the Christian pilgrims who began flocking to the city.

Bishop Eusebius' fears about replacing complex and abstract mysteries of faith with simplistic literal worship of places and objects would soon prove justified. At Easter in the year 381, less than fifty years after the consecration of the Anastasis, a Spanish nun named Egeria came on pilgrimage to Jerusalem and learned that the guard on the priceless relic had had to be reinforced after a pilgrim who had stooped to kiss the cross, 'bit off a piece of the Holy Wood, and stole it away'.[ix] A convenient notion, that the cross miraculously regrew itself however much of it was stolen, gained currency. By the beginning of the fifth century sections of the True Cross were to be found in Gaul, Syria, Asia Minor, Italy and Africa.

Sister Egeria gushed over the wonderful decoration around the tomb, at the piety of the crowds of pilgrims who wept and groaned with the pathos of Christ's Passion, at the glittering torch-lit processions from the Mount of Olives to the Anastasis, at the interminable night vigils and the magnificent church services. 'The decorations really are too marvellous for words,' she wrote home to her sisters in Spain. 'All you can see is gold and jewels and silk; the hangings are entirely silk with gold stripes, the curtains the same. You simply cannot imagine the number, and the sheer weight of the candles and the tapers and lamps and everything else they use for the services.'[x]

Both Judaism and paganism had favoured pilgrimage, but on a local scale. Now the half-ruined town on the road to nowhere was

* The Greek word for resurrection. The building did not become known as the Church of the Holy Sepulchre until the Crusader era.

attracting the world. People were converging on the place from far and near, to experience the incomparable thrill of walking in God's human footsteps in the land he lived and died in. A pilgrim from Rome informed his family back home that 'whoever is noblest in Gaul hastens hither, the Briton sundered from our world, leaves his setting sun and seeks the spots known only by rumour and the narration of the Scriptures. The Armenians, Persians, Indians, Ethiopians, Egyptians are to be found here, different in tongue but one in faith.'[xi] Christian Palestine's lingua franca was the Greek of the eastern empire, but every other language could be heard. Greek church services were faithfully translated into the language of the native population, Aramaic, but also into Latin for pilgrims from the western empire.

In the centre of the city pious and wealthy Byzantine widows built villas around the dazzling Anastasis and endowed churches and monasteries both inside and outside the city walls. The exiled Byzantine Empress Eudokia erected a gigantic copper cross on the Mount of Olives and a patriarchal palace in the city. There was any amount of work for icon-painters, marble-dressers, goldsmiths, jewellers and mosaicists in Byzantine Jerusalem. A marvellously pre-served floor mosaic of the era depicts Jerusalem on its side, with the colonnaded Cardo Maximus stretching, not north to south as it does on today's maps but – like a fat fish's backbone – the horizontal length of the city.*

Miracles abounded. An Italian pilgrim marvelled that whenev-er the True Cross was displayed a star appeared in the sky above the spot and remained there until the precious relic was locked away again. He was amazed by a cloud he saw shedding a miraculous dew over the city's churches every morning: 'In the hospices all the dishes are cooked in it and in the places where this dew falls many diseases are cured.'[xii]

St Jerome, in Jerusalem shortly after Sister Egeria, described how one Roman noblewoman of his acquaintance 'started to go around

---

* The Madaba Mosaic.

visiting all the [holy] places with such burning enthusiasm that there was no taking her away from one unless she was hurrying on to another'. And while venerating the cross and another remarkable archaeological discovery, the Stone of Unction – the slab on which Christ was anointed while awaiting burial – she was so transported by grief that 'her tears and lamentations' were heard all over Jerusalem.[xiii] The less exalted effects of this holy gold rush did not escape the irascible Jerome; he guessed that nowhere else in the world were people 'so ready to kill each other'.[xiv]

Religious toleration, especially where Jews were concerned, was conspicuously lacking in Byzantine Christian Jerusalem. Centuries of rivalry with Judaism and their own bitter schisms had bred in those early Christians a taste for rigid definition, a love of the strictest Orthodoxy, a hatred of 'the other'. In caves in the hills around the city hermit holy men, Jerome's brother monks, denounced the Jews on the grounds that they deserved to suffer for their wilful failure to recognize Jesus as their messiah and for having him put to death. St Jerome himself declared that Jews must be hated and their synagogue reviled as a 'brothel, a den of vice, the Devil's refuge, Satan's fortress, a place to deprave the soul, an abyss of every conceivable disaster or whatever else you will'.[xv] St John Chrysostom, the fourth-century archbishop of Constantinople, whose eight sermons against the Jews set the tone for centuries of anti-Semitism, described them as 'lustful, rapacious, greedy perfidious bandits', a people whose 'debauchery and drunkenness has given them the manners of the pig and the lusty goat', a race whose crime against Jesus Christ meant 'no expiation, no indulgence, no pardon'.[xvi]

By the sixth century the Byzantine Emperor Justinian was barring Jews from building synagogues, from reading the scriptures in Hebrew and from gathering in public places. Forbidden to own land or to live in Jerusalem, they were permitted one visit a year to their ancient capital, to weep over the ruins of the Temple.

～

Bishop Theophanis dismisses my questions about Byzantine Jerusalem with an impatient frown and a wave of his hand.

'Why are you speaking about this history? Everyone knows that our Byzantine Christianity was here first, that it has the deepest roots here among the people and so on, and that strictly speaking we Orthodox should be taking the lead in all Christian matters here. But the important thing – the *cru-cial* thing – is that effectively, with Orthodoxy, history does not exist – everything is now, *now*!'

Theophanis is speaking fast and furiously, in volleys of the broken theological English he learned while studying for a PhD at Durham. Bustling around his little kitchen, fixing me an impromptu meal of almonds, strong coffee and crimson-dyed hard-boiled egg, neatly sliced and sprinkled with pepper, he seems intent on quick-selling me Orthodox Christianity. From time to time he pauses midway between the sink and the fridge, or in the act of spooning coffee into the pot, while he racks his mind for the best formulation of his thoughts in English. There is no room for argument with him, but I am enjoying the drama of his lecture.

Giving me directions here, Rahme had explained that although Theophanis' bedroom window is only a step further down and across the alley from Arkhangelos, I would have to go the long way round, past the Internet cafe on Christian Quarter Street and take the first turning right up Greek Orthodox Patriarchate Street. About fifty yards ahead on my right I would see a big wooden door, which I must enter. Next I must climb a flight of marble stairs to arrive in a hall hung with almost life-size portraits of Greek patriarchs of Jerusalem, at the far end of which I would find another staircase that would bring me out onto a roof terrace rose garden. On the far side of that, by a heap of broken masonry, I would see Theophanis' little bungalow.

'God bless you, Victoria!' was how he greeted me, standing at his kitchen door with a dishcloth slung over his shoulder. He had barely paused for breath since.

'Our Orthodox liturgy, you see, is a constant re-enactment of history. It keeps everything present. When you're talking about history and Orthodoxy you must understand that in the context of our liturgy history is this moment – this bowl of red Easter eggs, the sun on the roses in the garden out there. Look, I've read the Desert Fathers and the writings of pilgrims like that Spanish nun Egeria, and St Jerome. Tell me something: what has changed in Orthodoxy? Anything? Nothing! Orthodoxy is always there; we just have to appro-priate it, you see? *Ap-pro-priate* it!'

I laugh appreciatively, and he continues. 'Some people say that we Orthodox are too relaxed. Just because we have the perfect true faith, we think there's nothing more to be said or done. Pah!' He shrugs. 'We all have our failings! But the Orthodox are going for the *es-sence* of the matter. At least we are not slaves of the pope like the Catholics. And the Protestants? Pah! We are more truly theological. Another egg, some cake?'

While he gulps his coffee I manage to slip in a question about the 'essence' of the Holy Fire miracle.

'Miracle? What miracle?' he counters. Startled, I wonder if this senior Greek hierarch is about to admit that the most effective and powerful weapon in the arsenal the Orthodox have been deploying for centuries against their fellow Christians here, as well as Muslims and Jews, is a base trick. I proceed with care. 'Theophanis, there are rumours about trouble at the Holy Fire ceremony on Saturday. *I* didn't see anything, but there was some violence, wasn't there?'

'Yes, yes,' he replies with an impatient flick of his dishcloth, 'I think Irineos and the Armenian hit each other, but it's quite normal here. Last year the Copts and the Syrian Jacobites were chasing each other around the tomb. I laugh at all this!'

'I know there are often fights, but inside the edicule?' I suggest that such a rumpus in the holiest place in Christendom is especial-ly shameful given the current crisis in Bethlehem, and enquire as to whether Patriarch Irineos is feeling a little embarrassed.

'Embarassed? Not at all. I think he's happy that he asserted him-self in there,' answers Theophanis, noisily slamming the fridge door. His tone has turned testy, dismissive. For all his charm and bon-homie there is an uneasy tension about him.

Crashing about at his washing-up, he fills in the background to the brawl for me. It seems that Patriarch Irineos' predecessor, an overweight and sick old man, gradually abandoned the correct order of the ceremony in favour of ease and convenience, thereby giving the Armenian priest free rein to usurp parts of his role and create a dangerous precedent that might soon be described as 'traditional'. Performing the ceremony for the first time this year, Irineos had determined to call a halt to this insidious encroachment on an Orthodox prerogative.

'You see, the Armenians do tricks . . . OK, OK,' Theophanis admits, pre-empting my protest, 'I know we all do wrong things, but they are worse than us. I tell you this frankly!'

'And what about the Holy Fire miracle?' I can no longer resist saying. The dragging of God to earth and the elevation of Orthodoxy above other forms of Christianity must be the oldest and boldest trick any established religion has ever perpetrated on its adherents.

Standing at the sink, his back to me, Theophanis coughs and pauses. He is planning another excursion into theology. 'Look, Victoria, I am sure that you know about the created world of man and nature but also about the *un*created world which sanctifies that created world and makes it immortal. Holy communion, for example, is not just bread or those wafers the Catholics have, but the body and blood of Christ, immortal and sacred! The same with baptism: water becomes a means of salvation . . .'

I can see where this is leading but doubt that Holy Fire qualifies as a sacrament, like either holy communion or holy matrimony. Perhaps I am thinking too rigidly. Theophanis attempts a further explanation: 'In this ceremony we are offering created fire and from it comes *un*created light, by the grace of the Holy Spirit. You see?'

'But how is that created fire created in the first place?'

'Oh,' he says, vigorously rubbing at a corner of the plastic table-cloth now, 'before the ceremony begins, a *kantila* – a little oil lamp – is placed, already lit, on the tomb. The patriarch lights his candle from it while he says a special prayer.'

He gives me a challenging look, as if to say, 'There! Are you satisfied now?' before hurrying out of the kitchen into his sitting room. When he returns, he is wearing a pair of half-moon spectacles and has a copy of the complete works of T. S. Eliot in his hands. Flicking through the book, furrowing his brow, he finds what he is looking for at last: 'Here we are – the chorus from *The Rock*. Wonderful!'

How can I drag him back down from this high heaven of fine feeling to the muddy matter at hand.

'Theophanis, the patriarchate's website is still presenting the Holy Fire as a miracle,' I begin, hastily riffling through the pages of my notebook in search of the relevant citation. 'Listen to this – "a wheeze is heard and almost simultaneously blue and white lights penetrate from everywhere, as though millions of photographic flashes turn on".[xvii] What would happen if Patriarch Irineos called a press conference and announced the simple truth you've just told me about the Holy Fire?'

Theophanis is impatient. 'Look, do you tell children of six years old the facts of life, all at once, just like that, suddenly? No, they get to know the truth little by little, don't they? The same with Father Christmas, the same with the Holy Fire.'

'But we're not talking about children. I'm thinking of my Greek diplomat friend who's in her mid-thirties. I'm thinking of Rahme, who must be almost sixty, and Nasra . . .'

He pauses to gaze out at the sunlight on the roses, thinking hard. 'If the patriarch made a declaration about the Holy Fire he would be like a pope trying to solve everything with encyclical letters, which only create more problems. No, no! And now, it is time for us to go!'

Striding back together through the patriarchate we hail a monk sitting tapping at a computer by an open window. On we go, passing some barking dogs and a washing line and climbing some stairs into an upper central courtyard, where suddenly we come face to face with Patriarch Irineos and a posse of monks. Theophanis introduces us and the patriarch responds in careful English, 'Good, good. I'm sure His Eminence is looking after you well.'

I wonder if Theophanis is feeling as sheepish as I am.

I remember my very first meeting with my Texan friend Father Athanasius and his solemn warning to me that distrust, disloyalty and suspicion are the air one breathes in Jerusalem. 'You just have to watch out,' he said. 'The air here is toxic.'

~

Home smells anything but toxic this evening.

After cooking a Palestinian pilaf Rahme is resting on her sofa, smoking. I help myself to some of the dish and join Nasra, who is sitting at the table pensively picking at a plate of watermelon. She tells me a friend of hers at the Greek patriarchate has just offered her a job there, translating old documents from Arabic into Greek. While reluctant to quit her post as an administrator at Bethlehem University, she is exhausted by the daily commute through the Israeli checkpoints and depressed by random curfews. She thinks she would like to help the Church, for a while at least and for free, because there is no telling if or when 'the situation' will improve sufficiently for her to return to her own flat in Bethlehem.

'I've been at the patriarchate too,' I say, seizing my chance while Rahme is otherwise occupied to test Theophanis' startling disclosure on her. Suddenly I feel sure that I have over-estimated Orthodox Christians' attachment to their Holy Fire. Nasra will probably just laugh and shrug. But no, she listens very carefully to my tale, her fork frozen in mid-air.

'My goodness! He told you that?' she shouts, shaking her head in angry disbelief. 'How can we believe in this religion now?' Her tone turns sarcastic. 'Did he also say that Mary the mother of God was never a virgin, that she had *sex*? And then did he happen to mention that *any* woman can be the mother of God?' Pushing the plate of melon away from her, she announces, 'You know, every Orthodox Christian believes in this miracle, every single one of us!'

I am dismayed by her distress and attempt to limit the upset I have caused. 'He talked about the created and the uncreated light and the symbolism . . .'

But Nasra is inconsolable. 'OK, OK, but that's *not* the way people believe it, is it? You know that!'

The pilaf-scented air tastes toxic now.

Nasra lights up the narghile and we bubble away ruminatively in a haze of cinnamon smoke while one set of neighbours rows and Rahme's television blares the latest bad tidings from the Church of the Nativity. And then it is Nasra's turn to shock me, by relaying what her friend and perhaps future employer at the patriarchate has told her about the Bethlehem siege.

'It's clear that the Catholics are using this crisis for their own purposes. The Franciscans don't control as much of the Church of the Nativity as the Orthodox, so they let the Palestinian gunmen into the church to make trouble.'

'I'm not following, Nasra.'

'It's simple,' she replies, exhaling a long plume of smoke. 'The Franciscans let the gunmen in because they, the friars, want to see the place destroyed by the Israeli tanks. When everything has been smashed up, the pope or some rich Catholics will offer to build a new church. Then, of course, the Franciscans will make sure that they have all the rights and control over it.'

'Do you believe that? Does Father Kiprianos really think that the climax of this intifada has been engineered by the Catholics to spite the Orthodox?'

'Of course,' she says.*

~

Neither theology nor miracles but physical space is what Bishop Theophanis would call the 'es-sence' of the trouble in this city, and over the wider area of what Jews, Christians and Muslims all view as holy land.

Walking down St Francis Road this morning, into the covered

---

* The siege of the Church of the Nativity lasted thirty-nine days and ended on 10 May 2002 with the exile of thirteen Palestinian militants to Cyprus.

gloom of Christian Quarter Road, I take the tiny second turning on the left – the cobbled alley of St Helena Road with its clutter of souvenir stalls and the Omar mosque at what looks like the dead end of it. The mosque's high minaret is catching the sun prettily but a sign on its fancy ironwork gate repels casual tourists with FOR PRAYER ONLY. Deliberately sited just there, where it still confuses Christian pilgrims in search of Christ's tomb, this tenth-century mosque was built to assert the supremacy of Islam over Christianity. Just past it, a sharp left turn will bring me to the steps leading down to the sun-filled parvis, an enclosed courtyard, and the dark entrance to the Church of the Holy Sepulchre.

Islam was not always as eager to emulate Byzantine Christianity's triumphalist exclusivity as that sign on the gate of the mosque would suggest. Mohammad believed that his divine revelation was only a refinement and expansion on the revelations granted by God to Moses and Jesus. 'Do not argue with the followers of an earlier revelation otherwise than in the most kindly manner,' he commanded his Muslims, 'say: "We believe in that which has been bestowed from on high upon us, as well as that which has been bestowed upon you: for our God is one and the same, and it is to him that we all surrender ourselves."'[xviii]

Jerusalem was not the capital of the promised land for Muslims in the same way that it was for Jews. Nor had Allah ever sanctified it in the way that Jesus Christ had, but Mohammad once dreamed he flew around the city as far as the ruins of the second Jewish Temple on a winged horse named al-Buraq in the company of the Angel Gabriel.* By means of that 'night journey' the Prophet had transferred a measure of Muslim sanctity to Jerusalem, rendering it Islam's third holiest city, after Mecca and Medina.

Mohammad had only been dead five years in 637 when one of his closest companions, Caliph Omar, arrived to besiege the city. Naturally, Omar tried to cajole Jerusalem's Byzantine Christian inhabitants into agreeing that Mohammad was God's apostle. In

---

* The second Temple, built by King Herod, was destroyed by the Romans in AD 70.

exchange for that declaration, he told them, they might rest assured that neither they nor their property would be harmed. But Patriarch Sophronius, who was leading the defence of the city, stood firm because, camped outside the city's western gate, the caliph's armies were obstructing his Christmas procession to Bethlehem. At last, in February 638, reassured to learn that Muslims also held Jerusalem in holy veneration, he bowed to the inevitable. A quarter of a century earlier the armies of the King of Persia had taken Jerusalem, ransacked the Anastasis and forced him into an eight-year exile. Sophronius was optimistic that Muslim Arab rule would prove just as temporary a punishment. He could be forgiven for underestimating the puritan energy and inexorable force of Islam in those early years. Seated on a camel, wearing the simplest of camel-hair robes and with his saddlebags of food, a leather water bottle and a wooden platter, Caliph Omar looked more like a common Bedouin than an all-conquering warrior chief. But Caliph Omar's conquest of Jerusalem marked the start of thirteen centuries of Muslim rule over the Holy Land, a period only briefly interrupted in the twelfth century and again in the thirteenth when western Christians, Crusaders, ruled Jerusalem.

The 638 transfer of power was accomplished without further bloodshed and Caliph Omar's first polite request to Sophronius was that he lead him on a tour of the city's holy places. At one of the hours of Muslim prayer, when they happened to be in the Anastasis, Caliph Omar begged his guide to be excused a moment. 'O Commander of the Faithful,' said Sophronius, at his most courteous, 'pray here.' But Omar refused, and nor would he pray in Constantine's basilica church. Instead, he insisted on performing his pious duty on the steps leading to the church and when he was finished, he asked Sophronius, 'Do you know, O Patriarch, why I would not pray within the church? Had I done so you would have lost your right to it, for the Muslims would have taken it from you after my death, saying, "Omar prayed here."'[xix]

Faithfully obeying Mohammad's injunction to respect the followers of earlier revelations, Caliph Omar instantly issued an order forbidding Muslims to build a mosque, or even pray, on the steps where he had prayed. It seems likely that were it not for Caliph Omar's scrupulous obedience to Mohammad's commands there would be no Church of the Holy Sepulchre here today. The mosque at the end of St Helena Road would stand not just uncomfortably close to Christ's tomb but fair and square on top of the site uncovered by Bishop Makarios. And the Anastasis would have been as thoroughly obliterated as the pagan Roman temple to Aphrodite that it replaced.

Next, Caliph Omar asked Sophronius to show him the Jewish Temple and, at last, after the proud prelate had tried and failed to distract the Arab's attention from the holiest place of the city's founders by taking him to church after Christian church instead, they reached a gate. Behind it was a flight of steps running with dirty water where the patriarch made one last attempt to prevent Omar paying his respects to the city's Jewish past by informing him that they were unable to proceed any further without crawling on their hands and knees through streams of sewage and mounds of garbage. Careless of his own camel-hair robe and Sophronius' costly finery, Omar commanded the old prelate to continue, to the top of the old Temple Mount. There, among the forlorn ruins of the Temple King Herod had built about twenty years before Christ was born, they were assailed by the foul stench rising from acres of Christian ordure but, instantly recognizing the place as that to which the Prophet had been transported on his 'night journey', the caliph joyfully exclaimed, '*Allahu akhbar!* By him in whose hands is my life! This is that which the Apostle of God – on whom be the peace and the blessing of God – described to me!'ˣˣ He set about clearing the place. Throwing handfuls of the revolting detritus into a sling improvised from the folds of his robe, he hurled it over the nearby stretch of city wall.

Palestine's new Muslim rulers would nickname the Anastasis the 'Dunghill'* in revenge for the Christians' arrogant desecration

---

* The Arabic words for Anastasis (al-qiyama) and for dunghill (al-qumamah) sound similar.

of the Jews' holy place but their treatment of Christians was generally exemplary. A written promise was given of 'security, to each
person and their property; to their churches, their crosses, to the
sick and the healthy, to all the people of their creed'.*ˣˣⁱ No church
would be damaged, no one forced to convert to Islam, no one
harmed. Fifty years after the conquest, in 688, work began on the
Dome of the Rock, a mosque so gigantic and gorgeously decorated
that the Christians in their Anastasis could not doubt that their revelation had been superseded and that Islam was in Jerusalem to stay.
An inscription over the arches of its inner arcade reminded all
Muslims that Jesus Christ was neither God nor a member of any
holy trinity, and that God was 'utterly remote' from having a son.

Jews were permitted to take up residence in the city again after
300 years of exile and, by the eighth century, Arab rule was so little
resented by the Holy Land Christians that they had jettisoned
Greek and Aramaic, and were speaking Arabic, as Rahme and Nasra
do today.

~

For all the crowd at the Holy Fire ceremony, Rahme and Nasra
cannot remember an Easter when the Christian Quarter was so
empty of pilgrims and the souvenir trade so slow; not 1948 when
Israel was born in the flames of war and not 1967, the year when the
six-day battle for the city raged.

The Church of the Holy Sepulchre's parvis is another unnatural
vacancy today. Two Israeli policemen loll on the shady steps leading
to the Franciscans' chapel, watching a lone pilgrim kiss a cracked
stone pillar to the left of the great door. Approaching, I glimpse
the gleaming white beard of an old Orthodox monk snoozing on a
bench just inside the entrance and, once my eyes have accustomed
themselves to the interior gloom, can just make out a high partition

* The document is probably not authentic but is in keeping with Muslim treatment of
conquered peoples.

wall covered with glittering mosaic. But I almost trip over a woman prostrated before the low, flat Stone of Unction. She yelps in angry Greek and a passing priest – instantly identifiable as Armenian by his black trapezoidal style of headdress – frowns and looks away.

The Greek woman is soon joined at her devotions by a Russian nun wearing a high velvet hat pulled down low on her brow like a helmet, and carrying a plastic bag full of linen cloths and towels. Frowning in prayerful concentration, she scatters them the length of the stone, before rubbing vigorously at the slab with each in turn, folding them neatly and packing them away. At her side a kneeling middle-aged man wearing a tweed jacket is performing an odd toilet. After dousing the stone in rose water, he applies some of the same to his hair and then, opening his shirt, to his bared chest.

A very small man wearing a fur-trimmed suede hat has appeared at my elbow.

'They are blessing themselves,' he tells me, and pauses a moment before introducing himself as Artin. 'If you are a fanatic of any religion you are an enemy of yourself,' he says.

'Are there many fanatics in here, Artin?'

He rolls his deep-set eyes heavenward to let me know I am more stupid than I look. 'Come with me,' he says, leading me past a couple of electricians in dirty vests kneeling by a large hole in the flagstones, surrounded by a tangle of wires and tools. We are headed towards the edicule and all that remains of the rock tomb uncovered by Bishop Makarios seventeen centuries ago.

In front of the shrine is a crowd of Ethiopian pilgrims swathed in pristine white gauze prayer shawls. Marshalled into an orderly queue by the commanding gestures of a young Greek monk with a mobile phone in one hand, they are quietly and reverently entering the holy of holies, one or two at a time. No sooner have they dispersed than suddenly, as imperiously as the voice of God, a thunderous organ chord sounds from the gallery above outgunning the Egyptian Copts' relentless low-calibre battery of *Kyrie eleisons* from their chapel at the rear of the edicule The discord swiftly spreads to the front of the edicule where a detachment of friars has lined up to sing a plain-chant. The two sets of voices do hideous battle.

Ugly discord, disagreements over when one service begins and another ends, the use of voices and musical instruments, and also church furniture, crosses and candlesticks as weapons, are all manifestations of the intense rivalry that mars relations between the Christians who share the stewardship of the church. But these incessant hostilities are only a pale imitation of the violence that defiled the early centuries of eastern Christianity, when disputes about the semantics of the words 'nature' and 'person' could flare into massacres, when losses in translation between Greek and Armenian, and discrepancies between classical Greek and Judaic ignited rebellions and launched wars. The denouncement of heresies and pronouncement of schisms were Orthodox Christianity's weapons of defence against all who would deny the impossibly brain-teasing truth about the God who was also a man. In addition to the Arian heresy that Bishop Eusebius had espoused, there was the Nestorian position that Jesus was not God and man but rather two entirely separate natures from the moment of his birth, one of them divine, the other human. On the other hand, the Oriental Orthodox, pejoratively known as Monophysites, believed that Christ had only one nature, at once utterly human and utterly divine. Oriental Orthodoxy has weathered the centuries a good deal better than Arianism or Nestorianism. The Oriental Orthodox churches of the Armenians, the Copts, the Ethiopians and the Syrian Jacobites have each retained a stake in the Church of the Holy Sepulchre.

Western Christians, Latins, owing spiritual obedience to a pope in Rome rather than to an Orthodox patriarch in Constantinople, did not arrive in the Holy Land until the early ninth century, at the behest of Emperor Charlemagne. Once precious gifts had travelled between Sultan Harun al-Rashid's famously sumptuous court at Baghdad and Charlemagne's magnificent new capital at Aachen, a few black-robed Catholic Benedictine monks were able to establish themselves on the Mount of Olives where they tended a garden of vines and vegetables, ran a hostel for western Christian pilgrims and built up a rich library.

Relations between the western and eastern halves of Christendom had been strained by an alteration which Charlemagne had made to the text of the creed agreed upon at Constantine's Council of Nicaea* so there could be no question of those Benedictines inserting themselves inside the Anastasis. Isolated and fearful, they penned a protest to Pope Leo III in Rome: 'We, who are Frankish pilgrims in this holy city of Jerusalem, so far from the seat of Rome, are a part of the flock confided to your care. John, a [Byzantine Orthodox] monk of St Saba, has dared to accuse us of heresy – we Franks of the Mount of Olives – and to suspect our orthodoxy. Nevertheless, our faith is that of the seat of Rome. That which we sing, we have heard it in the chapel of the Emperor Charles [Charlemagne].'[xxii] This letter is an early example of the bitter distrust that still mars relations between Orthodox and Catholic Christians. Bishop Theophanis' disparaging references to the papacy's nit-picking legalism are a more recent example of the same phenomenon.

Latin clergy did not win a foothold in the Church of the Holy Sepulchre until the conquest of Jerusalem by the First Crusaders in 1099 and Franciscan friars would not secure their place there until the fourteenth century. Thereafter the Catholics made up for lost time. Today by far the greater part of the Church of the Holy Sepulchre is minutely – to the last alcove, pillar and lintel – shared out between its three great powers: first the Orthodox Greeks, then the Catholic Franciscans and finally the Oriental Orthodox Armenians. The three remaining communities have been left with precious little. The Copts rejoice in the little chapel at the back of the edicule and the Syrian Jacobites have theirs, but the Ethiopians only maintain a tenuous foothold on the roof of the church. There, my guide Artin reminds me, they live in huts 'like in Africa'.

Texan Father Athanasius has kindly supplied me with a colour-

---

* The *filioque* clause, whereby western Christians asserted that the Holy Spirit in the Trinity 'proceeded from the father *and the son*', rather than only from God the Father.

coded plan of the Church of the Holy Sepulchre as detailed and
complex as a political map of Europe. No more than fifty paces from
Christ's tomb, up a steep flight of marble stairs, is Calvary with its
twin altars – one coded Greek Orthodox pale blue, one Roman
Catholic donkey brown. Before descending to the main church
again, at Artin's command I plunge my arm down a dark hole under
the first, to have a feel of the rocky spot where the cross on which
Christ died once stood. Behind the wide central space of the
Greeks' *catholikon* is a semicircle of dark chapels, the Chapel of the
Divi-sion of Garments, the Chapel of the Derision and the Chapel
of Longinus. The second is yellow Armenian property, the others
belong to the Greeks. Another flight of stairs descends to the
Chapel of St Helena, also tinted Armenian yellow on my map, and
on down, further still, to the dark place from which Constantine's
mother Helena unearthed the remains of the cross. This brown dun-
geon belongs to the Latins.

I have lost my way in a shadowy maze. What, if anything,
remains of the beautiful Anastasis that Bishop Makarios built on his
emperor's orders? Only the lower parts of the columns forming the
rotunda, says Artin, before he disappears.

I start back towards the edicule, intent on exploring it now that
the Franciscans and Copts have finished their service cum skirmish.
After waiting for a pair of nuns to finish their prayers and exit back-
wards from their holiest place, the Greek monk ushers me inside to
a tiny ante-room known as the Chapel of the Angels. It contains
nothing but the little that remains of the rock the angel rolled
away from the entrance to Christ's tomb on the morning of the
Resurrection. Generations of pilgrims, as hungry for holiness as the
fourth-century True Cross-consumer reported by Sister Egeria, have
furtively chiselled away at it for precious souvenirs. It occurs to me
that this ante-room is where, if Nasra's version of last Saturday's
Holy Fire fracas is to be believed, the patriarch and the Armenian
priest wrestled with each other.

Bending low for another doorway, I find myself in a still smaller
inner chamber. The dozens of oil lamps hanging from the ceiling

like creepers cast a murky jungle light over a cracked marble slab covering what little is left of the tomb Makarios' workmen discovered. The Cypriot Orthodox monk claimed that the Holy Fire emerges from a crack in this slab, but there is some disagreement about the matter. The earliest recorded reference to the miracle is Muslim and dates from the early ninth century. No particular mention is made of the Holy Fire's exit route; its author simply tells of a bright white fire spontaneously appearing inside the shrine as if sent from heaven, and of Christians lighting their candles from the Greek patriarch's Holy Fire before rampaging home in triumph, brandishing their divine favour and shouting 'Hasten to the religion of the Cross!'[xxiii] Not long afterwards, in 870, the first western Christian account, by a monk named Bernard, makes no mention of either a white fire or of flames rising out of the tomb. Instead, he writes simply, 'an angel comes and kindles light in the lamps which hang above the sepulchre'.[xxiv]

At the most, I calculated, standing in that dim-lit bunker with my head politely bowed, Christ's tomb measures no more than one and a half feet by two now. But responsibility for its drastic diminution cannot be laid at the door of overzealous pilgrims. Along with Arkhangelos' original church, Constantine's fabulous Anastasis and its precious tomb were horribly vandalized on the orders of a Muslim caliph at the start of the eleventh century.

~

The enthronement of the eleven-year-old Caliph al-Hakim in Cairo in 996 boded well for the Christians at first. The boy's mother was a Christian and two of his uncles were patriarchs, one of Jerusalem, the other of Alexandria. Even his grand vizier was a Christian. But then so was the scribe who would pen his fateful 1009 command to utterly destroy Constantine's Anastasis, making 'its sky equal to its ground and its length to its breadth'.[xxv]

What prompted the young caliph's thoroughly un-Islamic assault on the Anastasis? He may have been facing internal dissent on account of his Christian family connections. He may have calculated that an aggressive campaign against the followers of Jesus would be proof positive of his loyalty to Islam. The principal western Christian source on the subject – an eleventh-century French chronicle – scapegoats the Jews by telling of a rich rabbi of Orleans bribing someone to travel to Cairo with a letter hidden inside his walking stick. The letter, written in Hebrew, contained a warning to Caliph al-Hakim that the Christian powers were plotting to conquer Jerusalem and recover the tomb of Christ. 'The only way of averting this catastrophe, O prince of believers,' it allegedly advised, 'is to annihilate the Holy Tomb and the whole of the basilica.'[xxvi] Another, perfectly credible explanation involves the Holy Fire 'miracle'. A Greek monk, bitter at being passed over for promotion to a bishopric, resolved to avenge himself on the Patriarch of Jerusalem by exposing the annual marvel as a wicked fraud. He travelled to Cairo to tell al-Hakim that a priest of the Anastasis simply 'greased the chain of iron that held the lamp over the tomb with oil of balsam' and, once the shrine had been sealed, 'applied a match through the roof to the other extremity of the chain' so that 'the fire descended immediately to the wick of the lamp and lighted it'.[xxvii]

But both these explanations seem too crudely Christian in flavour. The true reason why Caliph al-Hakim found it expedient to destroy the holiest site in Christendom might have been that, having proclaimed himself a divine incarnation, he could not countenance competition from the Christians' far better established man-god. In the same year that he destroyed the Anastasis, al-Hakim unveiled the next phase of his lunatic vision: the abolition of the five central tenets of Islam* as well as chess-playing, honey, raisins and going out after nightfall. After provoking mass civil unrest, al-Hakim ended badly. One day in the year 1020 he went for his usual walk in the desert around Cairo and was never seen again. The coat he was wearing was found torn to shreds and

---

* God is one and Mohammad is his prophet, fasting, prayer, pilgrimage and charity.

the mule he was riding mutilated. His disciples – ancestors of today's Druze – believed that he had been murdered, that his soul had transmigrated to China, and that he would return to them one day.*

For most Muslims, al-Hakim was a mad and unwelcome but not particularly important aberration, but for Christians everywhere, mourning the glories of their Anastasis, he was the Antichrist. Although his efforts to utterly eradicate the holy tomb had failed, although his Christian mother oversaw the shrine's restoration and the celebration of Easter on the site within eighteen months of the calamity, al-Hakim remained a gigantic evil. Grief and fury at his crime would fester in the collective western Christian consciousness for the rest of the eleventh century to blacken the image of Islam in Europe and erupt in the late 1090s in the savagely vengeful First Crusade.

In the meantime, another Constantine was happy to fund the rebuilding of the Anastasis in the mid-eleventh century, although this Byzantine emperor's largesse did not extend to recreating the gigantic basilica church or the standard of adornment achieved 700 years earlier. There was another urgent call on Constantine IX's purse. Jerusalem needed a new city wall and the caliph of the time was demanding that the Christians pay for the section of it closest to their Anastasis. Constantine struck an advantageous deal on their behalf. He would pay for the wall on condition that no one but Christians lived in that north-western quarter of the city. The smaller church he built took in what had been the garden between the basilica and the shrine itself and, for the first time, Calvary and the tomb shared a single roof.

Less than fifty years later Crusaders would battle their way to the Holy Land, conquer the city of Jerusalem and rename the restored Anastasis the Church of the Holy Sepulchre.

* An estimated one million Druze worldwide – mostly in Syria, Lebanon and northern Israel – still await the return of al-Hakim. Unlike Palestinians, Israeli Druze are expected to serve in the army.

SUMMER 2002

*'Look at the Franks! Behold with what obstinacy
they fight for their religion, while we the Muslims
show no enthusiasm for waging jihad'*

– SALADIN, 1187

When the Old City's air is too poisonous to breathe, I escape up here to the roof of the Church of the Holy Sepulchre.

Today's noon sky is a burning blue and this sun-struck terrace empty but for one old monk seated in the generous shade of a eucalyptus tree. The small community of Ethiopian monks and nuns which inhabits this place must be praying or snoozing through the heat of the day in the cluster of low drab dwellings by the Gothic arches of the ruined Crusader refectory.

Their relegation to this miserable squat above St Helena's chapel would have astonished the Crusader-era monks who built and used the refectory. They would have known the empire of the Ethiopians to be powerful and wealthy beyond measure, and ruled by a fabulously rich Christian potentate called Prester John* who was descended from one of the magi who followed the star to Bethlehem to welcome Christ to earth.

Reports of Prester John, of his extensive realm, his astonishing wealth and his faithfulness to both Christianity and the Crusader cause first reached Europe in the mid-twelfth century when the four Crusader states in the east – Edessa, Jerusalem, Tripoli and Antioch – were as young as the state of Israel is today and facing mortal danger. All around them the native forces of Islam were ferociously resurgent and intent on their swift destruction. The County of Edessa

* Prester probably derives from the ecclesiastical office of presbyter.

had already been lost for a year when a German prelate comforted a
fearful Crusader bishop in Tripoli with the good news that Prester
John, who possessed a sceptre studded with emeralds and ruled over
the lands of seventy-two kings, was struggling to come to the aid of
his fellow Christians but had been sadly delayed by bad weather.

No matter that no one in Europe had discovered the precise
location of Prester John or his dominions. The news that his realms
were a paradise on earth, teeming with centaurs, phoenixes and
griffins, a place where no poisonous plants grew, where lying and
robbery were unheard of, where a fountain gushed with the elixir of
eternal youth and clothes were made from the incombustible skins
of fire-dwelling salamanders, was enormously heartening. If so great
a ruler, of such a wondrous land, was on his way to defend and
advance the Crusader cause in Palestine then all would surely be
very well. In September 1177, in a letter soliciting his aid against
Islam, Pope Alexander addressed Prester John as 'karissimo in Christo
filio Iohanni, illustri et magnifico'.*[i]

To no avail. Prester John did not reply to any letter and nor did
he appear in time to prevent the re-conquest of Jerusalem by
Saladin in 1187. But the myth of an elusive champion who would
one day arise to avenge the loss of Christ's holy sepulchre continued
to offer false hope to Crusaders and all Christendom for centuries to
come. It would also play a part in the resounding failure that was the
Fifth Crusade almost forty years later.

Cardinal Pelagius, a Spaniard and the pope's representative on
that predominantly German Crusade of 1219, was a good military
technician, which made a welcome change. The astounding success
of the First Crusade with its capture of Christ's tomb in 1099 and
the establishment of the Kingdom of Jerusalem had been followed
by a series of shameful failures. The Second Crusade of 1147–9 was
rendered a 'fiasco' by its leaders' 'truculence, their ignorance and
their ineffectual folly'.[ii] Some thirty years later Richard the Lion-
heart's Third Crusade managed to recover the coastal settlements,

* 'John, beloved son of Christ, illustrious and magnificent'.

but not Jerusalem. The abominable sacking of Constantinople in 1204 provoked the enduring distrust and wrath of Orthodox Christians towards all Crusaders and marked the abject collapse of the Fourth Crusade. It was followed by the horrifying folly of the Children's Crusade eight years later.* A break with the crusading movement's amateurish beginnings was long overdue. Instead of making straight for the Holy Land and Jerusalem, Pelagius and his Fifth Crusade would first try to conquer Egypt, the engine room of Muslim power.

A popular prophecy doing the rounds of the Crusaders' camp in Egypt in 1220 promised that a 'king of Abissi' – Abyssinia being another name for Ethiopia – would invade Arabia, attack Mecca and 'scatter the bones of Mahomet'.[iii] Another predicted a pincer movement on Islam, most likely by the armies of the Abyssinian Prester John and the Holy Roman Emperor Frederick II, who was expected to join the Crusade shortly. It clearly stated that the forces of the world's greatest Christian powers would meet, victorious over the Infidel, in Jerusalem, on Easter Sunday, 3 April. Rejoicing in every word, Pelagius discovered that Easter would fall on that day the very next year, and he determined to be present at the glorious reckoning. After hurriedly securing the Nile port of Damietta in early 1221, he and his army forged confidently on towards the Holy Land.

He might have been a good military tactician but Pelagius' failure to allow for the Nile's annual flooding would prove fatal to the enterprise. Drowning in mire and encircled by Muslims, the Fifth Crusaders were soon facing defeat. The Germans panicked and, refusing to abandon their barrels of wine, rendered themselves too drunk to retreat. While they blundered about in the blood and mud, the cardinal escaped by ship, and control of Damietta reverted to the sultan. The Fifth Crusade had failed, and still there was no sign of Prester John.

Shortly after this disappointment Christian Europe re-identified

* Thousands of French and German children set out for Jerusalem, inspired by charismatic preachers. Pope Innocent III sent the French home from Rome. The Germans got as far as Brindisi.

Prester John as the great Mongol leader from the steppes of central Asia, Genghis Khan. All Europe's hopes of a rescue mission to the Crusader states were immediately switched eastward to him, but were smashed when Genghis Khan's grandson, Batu, turned his horde on western Christendom in the mid-thirteenth century, torch-ing everything in his path – towns, villages, monasteries, churches. The search for Prester John switched back to Africa. In 1400 England's Henry IV addressed a letter to the 'king of Abyssinia, Prester John' praising his reputed desire to win back the Holy Sepulchre for Christendom and mentioning his own eagerness to set off for Palestine on Crusade. Might they be allies in such a worthy cause?[iv] It is not known if the letter ever reached Ethiopia.

The myth was fading, but at the end of the fifteenth century, when Christopher Columbus sailed west across the Atlantic, he was still dreaming of finding the kingdom of Prester John and of secur-ing an alliance between him and Spain for the purpose of defeating Islam, while Portuguese explorers were putting in at African ports and enquiring after the great emperor until well into the sixteenth century.*

~

'Oh!' exclaims Father Solomon, adjusting his purple velvet cap. He glances at me significantly over the golden rims of his black sun-glasses before saying, 'No, I never heard of Prester John.'

A figment of the western Christian imagination, a wishful dream shared by all who loved Christ's tomb in Jerusalem and prayed for the survival of the Crusader colonies, Prester John was still fascinating the writer John Buchan at the start of the twentieth century. But he meant nothing whatsoever to this young Ethiopian monk crouching in the shade beside me on the steps.

---

* Edward Ullendorff and C.F. Beckingham in *The Hebrew Letters of Prester John*, OUP, 1982 argue that tales of the phantom saviour were simply weapons in a complicated propaganda war the Roman popes were waging against the German Holy Roman Emperors from the eleventh to the sixteenth century.

We had met on my last visit, on Holy Saturday night while the Ethiopians were performing their own Holy Fire ceremony up here on their roof terrace. Amid the thronging crowds of ululating, drumming and singing pilgrims circling the dome of St Helena's chapel at a slow trot, with lit candles in their hands, Solomon had approached Nasra and me with a badly photocopied Easter greeting from the Ethiopian archbishop.

I had recalled Father Athanasius once telling me that from the point of view of their poverty and simplicity the Ethiopians were the real Franciscans in the city, 'but it means they're no good at lobbying and manoeuvring'. He had gone on to explain that one reason why they had been banished to the roof of the Church of the Holy Sepulchre 400 years earlier was their inability to speak any European language well enough to fight their own corner.

But there on that Easter night was Solomon, speaking not only passable English but fluent German. Amid the jostling uproar of his community's Easter celebration, he was urgently targeting visiting Westerners with his Easter greeting and drawing their attention to his community's miserable circumstances. Without any prompting, he had begun, 'We Ethiopians have had a hard life, oh a very terrible life here in Jerusalem. There is apartheid in the Holy Sepulchre. It is discrimination, a persecution! The Greeks and the Franciscans and the Armenians live in their palaces, while our nuns are sleeping up here in winter with clothes around their heads to keep warm! Look at our homes! Come with me!'

He had drawn us away from the dancing throng to show us the crumbling walls of the huts and roofs made of strips of corrugated iron held in place by bricks. We inspected rudimentary kitchen arrangements and stinking lavatories. 'You see? Not enough water even for our toilets! I am not accusing anyone. Oh! Please, no! I want to live in peace with my brother Christians! But in western Europe dogs and cats have a better life than we have here!'

We had listened and I had promised to return for an extended discussion about his community, its history and its grievances.

Today, two months later, his surprise at my having kept that promise is touching. 'In my country, if we say we will do something in one hour we mean one day, if we say one day maybe we mean one week or two. A month means next year! But here you are like a miracle! You said you would come on this day and you came – all the way from London! Oh you will save us!'

Solomon has worked me up into a fabulous Prester John in my absence. He is hoping I will remind the people who count that the Ethiopians once had charge of several chapels in the main church, as well as a starring role in the Holy Fire ceremony until as late as the seventeenth century. I assure him that I have heard of an early sixteenth-century Ottoman firman* stipulating that during the Holy Fire ceremony 'the first to enter the place where the Fire comes out would be the Chief of the Abyssinians'.ᵛ Am I aware, he asks me, that when Caliph Omar took possession of the city from Patriarch Sophronius in 638, he expressly mentioned the Ethiopians in his edict regarding the treatment of Christian minorities? Omar described the Ethiopians as 'living' in the city and almost everyone else, including the Catholics, the Copts and the Armenians, as only coming on pilgrimage. Yes, I am aware of that, but I am also aware that the authenticity of the firman is seriously disputed.

The mention of Egyptian Copts sets Solomon off on another train of thought. Since I was last in Jerusalem he and his brothers and sisters have become embroiled in a serious feud with the Egyptians of the next-door monastery, who jealously guard their right to use the Ethiopians' roof terrace as a short cut down to the parvis of the Church of the Holy Sepulchre.

'But they can only pass through! Not sit here. You see, over there?' Solomon hisses in my ear, indicating the old monk on the far side of the terrace who has been keeping so still I have forgotten his presence. 'For some days now that old Copt has come with his chair to rest there. Usually he sits outside our gate near his monastery. To come inside here is an invasion! Today he sits here with his chair, tomorrow another Copt will come with his chair and

---

* Decree issued by a sultan.

perhaps a table. One day the Egyptians will claim they have the right to be in this courtyard, and they will take our monastery!'

Solomon and his entire community are determined that the old Copt must never be allowed to park his chair and nap in their courtyard again.

'But you see he is here again today. This is a declaration of war.'

'Of war?'

Solomon collects himself a little. 'I know it is terrible for Christians to be fighting when the Israelis and Palestinians are at war. I only want to live in peace with my Christian brothers, but we cannot allow this invasion. We could lose everything!'

I am about to register a protest when I notice other members of Solomon's community emerging from the direction of the huts, taking stock of the situation and forming a huddle. To judge by their expressions they are planning battle tactics. A young nun wearing a royal-blue polo shirt over her long skirt crosses her arms and scowls challengingly at the sleepy Copt.

In the middle of this council of war, a pair of benignly smiling American tourists enters the courtyard from the direction of the Egyptians' monastery and exits down the dark stairs to the main church. Next, some lusty hymn-singing heralds the approach of a party of Italian pilgrims. They are led by a wimpled nun with a large wooden cross hoisted on her shoulder, and filmed by a man with a heavy camera on his. Oblivious to the rising tension on the rooftop, they pause for a few moments in the sun-struck centre of the terrace to listen to a gospel reading, before exiting stage right, like the Americans before them.

The Ethiopian monks have now armed themselves with sticks and are strutting about the courtyard brandishing their weapons, darting haughtily venomous looks in the direction of the old Copt. The young nun, grinning in anticipation of action, is barely bothering to hide a stone she is clutching in the folds of her skirt. A vanguard of bearded Copts, their embroidered cloth bonnets tied under their chins like costume helmets, is massing stage left, at the door leading onto the terrace from their monastery.

Apparently concerned to restrain his forces, Solomon approaches the old Copt with a peace offering of a plastic bottle of water and a final request that he abandon the field. But the monk sets up a piteous wailing. His agonized cries fill the courtyard and his brothers at the gate grow more restive, hurling challenges to the Ethiopians. Fresh members of the cast appear: three Israeli police – a young man and two young women – stroll towards the shade of the eucalyptus tree, mobile phones and guns bulging at their hips. The old Copt stops wailing. The Ethiopians act nonchalant, redeploying their weapons as walking sticks. The nun deposits her stone on the wall beside me and the Egyptians at the gate melt away.

After patiently listening to Solomon's frantically exaggerated explanation of the story so far, the policeman hands him his mobile phone and tells him to call the chief of police. 'Help! Help me!' Solomon shouts in English into the tiny instrument. 'I'm trying to stop a battle!' Four more police arrive but soon leave again, confident the worst is over. Solomon returns to my side and removes his purple hat to mop his sweaty brow. 'Oh! This is so hard! I have to use my brain, not my heart to stop a conflict with my Christian brothers. Egypt has more power with Israel than we do because Egypt shares a border with Israel and is important in the Arab world. We have no one to support us. Oh! So hard!'

He explains that the Copts' strategy is to stage a provocation in order to put a stop to the Ethiopians' most recent attempts to secure some improvements in their living conditions. 'Oh where is the justice? We must have hygienic toilets and electricity,' he says, repeating his powerful point about the luxurious circumstances of European pets. 'But you have some electricity, don't you?' I ask him, recalling their evening Holy Fire ceremony. 'Very little, and we had to arrange that in the middle of the night when the Egyptians were sleeping . . .' Just then another Copt appears at the top of the stairs with a plastic shopping bag in one hand. Glancing at me in passing, he cannot resist a little sally at Solomon. 'You Ethiopians, you let anyone, Christian or Muslim or Jew, sit on a chair here in this courtyard. Only our brother, because he is a Copt, is not allowed.' 'I don't want to fight,' says Solomon mollifyingly. 'We are all brothers in Christ!' 'No,' says the Copt. 'We are the father, you are the son.'

He is reminding Solomon that the Ethiopian Church was led by a Coptic archbishop for hundreds of years until 1948 when Ethiopia's Emperor Haile Selassie insisted on ecclesiastical independence. After sharing this courtyard and what is now the Egyptians' monastery for centuries, the separation had been about as painful and complicated as parting Siamese twins, the more so because the grander scheme of Middle Eastern politics had intruded on the drama. Between 1949 and 1967, during East Jerusalem's brief period of Jordanian rule, the King of Jordan had favoured first the Ethiopians and then, in a move dictated by the urgent need to break his country's isolation in the Arab world, about-turned to oblige the Egyptians. In 1970 the Israelis, ever careful of the balance of power among their neighbours, had suggested to the Ethiopians that they could regain control of the two chapels on the way down from the rooftop to the parvis of the Church of the Holy Sepulchre by replacing a few locks while the Copts were busy with their Easter services. The Copts only regained the right to cut across the Ethiopians' roof terrace in 1993.

This history of sly political manoeuvring as well as the recent close kinship between the two sets of African Christians means that the rooftop dispute remains the most intractable and inflammable of the many issues prohibiting peace among the Christian communities of the Church of the Holy Sepulchre.

~

In 1099 the victorious First Crusaders secured the freedom of the holiest shrine in Christendom from this kind of unseemly wrangling by the simplest and crudest of expedients: eviction of all the eastern Christians.

This had not been Pope Urban II's plan when he launched the First Crusade at Clermont in France in 1095, dazzling and inspiring the crowd of faithful with a vision of Jerusalem, telling them that on

Easter Eve the lamps in the Anastasis were extinguished and then 'relighted by divine command', and enquiring of them, 'Whose heart is so stony, brethren, that it is not touched by so great a miracle?'[vi] The Jerusalem that Pope Urban was planning on liberating from the Muslims, the home of such marvels, was to be the shared prize of a single Christian world, east and west. But his pious dream of unity was long forgotten by the time the brutalized and bedraggled First Crusaders conquered Jerusalem in the summer of 1099. The ousting of all eastern Christians from the Church of the Holy Sepulchre and the replacement of the Greek with a Latin patriarch were suitably thorough accompaniments to the Europeans' wholesale slaughter of some 10,000 Muslims and the incineration of all the Jews in one of the city's synagogues.

The Crusaders had no trouble justifying the conquest of a land so distant from their own. The First Crusade was no ordinary war; it was a pious duty, imagined and promoted as an armed pilgrimage, not a military campaign. Faith in their man-god sat comfortably with their feudal notions about property, hierarchy and justice. Palestine, the land their liege lord Jesus Christ had lived and died in, must be recaptured by them, his most faithful vassals, and restored to him. St Bernard of Clairvaux, the principal propagandist of the Second Crusade, was explicit on this point: 'The earth is shaken because the Lord of Heaven is losing his land, the land in which he appeared to men; the land made glorious by his miracles, holy by his blood.'[vii] Later, a cruder, more mercantile concept was formulated: Palestine belonged to Christendom 'by right of purchase and acquisition'[viii] because Christ had bought it with his blood. Old Bishop Eusebius of Caesarea could not have imagined what impious excesses the literal-mindedness of the *simplichiores** would lead to.

In 1099 it seemed only right and fitting to the First Crusaders that, having left their homes and risked their lives to win back Christ's tomb, they should take sole charge of the Church of the

---

* What the Greek Church Fathers called the simple faithful, those who lacked a higher, metaphorical understanding of the mysteries of Christianity.

Holy Sepulchre. It made sense from a practical point of view too; western Christian churchmen were trained to positions of management and authority, a legacy of the role the Church had been forced to play as the imperial Roman administration collapsed under the strain of invading German tribes during the early Middle Ages. The princes of the infant Crusader states also needed able churchmen to help them administer their new realms, but the quality of clergy prepared to endure the rigours of the almost four-year-long expedition to the east and stay to defend and extend the new colonies was poor. A chronicler described the only prelate of sufficient standing to qualify for the post of Latin patriarch as 'all but technically illiterate'.[ix]

Patriarch Arnulf was a renowned Norman womanizer and a butt of bawdy Crusader songs who had also once tutored William the Conqueror's daughter. He evicted the Orthodox from the Anastasis rebuilt by Constantine IX after al-Hakim's crazed assault on the original building and ordered that the custodians of the relic of the Holy Cross be tortured for refusing to reveal its whereabouts. His intolerance did not end there. Just as they had been under Byzantine Christian rule, Jews were again banned from entering the city. Muslims fared little better. Neither Arnulf nor any Crusader King of Jerusalem guaranteed the safety of the Muslims' holy places as Caliph Omar had the Christians' sites in 638. The Dome of the Rock became a church with a cross on its dome and the Al-Aqsa mosque* would become the headquarters of the new Templar order of knights.†

Arnulf and his successor Daimbert of Pisa, another venal prelate, would take turns on the patriarchal throne for the next few years, each contributing to the impression that top Crusader churchmen were a dangerous liability. Neither of them nor any of their successors was born in the east so none of them understood the

---

* The Crusaders believed the Dome of the Rock mosque was the temple in which Jesus was presented and disputed with the elders at the age of twelve. The Al-Aqsa mosque was thought to be King Solomon's temple and palace.
† The Poor Knights of Christ and of the Temple of Solomon, founded in 1118.

compromises and accommodations that could and must be made with the local Muslims, Jews, Armenians and Byzantine Orthodox Christians if there were ever to be peace and prosperity for all. Especially with the 'heretic' Greeks, they nourished and promoted confrontations that reinforced the schism that had formally split Christ's one true Church in two in 1053.* By the middle of the twelfth century, western Christians no longer regarded Byzantine Christians as their spiritual brothers and natural allies. The familiarity brought about by the Crusades had bred contempt on both sides.

Crusader churchmen also siphoned off much of the new colony's riches. They harvested revenues from sixty churches all over western Christendom and profited by bequests of land in Outremer as well as drawing large incomes from their near monopoly on Jerusalem's bread ovens. Early on in his eastern sojourn the greedy Patriarch Daimbert almost provoked a civil war among the Crusaders and the collapse of the Kingdom of Jerusalem by insisting that, if its first ruler Godfrey de Bouillon died without heirs, the entire city should become the property of the patriarchate and submit to his control. When the childless Godfrey duly died in 1100, the city's French garrison, appalled by the prospect of rule by Daimbert, revolted and invited Godfrey's brother Baldwin, Count of Edessa, to be the Kingdom of Jerusalem's second ruler.

While the Catholic clergy prospered, King Baldwin I and his successors were always perilously short of funds. Simple economic necessity was what eventually forced the monarch to overrule his patriarch's protests and invite disaffected eastern Christians back into Jerusalem to repopulate and supply the almost abandoned city. To all those willing to bring 'grain or vegetables, beans, lentils, or peas through the gates of Jerusalem'ˣ he offered tax breaks. Mercenary considerations seem to have informed Baldwin's attitude to the Holy Fire ceremony too. Crusader Jerusalem would be as economically dependent on the pilgrim trade as it had ever been

* Pope Paul VI and Patriarch Atenagoras of Constantinople lifted the formal anathemas in 1965, but the schism remains, and much of the hostility too especially on the Orthodox side.

under the Byzantines, and there was no more powerful attraction than the Orthodox Christians' annual spectacular.

On Easter Saturday 1101 all the Crusader inhabitants of the city and thousands of Christians from all over Christendom, east and west, gathered in the Church of the Holy Sepulchre to witness the miracle. But to the crowd's great dismay hours passed and no Holy Fire was kindled. When solemn processions around the edicule and incessant prayers for mercy made no difference the ousted Greek clergy seized their chance. Naturally there had been no miracle, they declared, because God favoured only the Orthodox in this matter; no Latin patriarch would ever receive the gift of Holy Fire. Swiftly calculating the potential loss to his coffers, King Baldwin conceded the point. Thereafter the Byzantine Orthodox were readmitted to the great Church of the Holy Sepulchre.

In 1104 a Russian Orthodox abbot named Daniel travelled to Jerusalem to attend the ceremony.[xi] Eager that his beloved homeland and its princes should receive their due dose of grace in the form of Holy Fire, Abbot Daniel asked for an audience with King Baldwin – 'a very kind and humble man and not in the least proud' – and begged leave to hang a lamp in the tomb. Permission granted, Daniel then invested in 'a very large glass lamp', which he filled with oil before going to the church to place it at 'the most pure feet of Our Lord Jesus Christ'. While there he happily observed that the Greek clergy's lamp was in pride of place where Christ's head would have been. Others, belonging to the big Greek monasteries outside the city, were similarly well placed, on a level with Christ's heart. He was gratified to note that those of the 'Franks', the Latins, were hanging at a suitable distance from the tomb.

Early the next morning the church's immediate environs were already thronging with the faithful 'from every land, from Babylon and Egypt and from every corner of the earth'. A terrifying scene, one that would be repeated annually until well into the twentieth century, astonished the old Russian, who observed that 'many are suffocated from the pressure of the vast number of people'. The doors of the edicule were sealed, the Orthodox sang and the Latins began 'mumbling after their own fashion'. Abbot Daniel waited, weeping with worry that the miracle would not happen on account of his sins. It was mid morning when at last 'the holy light shone in the holy tomb and a fearful bright flash' appeared. 'The Holy Light is not like earthly fire for it shines in a different and wonderful way and its flame is red like cinnabar and it shines in a way which is quite indescribable,' he wrote, listing the names of various fellow countrymen, 'Izyaslav, Ivanovich, Gorodislav, Michailovich and two Kashkiches and many others' who could vouch for this fact.

The next morning the Russian abbot was back inside the edicule checking his lamp and noting that although the Catholic lamps had been lit with Holy Fire, the light they cast was not as bright as that of the Orthodox lamps, 'which were burning particularly wonder-fully'. A generous tip to the doorkeeper earned him a special favour: 'seeing my love for the Lord's tomb, [he] pushed back for me the slab which is at the head of the holy tomb of the Lord and broke off a small piece of the blessed rock as a relic and forbade me under oath to say anything of this in Jerusalem'.

Some forty years later the Holy Fire ceremony was continuing to attract pilgrims. A far-faring Icelandic bishop visited the Holy Sepulchre and reported that 'men receive light down from Heaven there on Easter eve'.[xii] By that time however there were murmurs of disbelief among the Crusader settlers, and pressure was mounting to sideline the eastern Christians again. Furthermore, the miracle's dazzlingly demoralizing effect on the Muslim infidel was waning. In 1173 a Muslim gave brief but eloquent expression to his own doubts: 'As for the descent of the fire, I lived long enough in Jerusalem at the time of the Franks to know how it was done.'[xiii]

Jerusalem was sunk in iniquity. By the late twelfth century the city was so far from being the holiest kingdom on earth that the catastrophe of Saladin's reconquest in 1187 was viewed by many in Europe as well-deserved punishment for the creation of a foully degraded society of 'criminals on the run, excommunicated people . . . wicked men, impious, robbers, sacrilegious homicides, liars, adulterers'.[xiv] Second-generation Crusader settlers had 'gone native' in a way that shocked and disgusted newcomers to the king-doms of Outremer. The memoirs of one Arab gleefully recount a tale told him by the keeper of a bathhouse visited by one such Crusader: 'The Franks disapprove of girding a cover around one's waist while in the bath. So this Frank stretched out his arm and pulled off my cover from my waist and threw it away. He looked and saw that I had recently shaved off my pubes . . . "By the truth of my religion, do the same for me!" [he said, and] . . . lay on his back and I shaved it off. Then he passed his hand over the place and, finding it smooth, he said "By the truth of my religion, do the same to madame."'[xv]

An outraged French clergyman described late-Crusader Jerusalem as teeming with 'apostate monks, nuns that are common harlots and women who have left their husbands to live in brothels, or men who have run away from their true wives'.[xvi] He also hated the way some of the Crusader settlers locked up their women so strictly that they could not even go to church to hear 'the wholesome preaching of God's Word',[xvii] although they were permitted to go to the baths three times a week. He lambasted the kingdom's clergy for a whole catalogue of faults, adding for special emphasis, 'and this when God said to St Peter: "Feed my sheep," and we never found him saying "Fleece my sheep."'[xviii] By the second half of the twelfth century the city's notoriety was being blamed for significantly delaying the annual miracle of the Holy Fire.

The famously venal Latin patriarch during the few years prior to Saladin's conquest kept a mistress who was the wife of a draper from Nablus but known to all as 'madame la patriarchesse'. On her Patriarch Heraclius lavished such fine silks and jewels that, according to one chronicler, she was frequently mistaken for a noblewoman. Heraclius himself maintained such an opulent establishment that, during a begging expedition to England, he shocked at least one Englishman with how grotesquely corrupt and wealthy the Latin Patriarchate of Jerusalem had become in the less than a hundred years of its existence: 'I saw the Patriarch of the Jerusalemites when he came . . . with such a pomp of golden and silver equipment that it was sickening to hear his request because of the constant jangle . . . If we have to judge the luxuries of that land [the Kingdom of Jerusalem] according to what we saw, we can safely presume that there is a great deal which is odious to God.'[xix]

Viewed against this background of luxury and moral degradation, Saladin's clemency towards the city's conquered Christians in 1187 is impressive. Instead of unleashing an avenging slaughter on the Crusaders he allowed them, garrison included, to ransom themselves. A few knights of St John were permitted to remain in the city to care for the sick in their hospital and, in spite of having paid his soldiers to defend the city with silver stripped from the edicule of Christ's tomb, Patriarch Heraclius was permitted to leave with wagonloads of riches. When one of Saladin's aides protested at such leniency the great commander sagely replied, '"Let them be, otherwise they'll accuse us of lacking a conscience. It will force them to sing the praises of the mercifulness of our religion."'[xx] The Byzan-tines abhorred the Crusaders' habit of sending their clergy into battle, but the great sultan could not help feeling some regard for his Crusader foe and had exhorted his men into battle with the words, 'Look at the Franks! Behold with what obstinacy they fight for their religion, while we the Muslims show no enthusiasm for waging jihad.'[xxi]

Saladin had his soldiers use rose water to swill out the Dome of the Rock mosque, which the Crusaders had turned into a church called the Temple of the Lord. Its white marble altar and a lamp the Crusaders had believed to be filled with Christ's blood were torn out and the great gold cross removed from the roof. For two days the latter was beaten with clubs and dragged through the streets to joyous cries of '*Allahu akhbar!*' But credit was given the western Christians where credit was certainly due. One Muslim *qadi* wrote admiringly of the Jerusalem Saladin had reconquered: 'Islam received back a place which it had left almost uninhabited, but which the care of the unbelievers had transformed into a paradise garden . . . those accursed ones defended with the lance and sword this city which they had rebuilt with columns and slabs of marble, where they had founded churches and the palaces of the Templars and the Hospitallers . . . One sees on every side columns decorated with leaves, which makes them look like living trees'.[xxii]

The Church of the Holy Sepulchre also lost its rooftop cross and was locked for three whole days. Only once all its bells had been removed and a pilgrims' poll tax agreed was it reopened by Saladin and the Orthodox fully reinstated thanks to some generous gifts from the Byzantine emperor. In the archives of the Greek patriarchate today is Saladin's firman stipulating that 'The Patriarch of the Greeks should be the head of all the Nazarene [Christian] nations which come to Jerusalem . . . The nation which should dominate in the Church of the Resurrection [the Holy Sepulchre] should be the one who enters into the tomb of Jesus to take the Holy Fire'.[xxiii] Ethiopians were exempted from paying the pilgrims' tax and graciously granted two chapels in the Church of the Holy Sepulchre.

Jews were readmitted to the city; in the happy words of one medieval Jewish historian, 'God stirred the rabbis of France and the rabbis of Angleterre to go to Jerusalem; and they were more than three hundred.'[xxiv] Saladin was persuaded to allow a few western Christian pilgrims to visit the city in 1192 but Latin clergy remained strictly excluded from the Church of the Holy Sepulchre.

~

The sun is now low in the sky and most of the roof terrace in shade; I have spent all day up here with Solomon. Stumbling back down the dark narrow staircase and out into the courtyard, I find Artin, the tiny Armenian guide.

'So, you came back to us. You heard about the battle of the chair up there?' he asks, without interest because his roving gaze has locked onto the sexily swaying backside of a young woman in a diaphanous summer dress. 'Russian tourist!' he murmurs admiringly and then frowns as a younger guide wins her custom. Artin is eager to display his skill at guessing the nationality of every pilgrim and tourist but there are pitifully few of them, fewer even than there were at Easter.

The souvenir shops along Christian Quarter Road are almost all shut. With the intifada still raging and the heat of high summer fast approaching, trade is dead. From the only open stall I pass a desperate young man calls out, 'Come in! Everything is free today!' Through the door of the strip-lit Internet cafe across the way I see bored youths slumped in front of screens, mouse in one hand, cigarette in the other. Resisting the lure of its air-conditioned chill I turn right at the end of the street. If I buy Rahme some cigarettes she may spare me a lecture on the perils of spending complete days in the company of Africans. I pass a photographic shop displaying an enlarged black and white print of Germany's Kaiser Wilhelm II being hailed by cheering crowds in Jerusalem in 1898. Inside sits the proprietor, drinking tea with a friend.

'Come in! I've seen you walking up and down this street many times,' he calls out to me. 'You're staying in Arkhangelos?'

'That's right,' I say, admiring his powers of detection while I study another photograph, of an Indian soldier of the British Mandate, the most recent spell of Christian rule over the Holy Land.* The soldier is wearing turban and puttees, and frisking the flowing robes of a Greek Orthodox priest. A small Jewish boy in a skullcap watches with interest.

'My father took that one in 1937,' says the proprietor, fetching me a chair, laying out a selection of prints for me to inspect and telling a boy to bring me tea. 'So what brings you here at this terrible time?'

I describe my business and the scene I have just witnessed on the rooftop. He looks unsurprised and shrugs as if to say what does any of that matter when our tourist trade has dried up, when our lives are paralysed, when Israeli tanks are roaring into West Bank towns and helicopter gunships bombing Gaza? But his friend, a man with a large belly and handsome moustaches, is interested. This pillar of the local Christian community tells me that he once helped the Ethiopians. 'I telephoned the electricity company,' he says, 'to per-

* Britain ruled Palestine from 1917 until 1948.

52

suade them to connect the electricity for them in the middle of the night, while the Egyptians were sleeping. Someone had to help those poor people. The other communities of Christians in that church are too selfish . . .'

I buy Rahme's cigarettes next door to the photographer's, in the little supermarket she likes me to patronize because it belongs to a fellow Orthodox. Tacked to the window by the till are two colour photos I have not noticed on previous visits. One shows the shopkeeper with a smiling Patriarch Irineos. In the second he is shaking hands with a grinning Yasser Arafat.

Trudging up the alley in the dark gold evening sunlight, past the skinny cats sniffing around the rubbish bags, past the little mosque and the Franciscans' great orphanage for girls, I feel happy to be back in Jerusalem, quite at home. Two young lads sitting puffing on a narghile in the cool gloom just inside Arkhangelos' low doorway smile and nod as if they recognize me.

Rahme is too happy inspecting the sumptuous gifts that her eldest nephew George has just bought for his fiancée to berate me for being gone all day. Displayed on her sofa in the living room are a silk and taffeta evening dress and a gold box containing a full set of gold jewellery – to be worn by the bride-to-be at the engagement party. A king's ransom has been spent. Rahme is bright-eyed and flushed with excitement. The groom-to-be looks dazed.

George's job at the electricity company is respectable and steady but far from lucrative. The young couple need help with finding a home of their own. Fortunately, Nasra has almost managed to persuade her friend at the patriarchate that the best way to prevent what little remains of Jerusalem's Orthodox flock from emigrating is to make sure that decent young Orthodox couples like her nephew and his bride have access to generously subsidized housing from the patriarchate's portfolio of prime real estate.*

George departs with his armful of treasure and Rahme settles

---

* The Greek Orthodox patriarchate owns approximately 20 per cent of the Old City. The land the Knesset is built on in West Jerusalem is leased to Israel by the patriarchate.

down on her sofa to knit. But no sooner have I retired to my cell to read than the screams of multiple ambulance sirens drown out the neighbours' arguments, the Arab Catholic Scouts band rehearsal and the bells of San Salvatore, and I am back in the sitting room alerting Rahme to the likelihood of another suicide bomb. 'No, no – there was that big one on a bus yesterday morning. Nothing today, *Hamdulillah!* Thanks be to God,' she says, but she puts down her knitting to aim the zapper at the television, just in case.

A newsflash. A Palestinian suicide bomber has blown up a bus at a busy junction on French Hill, only two miles north of here. In silence we watch the live coverage of flashing lights, neon-orange-clad emergency workers, white-faced bystanders and traffic chaos. A hospital entrance begins ingesting laden stretchers. The death count steadily mounts. Two dead and thirty-five injured, then six dead and forty injured, then seven dead and eight more hopeless cases. The bomber is too mutilated to be identified as man or woman. The bomb was packed with metal screws.

'I think this is the end of the world,' says Rahme.

Two days, two bus bombs. I retreat to my cell again and the consoling tale of the only Crusade that achieved its goal of recapturing Jerusalem without bloodshed.

~

Only seven years after the shameful fiasco of Cardinal Pelagius' venture another mighty expedition, the Sixth Crusade, set sail for the Middle East. At last the great Holy Roman Emperor, Frederick II, was fulfilling his thirteen-year-old pledge.

In 1228 the mood of western Christendom should have been buoyant, joyful. If anyone could win back Christ's tomb for Christendom, Frederick, '*Stupor Mundi*', could. The 'Wonder of the World' was offering free passage and all expenses paid to anyone who joined his pious enterprise. But there was no joy because Frederick was locked in deadly dispute with Pope Gregory IX and all Catholic Europe was in turmoil. The long struggle between the

Holy Roman Empire and the papacy over whether emperor or pope reigned supreme over western Christendom had reached one of its frequent climaxes.

Papal propaganda painted Frederick as black as the Devil. Not only had he delayed his departure on this Crusade for over a decade, he was also resisting the pope's attempts to wrest control of southern Italy away from him. Furthermore, in his Kingdom of Sicily, where both Catholic and Orthodox Christians and Muslims had been coexisting happily for the past century or so, Frederick was dangerously prey to Muslim influence.* His elite bodyguard was Muslim and so were many of his chief courtiers. He kept a harem of concubines and bathed every day. Worse still, he was in close touch with one of the Sultan of Egypt's confidants, and splendid gifts – apes, camels, a pair of leopards, a giraffe and an elephant – had travelled from Cairo to Palermo. Most heinous of all in the pope's eyes, by marrying the daughter of the exiled King of Jerusalem and fathering a child by her, he had a claim to the Crusader throne of Jerusalem. Frederick, the papal propaganda said, was the Antichrist, the Beast of the Book of Revelations, a sodomite who had once emptied his bladder on an altar, a shameless infidel who had opined that Moses, Jesus Christ and Mohammad were the world's three greatest impostors and deceivers† and a faithless rationalist who thought that anyone who believed that Christ was born of a virgin must be an idiot since 'no one can be born whose conception was not preceded by coitus between a man and a woman'.[xxv]

One fact was clear to Pope Gregory: Frederick had not turned Crusader for love of the papacy or of Christendom. When ill health forced the great emperor to delay his departure for the east once again, Gregory seized the opportunity to excommunicate him.

Nevertheless, the late 1220s were a propitious time to be seeking to recapture Jerusalem for Christendom. Disunity between the

* Frederick was King of Sicily as well as Holy Roman Emperor of the German lands and much of mainland Europe. He inherited Sicily because his grandfather was the Norman King of Sicily, Roger II.

† In fact, the saying has been traced back to the Islamic world in the tenth century.

temporal and spiritual branches of western Christendom was an embarrassing disadvantage, but still greater disunity among the multiple rulers of the Islamic world augured well for the Holy Roman Emperor's Crusade. While Arab princes were more murderously intent on fighting each other than on battling western Christians, Frederick had high hopes of striking a deal with Saladin's nephew, Sultan al-Kamil. Surely two such famously learned men as they could avoid the sort of barbarous bloodletting that had characterized previous Crusades by arriving at a civilized compromise. Some superior falcons and a magnificent white charger with a jewelled saddle were dispatched to Cairo, to propitiate the sultan who was wont to contemplate philosophical questions while 'fifty scholars reclined on divans round his throne'.[xxvi]

Unfortunately for Frederick the situation, always fluid, had altered by the time he reached the Holy Land and set up his camp at Acre, the last Crusader stronghold in the Levant. The sultan was no longer interested in a deal or, as one Arab chronicler put it, 'al-Kamil had no further need of the emperor'.[xxvii] Frederick received some more splendid gifts – jewels, ten thoroughbred camels, an elephant, Arab mares, bears and monkeys – but no promise of Jerusalem. He humbled himself to plead with the sultan: 'I am your friend. You must be aware that I am supreme among all the princes of the west. It is you who caused me to come here. The kings and the pope know of my expedition. If I return without having obtained something, I shall lose all respect in their eyes. After all, is not the city of Jerusalem the place of the birth of the Christian religion? Give it back to me in the condition in which it is so that upon my return home I may hold up my head among kings.'[xxviii]

Frederick was in a frustrating bind. The pope's armies were threatening his lands in southern Italy. He needed to do his duty in the Holy Land and hurry home again, but he now faced another problem. The Templars and Hospitallers were so jealous of the favour he was showing the German Teutonic order they were refusing to fight for him on the grounds that he had been excommunicated. After solving this problem by declaring that all military commands would be issued in the name of God or Christendom rather than in his own, Frederick applied pressure to Sultan al-Kamil by marching his Crusaders south as far as Jaffa. But disaster struck again: the Crusaders' supply ships all foundered in a storm.

It was the sultan's right-hand man and Frederick's personal friend who eventually rescued the entire enterprise from ignominious failure by suggesting that the Emperor of the West humble himself yet again to send another embassy to the sultan. The time was right and Frederick's luck turned. In February 1229, an equitable and astonishingly gentlemanly truce was arranged. Jerusalem, Bethlehem and Nazareth would be returned to Crusader rule, but not much of their hinterland. There must be no defensive rebuilding of Jerusalem's ruined walls, but the Crusaders would get a narrow corridor to the sea, a couple of their old castles and some coastal towns. Muslims would retain control of their holy places on Jerusalem's old Jewish Temple Mount, their Haram al-Sharif.

Frederick took formal possession of Jerusalem the following month. Entering the Church of the Holy Sepulchre in his weighty royal robes and seating himself high on a throne, he tactfully dignified himself with the crown of the Holy Roman Empire rather than that of Jerusalem. His close confidant, the Grand Master of the Order of Teutonic Knights, then delivered a pious and conciliatory speech on his behalf. Again, in order not to rile the pope, no mass of thanksgiving was said. The Teutonic Knights bowed deeply to kiss the hem of their emperor's cloak.

His duty done by the tomb of Our Lord, Frederick requested – just as Caliph Omar had done of the Byzantine Christians 600 years earlier – a tour of his opponents' holy places. With exemplary politeness he asked the *qadi* who accompanied him why the Muslims' call to prayer had been silenced. When the *qadi* explained that it was in his honour, Frederick protested. '"You have done wrong. Why do you deprive yourself because of me of your normal obligation, of your law, of your religion?"'[xxix] He also ticked off a priest for entering a mosque with a Bible in his hand, saying, '"It was through the grace of the sultan that he has restored to us our churches – let us not abuse it."'ˣˣˣ His easy familiarity with Islam and religious tolerance, bred in him by a boyhood spent among the Arabs of Sicily and then nurtured by his contacts with the sultan's court, seems to have made him a regretful sort of conqueror. When he asked why the windows of the mosques were all covered with grilles and was told that they were there to keep sparrows out, he ruefully joked, "'Yet Allah has brought the swine amongst you after all,'" swine being the Muslims' rudest term of abuse for Christians.ˣˣˣⁱ

After a break of almost half a century, the blessed tomb of Jesus Christ, his birthplace in Bethlehem and home town of Nazareth were back in Christian hands, by courtesy rather than carnage. The church bells should have rung out all over Europe at the gladsome tidings. Pope Gregory might have thanked Frederick for his services to Christ, to himself and to Christendom. But instead, there was an outcry. What kind of a Crusade cheated its participants of their rightful share of penitential suffering, let alone booty? How could Frederick have lowered himself to treat with the wicked infidel in such a subtle, slow and devious fashion? The holy places had been regained but without a wall or hinterland Jerusalem, Bethlehem and Nazareth could not be defended. Furthermore, troops of Muslim pilgrims to the Haram al-Sharif and muezzins wailing from minarets would spoil the Christian character of Jerusalem.

The Templars were so angry at not being able to reclaim their headquarters on the Temple Mount and all their castles that they invited the sultan to have Frederick assassinated. He refused and honourably alerted Frederick to the danger. The furious Latin patriarch, a loyal servant of the pope, trumpeted his own opposition to the truce by instructing pilgrims to boycott the Church of the Holy Sepulchre. No masses were to be said there, so no indulgences could be gained as the culmination of long, arduous pilgrimages. All in all, *Stupor Mundi* made so many enemies in his new kingdom that the butchers of Acre would pelt him with offal when he took ship for home.

The one European sovereign Frederick could rely on to applaud his remarkable achievement was Henry III of England, whose clergy had been outraged at the Pope's demand that they finance his wars against Frederick in southern Italy. In a letter to Henry, Frederick pointed out the simple boast-worthy fact that 'in these few days, by a miracle, rather than by valour, that undertaking has been achieved which for a long time numerous princes and various rulers of the world have not been able to accomplish by force'.[xxxii] The truce was still holding in 1238 when the intemperate Pope Gregory IX spoiled a lucrative business and a thrilling custom by banning western Christian involvement in the Holy Fire ceremony. Frederick the rationalist might have applauded this move, but there is no record of his reaction.

Only five years after Frederick's truce expired, in 1244, Jerusalem was lost to western Christendom again. The Orthodox clergy returned to the Church of the Holy Sepulchre with all the rights granted them by Caliph Omar in the seventh century restored. Although the Crusading movement did not finally exhaust itself until the end of the sixteenth century, the Crusaders' single experi-ment with tolerant compromise was over and Jerusalem denied to them for ever.

When the Wonder of the World died in 1250 Rome rejoiced but many Germans felt so bereft they comforted themselves with the thought that Frederick must be merely sleeping awhile in the fiery bowels of Sicily's Mount Etna. Even a hundred years after his death there were plenty who insisted that he was on his way to recapture the Holy Sepulchre for western Christendom again, equipped with an asbestos robe, a magic ring and a rejuvenating drink given him by none other than Prester John.

~

Solomon must have sensed my disappointment at his ignorance of Prester John. Instead he is telling me everything he knows about the Queen of Sheba.

We have retreated out of the searing heat into the cool gloom of a hut whose flaking green walls are covered with cheap poster reproductions of icons. We are sitting side by side on an untidily made bed, beside a fridge and a table strewn with medicine bottles and toilet rolls, while one radio burbles an Amharic news bulletin and another drones a church chant. Towards the end of the thirteenth century, some forty years after Emperor Frederick's death, a friar admiringly described the Ethiopians in Jerusalem as 'the most pious' among all the Christians on account of their rigorous fasting and forbearance from spitting on the days they took holy communion.[xxxiii] Seven hundred years later they enjoy a similarly enviable reputation.

One of Solomon's brothers, the occupant of this hut, serves me a plastic bottle of lemon squash from the fridge and two hard-boiled eggs floating in a bowl of hot and spicy tomato sauce. A greyish substance as soft and spongy as fungus is Ethiopian bread, which Solomon orders me to dunk in the fiery liquid. While I eat he reminds me that there were Ethiopians living in Jerusalem before the Church of the Holy Sepulchre was even built, when Jerusalem was ruled by the Jews. The Ethiopians, he explains, worshipped the Jewish God too until they were converted to Christianity in the fourth century, and to this day they retain many Jewish customs. Ethiopian boy babies are circumcised after eight days, and Saturday as well as Sunday is the Sabbath, he informs me. His own name, Solomon, is Jewish of course, as is his surname.

'Maybe you know the story about how our great and beautiful Queen of Sheba* came to Jerusalem to visit the great Jewish King Solomon and they did sex?'

'No?'

'Oh, a very important story! The Queen of Sheba came here and ate a dinner with King Solomon. After dinner he asked her to lie down and sleep in the same room with him – on a different bed, of course! And she told him not to do any sex with her when she was sleeping. He said, "OK, no sex, but you too must not steal anything

---

* The Ethiopians equate Sheba with the lands comprising modern Ethiopia, but modern Yemenis also claim the Queen of Sheba as their ancient ruler.

from me in the night." She said, "OK." But the food they ate was very hot and spicy and in the middle of the night she was thirsty, oh very thirsty, so she drank from a water jar near the bed. Of course, King Solomon was waiting for this and he was very happy! He said, "You take my water from me! Now we must do sex." They made a baby.' Suddenly bashful, Solomon removes his purple hat and mops his brow with a sleeve of his cotton robe. 'This baby was our first great Emperor Menelik. Now, you see, Jews say that when the Queen of Sheba came to Jerusalem she said to King Solomon, "Give me what I want," and that was a baby. But we Ethiopians know that she did not mean a baby. She meant some land for some of her people to live here in the holy city.'

In the Ethiopian version of the story, Solomon's royal namesake had given the Queen of Sheba a plot of wasteland, a rubbish tip which happened to be the very spot where Christ's cross would be thrown many centuries later, before being dug up by the Byzantine Empress Helena 300 years after that.

'Now you can see how the Ethiopians were in this place even before Christ was born. St Helena's Chapel is below us of course so that is why we must stay here and never let the Egyptians have it. Come with me now,' he said. 'We must sit outside because I am waiting for a visit from the Israeli minister in charge of Christian affairs and a deputy foreign minister. They will resolve our problem with the Copts.'

Back on the shady steps, I ask him to tell me how a first meeting with the ministers went yesterday. Not smoothly, he admits. The two delegations – one of Copts, the other of Ethiopians, including Solomon and two bishops – made their way to the Department of Religious Affairs and were ushered into separate waiting rooms. The Copts' room, he tells me, was comfortably air-conditioned, while the Ethiopians' was small and horribly overheated by a blazing radiator. After the Copts had spent forty-five minutes with the minister pleading their case it had been the turn of the Ethiopians to air their grievances.

'But the minister was not serious! He looked around smiling and then he asked me why I was wearing a purple hat! Oh, not serious! But after that our bishop was not very wise. He talked for a long, long time about our history here in Jerusalem. At the end – we stayed there for three hours – the minister asked, "If I, an Israeli, bring a chair and sit down in your courtyard, will you let me stay?"'

I am marvelling that any member of the Israeli government is free to worry about a Copt and a chair for three hours and more, but Solomon is clearly deeply offended by what he deems the minister's facetious attitude and admits that he vented his anger by issuing an impolitic string of threats. 'I told the minister that the conflict with the Egyptians goes back almost two hundred years. I said that there is no more apartheid in South Africa but it still exists here in Jerusalem. I told him he should be careful not to upset the family of black peoples. I told him I would go to Prime Minister Sharon to discuss our problems. I said we would take the problem to the international court of human rights! I asked him, "Do you know the meaning of discrimination?" He said to me – then he was angry, oh very angry – he said, "Are you trying to tell a Jew about discrimination?"'

We are interrupted by the arrival in the courtyard of three bespectacled middle-aged men wearing *kippot*.* I busy myself with my notebook while straining hard to overhear their talk. 'How come that woman can sit here in your courtyard and the Copt can't?' asks one of them. 'Who is she anyway? The Queen of Sheba?' When Solomon unwisely describes me as a 'special friend of Ethiopia' the deputy foreign minister asks me my name and nationality. Then they all move out of earshot to continue their conference.

Three more Ethiopian monks arrive to join the discussion. After a few minutes the Israelis exit, stage left, to visit the Copts in their monastery, but they have promised to come back. Solomon returns to my side. He seems suddenly blithely confident that his people will triumph in the dispute, convinced that the Israelis are acknowledging the justice of the Ethiopians' case against the Copts. 'I love the

* Skullcaps.

Jewish people with all my heart! Oh so much! They are the people of the Old Testament. The Arabs have so many different countries to live in but the Jews have only one!'

I leave the rooftop and hurry home to Arkhangelos, where I find Rahme angry and upset by two new developments. First, she has just listened to President Bush announce his long-awaited peace initiative on the radio and is bitterly disappointed.

'What did that man say? He said nothing, nothing! He understands nothing! He says we must change Arafat if we Palestinians want our state, but the Jews can keep Sharon! What peace is that? No peace, no *peace*, until we have no Arafat and no Sharon!'

Second, Nasra had failed to screw the lid of a jam jar on properly and it tumbled out of a cupboard when Rahme opened it, tipping sticky strawberries down her nightdress.

~

'Idiot!' hisses Nasra with a gleeful grin. 'You've just missed another fight.'

We are standing in a small crowd of Orthodox Christians gathered around the edicule in the Church of the Holy Sepulchre to celebrate the ordination of an Orthodox priest on this great feast of Pentecost.

I have arrived halfway through the four-hour service the start of which happened to overlap with the Copts' service in their chapel at the rear of the edicule. According to Nasra, there had initially only been some angry shushing but a full-blown fracas had erupted when, while processing around the shrine, an alert Greek monk had spotted the scruffy doormat on the threshold of the Copts' chapel protruding some two inches into the ambulatory. The very same infringement of the intricate rules governing every object and action in the Church of the Holy Sepulchre had led to violence as recently as Palm Sunday. Conscious that another skirmish coming so soon after the Holy Fire fracas would reflect badly on him, Patriarch Irineos has reined in his cohorts on this occasion. Seizing the moral high ground, he has just delivered a little sermon about the need for brotherly love in this place at this time of crisis, and embraced the Coptic bishop.

The interminable service is beginning to take its toll on the faithful. Stomachs are rumbling and tempers fraying. An elderly nun on the other side of Nasra raises her voice high in pious song only to be reprimanded by another nun with an angry 'Quiet! Did we come here to listen to your cretinous croaking?' Unable to follow the liturgical chanting and my mind full of Crusaders, I wander away from the service.

Crusader Jerusalem survives best in this Church of the Holy Sepulchre, which the French historian Perry Benoist-Mechin has described as a 'western building departed for the east'. From the look of 'its square Romanesque tower,' he writes, 'one might have guessed it a parish church of any French village, built by a humble Norman or Ardennes architect. All that marked it out was a large cupola which one couldn't have seen in France because it had been copied from the Dome of the Rock.'[xxxiv] That same square Romanesque tower, erected by the Crusaders after destroying an arch of the church that replaced the one al-Hakim had vandalized, is wrapped in scaffolding today.

I make a wide detour around the back of the Pentecost service to inspect the lifelike stone leaves in the capitals of the marble columns, the same ones the Saracen chronicler had admired so much. It was King Baldwin I's half-Armenian granddaughter, the pious and energetic Queen Melisende, who initiated the expansion and redecoration of the church in the mid-twelfth century and worked hard to sweeten the soured relations between the Crusaders and the Oriental Orthodox community she belonged to. Melisende also established a scriptorium in the church, staffed by monks so artful they produced the incomparable Melisende Psalter, which is now in the British Museum.

High in the gallery above the main entrance, in Armenian territory, I discover a length of fancy metal grille-work dating back to Crusader times. It was first installed in the Dome of the Rock during its period as a church to discourage Latin monks from chiselling off fragments of the rock as relics for pilgrims. And there it had remained until the 1960s when it disappeared, apparently without trace, before surfacing once again amid the junk of a blacksmiths' shop. An Armenian who instantly recognized its provenance and value acquired it and allowed the three great powers of the Church of the Holy Sepulchre – the Greeks, the Latins and the Armenians – to divide the treasure between them. Each community fixed a portion of the grille to one of its possessions in the church. But then the Muslim *Waqf** demanded its return to its original home in the Dome of the Rock. Only the Armenians succeeded in retaining their portion of it.

Otherwise, the only trace of the Crusader era I can find up on Calvary is a ceiling mosaic of Jesus' face. For all their distrust of Byzantine Christians the Crusaders had to applaud their skill at what they called 'Greek work' and covered the entire church interior with mosaics. The styles of East and West have blended beautifully; the glittering gold tesserae of this Christ's Byzantine halo frame the face of a Crusader Christ – low of brow, dark of eye and stubborn of chin.

Outside, I cross the dazzling white expanse of the parvis and exit in the direction of the oldest section of the souk. I am making for the triple line of interconnecting covered alleys which the bountiful Queen Melisende had built – the herb market, the textile market and the market where medieval pilgrims were able to shop for food in breaks from their gruelling tours of the holy places. Pandering to every palate, Western and Eastern, this market apparently smelt atrociously bad. It still reeks of the offal sold here today. But there is another, more tangible, Crusader legacy here. Etched into the stone lintels of some of the shops are letters – TD or ANNA. The former stands for *Templum Domini*, which means they were owned by the Latin clergy in charge of the converted Dome of the Rock mosque, the Temple of the Lord. ANNA signals former properties of the

---

* Muslim charitable body overseeing the management of religious property.

wonderfully preserved Crusader church of St Anne, yet another of Queen Melisende's foundations, in what is now the Muslim eastern quarter of the old city.

South of the Muslim Quarter and across the vast open space in front of the Wailing Wall, I enter the Jewish Quarter, pristine and landscaped and less than forty years old. There are some archaeological proofs that Jews inhabited this city millennia before either Christ or Mohammad was born and the one Crusader Church of Sancta Maria, but little else to show for the intervening period. I find a more vivid trace of what I am seeking for on a handwritten notice untidily tacked to the window of a bookshop: SPACE FOR RENT IN A 900-YEAR-OLD CRUSADER BUILDING.

~

The frown lines above Solomon's nose hint at anxious eyes behind his fashionable shades. For the first time in our acquaintance he is wearing a dusty black cotton hat instead of his purple velvet one. The impression of desolation seems complete when I notice that under his grubby white robe a strap of his vest has slipped down his arm.

The war with the Egyptians is not over. The monk is still parking his chair under the eucalyptus tree and the Israeli authorities are still shuttling between the two communities. A minister called earlier to say, 'The Copt's not there this morning, is he?' But he was. Solomon tells me that he and his brothers feel discouraged and confused. 'Perhaps you have to be patient,' I say lamely. 'Perhaps everything will be solved by the time I come back in September . . .'

'If you are a monk and you spend your life praying like we do, you must be very patient. But it is hard, oh very hard! Jesus Christ said we should give everything away and follow him but this is a holy place for us. We cannot give it away!' He tells me he has been plunged into doubt and sadness since yesterday when an Anglican priest he spoke to seemed irritated by his attempts to lobby support for the war against the Copts.

'Maybe he didn't understand your feelings for this place,' I say, more concerned with alleviating Solomon's suffering than with the rights and wrongs of the matter. 'After all, the Anglican Church only arrived in Jerusalem in the nineteenth century, far too late to get a place here in the church. How can any Anglican know how you feel?'

'Oh! You are right!' says Solomon, visibly cheered.

~

Weeks later, back in London, I recall that last meeting with Solomon and my clumsy attempt at comfort. A front-page news story in the *Daily Telegraph* reads:

MONKS FIGHT ON THE ROOF OF HOLIEST PLACE
Eleven monks were treated in hospital after a fight broke out for control of the roof of the Church of the Holy Sepulchre in Jerusalem, the traditional site of Jesus's crucifixion, burial and resurrection. The fracas involved monks from the Ethiopian Orthodox Church and the Coptic Church of Egypt, who have been vying for control of the rooftop for centuries . . .[xxxv]

A quick call to Nasra reassures me that Solomon is not among the injured.

AUTUMN 2002

'From their number, wealth and influence, they are able to effect almost any object they please and defeat anyone that falls under their displeasure'

– An early nineteenth-century English clergyman, describing Jerusalem's Christian establishments

After three months away I see the façade of the Church of the Holy Sepulchre afresh, in the shadowy light of an autumn early evening.

Its twin Crusader lintels are a pair of eyebrows raised in polite distaste and its twin entrances eyes, one of them open in a black stare, the other blind. It was Saladin who decreed the bricking up of the second door and the appointment of Muslim doorkeepers to supervise traffic in and out of the holy place. The keys of the church have been in the hands of two Muslim families since the thirteenth century.

Mamluk Egyptians finally succeeded in expelling the last Crusaders from their stronghold of Acre in 1291.* But they, and the Ottoman Turks who succeeded them as rulers of the Holy Land in the early sixteenth century, were faithful to the law of their Prophet and emulated the clemency shown by Caliph Omar and Saladin. Both these Muslim empires safeguarded the Christian holy places in Palestine and the Christians' freedom to worship at them. Christians, like Jews, were second-class citizens, forbidden to ride horses or bear arms, subject to a special poll tax and a distinguishing dress code, but as long as they forbore from building or extending churches and synagogues and from advertising their faith with

* The Mamluks were originally non-Muslim slaves from the Caucasus region around the Black Sea and Central Asia converted to Islam as youths. Raised as soldiers, they were a military elite and ruled Egypt and much of the Middle East for long periods between 867 and 1517. They controlled the Holy Land continuously from 1290 to 1517.

71

showy processions or bell-ringing, their status was assured and safe. With their affairs – legal and educational as well as religious – regulated by their own religious leaders, Christians even enjoyed a degree of autonomy.*

But through the next five centuries of Muslim rule in Jerusalem the Christian custodians of the Holy Sepulchre would dismally fail to regulate their affairs within the church. Brute force, base trickery and crude commerce became the accepted means of attaining and maintaining their positions around the shrine. From time to time regional politics exacerbated the disorder. Alarming reports of Prester John's magical ability to reduce the Mamluks' Egyptian heartland to a desert by reversing the course of the Nile secured the Ethiopians a plethora of possessions in the Church of the Holy Sepulchre, and their crucial role in the production of Holy Fire dates back to the Mamluk period. As late as the mid-seventeenth century a French priest who witnessed wild scenes of childless women applying Holy Fire 'to their shameful parts' also observed an Ethiopian priest 'expressly sent by Prester John' entering the edicule to create the Holy Fire 'with a gun which he has secretly brought in for the purpose'.¹ It was 1668, and the Ottoman Turks had been ruling Jerusalem for over a century, before the impoverished Ethiopians retreated to the roof.

Just as I am about to enter the church an anxiously smiling woman intercepts me, asking directions to San Salvatore. Our status as outsiders there in an Old City empty of pilgrims and tourists is a natural spur to further conversation. An eminent archaeologist from the former Soviet republic, now independent state, of Georgia, Dr Tamila Mglaloblishvili has forty years passionate study of her people's historical links with the Holy Land behind her. She informs me that although her devoutly Orthodox Christian ancestors from the rich lands between the Caucasus mountains and the Black Sea had benefited more even than the Ethiopians by Mamluk rule in Jerusalem, they had fared far worse in the long run.

* Each semi-autonomous religious minority was known as a *millet*.

'We Georgians had so much here, so much!' she begins. 'Everything started in the fourth century for us, when the Emperor Constantine gave our king some land to build a monastery. After that, all our medieval kings loved to build churches and monasteries in the city and to come on pilgrimage. The Mamluk period was wonderful for us! At that time we Georgians were free to enter the city without paying tax, and to bear weapons and wave flags, and our noblewomen were famous for carrying weapons like men. We had plenty of possessions in there,' she says indicating the dark church interior, 'St Helena's chapel, the Chapel of Our Lady by the edicule, the one under Calvary where the Crusader kings were buried, and the Stone of Unction too. In the fourteenth century, we even held the keys to the edicule! We know that because a German pilgrim mentioned that Georgian monks refused to take bribes from people who wanted to steal parts of the tomb.'

Tamila beams with recollected pride, but only momentarily.

'Unfortunately, when the Mamluks became weaker so did we. We have the testimony of an Italian monk who says that Georgians were living in such misery before the Ottoman conquest at the beginning of the sixteenth century that they had to sell the Stone of Unction to the Catholics. There were only five of us left here at the end of the sixteenth century. Georgian pilgrims still came after that – we are a very, very Christian people – but they forgot all about our greatness here. Have you heard of our writer Timothy Gabashvili? No? He was here in around 1750 and he was so upset and he wrote, "Nobody knows what Jerusalem is for Georgians and I myself was unaware of it. Alas! How ignorant our countrymen are!"'[ii]

Her eyes, magnified behind thick-lensed spectacles, have turned misty, but she shrugs and smiles. 'Isn't this the way of the world – ups and downs? But come with me now if you have time. Not everything we had here is lost for ever. There is something I would like to show you.'

Hurrying me out of the courtyard, along the covered market and left into Greek Orthodox Patriarchate Road, she leads me through the great wooden door of the patriarchate, straight up the stairs to

Bishop Theophanis' roof terrace and across the rose garden to the back wall of the Church of St Nicholas – another ancient Georgian foundation, she informs me – where a muscular young man wearing a white T-shirt and safety goggles is busy chiselling an inscription. The letters, as decoratively curly and utterly indecipherable as runes to me, are in Church Georgian but Tamila is already explaining,

'Now this is a real treasure. It's about a Georgian queen of ours called Elena who arrived here on a pilgrimage in the seventeenth century and became a nun called Elizabeth. She is asking St Nicholas to help her . . .'

Bewildered, I cannot imagine why this young man should be chiselling a brand new inscription in this place.

Had the battle for land and memory in Jerusalem really reached so frenzied a pitch? Were Christian archaeologists and patriotic historians now brazenly faking history to suit their national needs? Solomon had regaled me with a peculiar Queen of Sheba legend to substantiate his community's claim to the roof of the Church of the Holy Sepulchre. Archaeologists and historians on both sides of the present conflict between Jews and Arabs have certainly been accessories to the politicians' battles to prove the longevity of their peoples' habitation in this land and thus their right to it; one people's relics have been conserved, the other's destroyed. Perhaps there was nothing very surprising about an impoverished new state such as Georgia boosting its morale by manufacturing a few marks of its glorious past.

It is a while before Tamila can make me understand what I am seeing. I need a historical context and she gives me one. On a first visit to Jerusalem a few months ago she and her team of experts dis-covered the church wall with its rare and precious evidence of a female ancestor's devotion to the Holy Land. Thrilled, they had carefully made a template of the inscription and photographed it for later study back home in Tbilisi. Just as well, because on returning a month later they had found all trace of the inscription erased, in its place only a smooth blank surface.

'We were so shocked. Almost we couldn't believe what our eyes were telling us!' Tamila continued breathlessly, her hands clasped to her bosom as she relived the agony of the loss. 'Someone used a machine – look how smooth it is here – to remove every letter. It was hard for us to believe that it ever existed – so terrible!'

They had swiftly surmised that someone inside the Greek patriarchate must be responsible for the shocking crime, someone worried that the Georgians were back in the city for the first time since the end of the Cold War to reclaim their old possessions. After re-photographing the blank spot, Tamila had presented Patriarch Irineos with the irrefutable before and after evidence.

'We told him again, "Please! We are scholars. We want nothing from you. Hundreds of years have passed now and we do not claim anything back. You have nothing to fear from us." He was embarrassed because it was also clear to him that someone from here in the patriarchate was responsible. How could anyone else get to this place? He believed it was someone who wanted to undermine his authority as the new patriarch.'*

'So now he's allowing you to recreate the inscription,' I said, slowly making sense of a story that was at least as shocking as my earlier hypothesis. Not the Georgians but the Greeks, who still own so much land and property in Jerusalem today, seemed to be intent on re-fashioning history to their advantage.

'That's it! Irineos begged us not to say anything more about it and to recreate it quickly. Luckily, we had the photograph and the template we made on our first visit, so this is an exact copy. Isn't it beautiful?'

~

Almost home, passing the Franciscans' San Salvatore, I am so intent on recalling what Tamila has told me about a Georgian monastery occupying the site until the mid-sixteenth century, when the

* Patriarch Irineos was elected in August 2001 after an acrimonious election campaign. For reasons that are unclear the Israeli government did not recognize his appointment until March 2004, which may have contributed to his sense of insecurity.

Franciscans had acquired it for a derisory sum, that I almost collide with Father Athanasius.

'Good to see you back again,' my Texan friend drawls politely, but he seems uneasy, preoccupied. The tale of the vanishing inscription elicits only a shrug. He is busy, he explains, so busy that his blood pressure is 'way too high'. Overseeing maintenance work on water pipes and drains in the Church of the Holy Sepulchre is stressful and not what he became a friar to do. 'Anyone could do this stuff, with pipes and sewers. You could do it!'

Father Athanasius has spent a total of eight years in the Middle East, in Syria and Jordan as well as Israel, but the story of the Franciscans' presence in the Holy Land and the Church of the Holy Sepulchre begins all the way back in the early thirteenth century. A first Franciscan missionary arrived in Jerusalem in 1215, and four years later, at the start of Cardinal Pelagius' failed Fifth Crusade, St Francis himself led a brave peace mission to Emperor Frederick II's learned friend, Sultan al-Kamil.

Al-Kamil's courtiers were reportedly so disgusted by Francis's foolish and filthy appearance that they set out to undo him. A whore was supplied to test his virtue but he easily avoided that trap. Carpets, gorgeously patterned with the sign of the cross, were laid for him to walk on as he approached the sultan, because surely trampling on the emblem of Christ would constitute a gross sacrilege. Francis calmly explained that Christians carried the sign of the cross in their hearts and nowhere else. To the courtiers' dismay the grimy Italian was welcomed kindly and, although he failed to convert his host to a belief in Christ, they parted friends. Francis returned to the Fifth Crusaders' encampment with rich gifts, a grand escort and a letter of introduction to the governor of Jerusalem.

The story goes that it was the middle of the night when the saint-to-be and his friar companion arrived in Jerusalem, but they made straight for the Church of the Holy Sepulchre. Finding it locked, they roused the Muslim doorkeepers, who demanded an extortionate entrance fee. When they replied that they had no money, they were denounced as spies, beaten up and hauled before the city's governor. Just in time Francis produced Sultan al-Kamil's letter. The governor turned deathly pale on reading it and began pressing refreshing sherbets and a purse filled with gold on the prisoners. St Francis politely refused the money and instead cunningly engineered a western Christian return to the holy city by petitioning the governor for a house in which to settle some friars. Other, perhaps more reliable sources relate that the Franciscans were simply bought their residence in Jerusalem just over a century later.

In 1333, a pious King and Queen of Naples and Sicily, Robert and Sancha, paid Palestine's Mamluk rulers a gigantic sum for the right to install twelve Franciscan friars on Mount Zion, in the place where Christ was believed to have hosted his Last Supper. Such mercantile transactions between Christian princes and Muslim Mamluks were not uncommon; always fearful of another Crusade and lacking timber from which to build a defensive fleet, the Mamluks approached the businesslike Republic of Venice for help. The Catholic Doge declared himself happy to flout the papal ban on selling metals and wood to the infidel in return for a small favour to the Franciscan order. The Mamluks gained a commodity as useful then as enriched uranium is today and a few friars, the first since the late twelfth century, were comfortably installed in the Church of the Holy Sepulchre, in possession of two chapels.

The Mamluks' terror of fresh Crusades on the one hand, and Catholic Europe's fear of Islam on the other, did not much affect trade or the flow of pilgrims to the Holy Land, which was also profitably handled by the Republic of Venice. Indulgences, the currency of Catholic salvation, were the principal prize of the arduous pilgrimage to Jerusalem; if in 1163 a visit to Christ's tomb reduced a person's stay in purgatory* by a year, by 1301 the same devotion spared him or her 5,000 years in that miserable ante-room to heaven. Plenary indulgences – fast-track entry tickets to heaven with the cancellation in full of every sin – were easier to win in

---

* A Catholic, not an Orthodox, doctrine: a place of purification in which sinful souls pay for their sins before gaining admission to heaven.

Jerusalem than anywhere else in the world. A person could pick up one at the Church of the Holy Sepulchre, another at the Church of the Annunciation on the Mount of Olives, and so on, and hold some in reserve, like spiritual savings bonds, in case he or she sinned again before death. For hundreds of western Europeans a pilgrimage to Jerusalem was the most efficient and economical route to a happy hereafter as well as a thrilling adventure.

The Holy Land Franciscans, honoured by a pope with the presumptuously pompous title *Custodia Terrae Sanctae*, flourished on the pilgrim trade. Assuming full responsibility for western Christian pilgrims from the moment they disembarked from the Italian pilgrim ships putting in at Jaffa twice a year to the moment they re-embarked for home, they guided, instructed, fed and lodged their charges in exchange for a generous contribution to the upkeep of the holy places. The wealthy – nobility, senior churchmen and sea captains – lodged more or less comfortably with the friars at their house on Mount Zion and drank the 'most delicious wine in the world'[iii] while common pilgrims were less comfortably stabled in the derelict former headquarters of the Knights of St John Hospitaller, opposite the Church of the Holy Sepulchre.

Pilgrims complained of their treatment by both Mamluks and Franciscans, but the friars were in a delicate position. Like the Crusaders before them, they were forced to discover the virtues and uses of tactful compromise. Early efforts to win themselves 'the glorious bays of martyrdom in the Holy City of Jerusalem' by appearing at the Dome of the Rock mosque on an important feast day to preach to the 'blind multitude' about the 'errors of the false sect of Mohammad'[iv] had, not unnaturally, only imperilled their position in the Holy Land. A later crisis, provoked by the Franciscans' right to drink alcohol but never, on pain of death, to give it to any Muslim, almost caused them to abandon their sacred trust. Two Turks came banging on the gates of San Salvatore one night, demanding wine. In vain the head of the community, the *custos*, strove to appease their cravings with bags of sugar, and the intruders had set upon three friars by the time the cook emerged from his kitchen to hurl a roasting spit at them. Undeterred by this doughty defence, the thirsty robbers climbed out onto the roof and entered the kitchen through a skylight to continue their quest for wine. The *custos* and his injured friars meanwhile managed to escape down a secret passageway to lodge a complaint with the city's governor. Instead of preaching a fiery sermon about Mohammad's 'errors' or demanding the punishment of the rascals, the chief of the Franciscans spoke about turning the other cheek, and the governor was apparently 'very satisfied and edified'.[v]

If the friars wanted to maintain and expand their presence in the Holy Land – a task they accomplished during the Mamluk era by a blend of single-mindedness and iron discipline that did not come easily to the eastern Churches – every *custos* had to ensure that western pilgrims did not offend Muslim sensibilities. A list of twenty-seven dos and don'ts was read to all pilgrims on arrival. There must be no chipping off parts of Christ's tomb or scrawling of graffiti in the church because those activities 'give great offence to the Saracens and they think those who do so to be fools', no laughing at praying Muslims 'for they themselves refrain from molesting or laughing at us when we are at our prayers', no giving of wine to a Muslim because 'after one single draught thereof he becomes mad', and no tugging at Muslims' beards because it enrages them.[vi]

Medieval pilgrims to Jerusalem could be hysterically pious as well as boisterous. A woman from Norfolk who travelled to Mamluk Jerusalem in the early fifteenth century suffered such terrifying paroxysms of devotion in the Church of the Holy Sepulchre that she 'could not stand or kneel on Calvary'. Instead, in the place where Christ had hung on his cross Margery Kempe 'rolled and wrested with her body, spreading her arms abroad'. She 'could not keep herself from crying and roaring' and 'cursed and made wondrous faces and expressions'[vii] until her companions wished her 'on the sea in a bottomless boat'.[viii] In thrall to her wild ecstasy, Mrs Kempe did not find time to observe Mamluk Jerusalem and its majority of Muslim inhabitants or the Franciscans, except to say that everyone she met was 'good to her and gentle, save only her own countrymen'.[ix] A few decades later an Italian pilgrim, Pietro di Casola, cursed the Muslims he met as 'mastiffs' and 'dogs' and the lazy Franciscans who, between them, were rendering his pilgrimage so arduous that 'one hour seemed a year'.[x] He did admire the Dome of the Rock, however, and considered it nothing short of a miracle that the Muslims had generously left the dome of the Church of the Holy Sepulchre intact.

At much the same time, Felix Fabri, a jocular German Dominican friar, complained of the Franciscans' lackadaisical treatment of pilgrims and the squalor of the Church of the Holy Sepulchre. The church of his time was swarming with fleas 'jumping about', which he imagined were 'bred naturally from the marble'.[xi] He saw loutish pilgrims scratching their names and professions on walls, gossiping noisily about their business affairs and baring their arms to show off new tattoos drawn in gunpowder and ox gall. By contrast the Muslims' Dome of the Rock, topped with the symbol of a 'moon on its back like a boat',[xii] moved him deeply and he liked the orderly way the Muslims said their prayers, 'as if they had been monks of the same rule'. Whereas all the Christian churches he knew in Europe were 'dirty, with people walking through them as though they were inns and befouled with filth', mosques, he noted approvingly, were barred to children and animals. Felix believed that the Muslims' teetotalism was what rendered them more dignified than most Europeans and he wistfully concluded that 'easterners are men of a different kind to us . . . they have other passions, other ways of thinking, other ideas . . . they are influenced by other stars and a different climate'.[xiii]

Felix belonged to the period shortly prior to the Reformation. He took the Holy Fire miracle at face value; 'a sudden lightning comes down from Heaven and lights the Easter wax candle and all the candles and lamps' he wrote simply, and he wonderingly noted that while celebrating a mass inside the edicule his singing voice was 'much clearer and louder than usual'.[xiv] But his appetite for marvels was limited. The news that one of his fellow pilgrims was doing business with a Muslim who was passing off a dead baby he had slashed with a knife as the mummified relic of a Holy Innocent slain by King Herod disgusted him. And he laughed at prima donnas of piety like Margery Kempe, in his case a Lady Hildegarde whom he almost tripped over as she crouched sobbing over the Stone of Unction.

It would not be long, less than forty years, before Martin Luther's rebellion launched the great sixteenth-century Reformation in the Roman Catholic half of Christendom. In the eyes of northern Europe's new Protestants, showy transports of emotion like those of Margery Kempe and Lady Hildegarde, miracles as dazzling as Holy Fire, pilgrimages all over Europe and the East, but especially the currency of indulgences and relics for the trade in eternal salvation were the loathsome marks of the corrupted Roman Church. Luther sternly advised that the money and effort spent on pilgrimages would be 'used a thousand times better for the maintenance of one's family and for the poor'.[xv] Scoffing at Christ's tomb in Jerusalem, he calculated that God cared as much for Christendom's holiest shrine as he did 'for all the cows in Switzerland'.[xvi] Careless of the fact that he was dividing and weakening Christendom at precisely the fateful moment when the Ottoman Turks looked mighty enough to conquer all of Europe – they would reach the gates of Vienna by 1529 – Luther proclaimed the pope as great an enemy as the Turk. 'Both,' he thundered, 'are of one lord, the devil – since the pope is a liar and the Turk a murderer.'[xvii]

The Reformation and the wars of religion that followed would slow Holy Land pilgrimages to a trickle and leave the Franciscans, who had by then secured control of both the edicule in the Church of the Holy Sepulchre and of the Church of the Nativity in Bethlehem, in reduced circumstances. But the Protestant challenge only magnified their devotion to Christ's tomb and doubled their determination to ensure that if Catholics could not be first in Europe, they would be first in the Holy Land. Their contempt for their fellow Christians in the Church of the Holy Sepulchre knew no bounds. A *custos* of the period counted ten different Christian communities in the church, among whom the Greeks were the 'worst and most atrocious enemies' and the Georgians 'the worst heretics, like to the Greeks and equal in malice'. The Armenians, having once upon a time surrendered their Oriental Orthodoxy and recognized the authority of the pope, had since 'returned to their vomit'. And while the Ethiopians were 'a malicious, almost black and very ugly people', the Syrian Jacobites were simply 'the most perfidious of all heretics'.[xviii]

Before long an uncommonly energetic *custos*, Bonifazio of Ragusa,* won permission from the city's new Ottoman Turkish rulers – the Ottoman Turks had conquered Jerusalem from the Mamluks in 1517 – to rebuild the edicule in the current Renaissance style. The Crusaders' glittering mosaic-covered structure with its crowning gilded statue of Christ was torn down, doubtless for the sin of being too Byzantine in style. After Bonifazio had seized the opportunity to peer inside the tomb and watched the cloth used to wipe away Christ's sweat dissolve into a few gold threads on contact with the air, an opulently marbled monument to the pious largesse of Holy Roman Emperor Charles V and his son Philip II of Spain was erected. It would last almost 300 years, until its destruction by fire in 1808.

Bonifazio's record of service in the Holy Land was remarkable in other respects. It was Bonifazio who wrote a letter to the pope of the day asking him to bar Jews from travelling to the Holy Land on Italian pilgrim ships; he worried that far too many of them were seeking refuge in their ancient homeland after their expulsion from Spain by King Ferdinand and Queen Isabella in the last decade of the fifteenth century. Neither the Orthodox clergy nor the Franciscans profited by the Muslims' example of tolerance towards people of different faiths. It was also Bonifazio who tried to barge his way into the edicule ahead of the Greek patriarch during a Holy Fire ceremony. Whether he intended to expose the fraud or to hijack the management of the miracle himself is unclear, but his bold sortie,

---

* Then a possession of the Republic of Venice, now Dubrovnik on Croatia's Dalmatian coast.

witnessed by a Russian envoy from the court of Tsar Ivan the Terrible, was immediately halted by a posse of vigilant Orthodox monks.

~

In his tobacco-brown habit and open sandals Father Athanasius is far less conspicuous than I am in the courtyard of this pleasant restaurant by the Old City walls at Jaffa Gate. We are surrounded by other churchmen.

At a table behind us a young Greek monk wearing a regulation black chimney-pot hat is laughing with family and friends. In a corner two dog-collared Anglicans and a young Italian priest in an elegantly buttoned soutane are ordering another bottle of wine. While the lilac sky darkens above us and the candle on the table flickers in the lightest of autumn breezes, Athanasius tells me about an Israeli historian who views the shared management of the Church of the Holy Sepulchre as a model for conflict resolution. When I laugh, incredulous, Athanasius favours me with a slow, lop-sided smile before taking another swig of Maccabee beer from the bottle and insisting: 'No. He's serious. This just happens to have been a very bad year for disputes in the church. We've had Greeks and Egyptians fighting about a rug, Greeks and Armenians brawling over the Holy Fire, Egyptians and Ethiopians going to war over a chair, and it's only September . . .'

When his second cold beer arrives Athanasius begins to tell me about a new project of his. In order to limit occasions for argument in the church, he is carefully compiling a video-record of every service, ritual and ceremony. 'It's a way of codifying practice, something that's never been done before,' he says.

I ask him if he is telling me that there is no document detailing who does what when, and who owns what and where in the church.

'There is the Status Quo agreement – not a document but a freezing of the situation as it was in 1852 when the Ottomans ruled the Holy Land and the Greek Orthodox dominated in the holy places. But that's more like a ceasefire than a settlement, which is why the six communities in the church act more like rivals than partners. Roughly speaking the Status Quo gives the Greeks about 40 per cent of the place, us about 35 per cent and the Armenians – don't ask me to explain how they snuck in – about 25 per cent.'

'But that leaves nothing at all for the Egyptian Copts, the Ethiopians and the Syrians?'

'I'm speaking here about the three great powers in the church, the ones that really count. Anyway, in the past fifty years or so all six of us, the communities who share the place, have signed hundreds of bi- and trilateral agreements. So one way and another probably 90 per cent of all the rights are defined by now.'

I point out that if there is no definitive document then, by rights, there should be anarchy in there. Perhaps his Israeli professor friend has a point.

'Actually, rights is what it's all about,' he answers. 'It's important to understand that there are three different sets of rights governing everything inside the church and everything that happens there: rights of property, rights of use and rights of cleaning. Having the right to clean somewhere doesn't presuppose a right to use it and the right to use it doesn't necessarily entail ownership, because ownership can be shared. Think of it like a delicate ecosystem. Everything closely depends on everything else. It means there has to be a very tight schedule of who does what service in the church for how long. Let me give you an example: if the Copts overrun with their *Kyrie eleisons*, we go right ahead and start our service.'

I recall the battle between the Copts' steady small-arms fire of *Kyrie eleisons* and the cannon organ.

'Let me give you another example,' he continues. 'Although the Greeks and us and the Armenians all share property rights to the courtyard in front of the church, only the Greeks get to clean it. If the Franciscan who sweeps the steps up to our chapel from the courtyard happens to sweep below the bottom step, it could mean trouble. It did in 1901, when a battle with the Greeks left eight of our guys dead. You want another example? No one but the Greeks get to clean the bathrooms . . .'

Precedent and custom are all while a centuries-old Ottoman Status Quo is the only framework the six groups can even begin to agree upon. An apparently generous offer to foot a repair bill by one community, the chance prolongation of a service by another, the removal of a candlestick or the repositioning of a rug are all occasions for friction, each of them the thinnest end of the thickest wedge imaginable. The logic of Ottoman law dictates that unless an immediate objection is registered, two inches of Coptic doormat protruding into the ambulatory one year will become four inches the following year and be joined by a lectern or a candlestick the year after that. If the Armenian is allowed free rein inside the edicule at this year's Holy Fire ceremony, next year he could – like *Custos* Bonifazio of Ragusa – try barging into the shrine ahead of the Greek patriarch. If the old Copt is permitted to park his chair under the Ethiopians' eucalyptus tree, what is there to stop one of his brothers doing the same, and then another, and all the rest?

Athanasius continues: 'Things go wrong when, let's say the Copts, behave like kids reaching for the candy jar. The smaller communities are always trying things, so you slap them down, but they creep back and try again. You only get a real crisis when there's no bi- or trilateral agreement about something, when no precedent has been established. For example, there's a manhole cover a short way from the Stone of Mockery – you probably haven't noticed it?'

'No.'

'Never mind. Five years ago it broke and the question of who got to repair it blew up into a crisis. Why? Because it's situated right on a line where property held by all three main communities intersects. Right away the Armenians claimed the exclusive right to repair it but that implied a territorial claim over the whole manhole cover, not just the largest portion of it. There was no way we or the Greeks could let that pass. But that manhole was a safety hazard. In the end, after five years of stalemate, the Israelis stepped in to fix it. That's what happens when there's deadlock. Like in Ottoman times, the ruling power in the land has the final say.'

I ask Athanasius to explain the significance of the church's hundreds of oil lamps.*

'The lamps are nothing, it's just like cats and dogs marking out their territory with piss,' he says, signalling to the waiter for another beer. 'Of course, there are times when we have to compromise, but that's not easy. Here's what happened when the interior of the little dome above the edicule needed fixing up. The Greeks wanted some kind of Byzantine mosaic in there, the Armenians demanded a fresco of some kind and we Latins wanted it bare. Well, you won't believe this but it took twenty-three years to agree on that hideous and totally meaningless golden ray effect! I'm not kidding! My nightmare is what happens when we finally get around to discussing how to fix up the edicule itself – an urgent job, but it could take centuries to get an agreement and we haven't even started talking.'

Father Athanasius is more relaxed than I have ever seen him. His conversation begins to stray beyond the maddening confines of the Church of the Holy Sepulchre.

'You have to understand that what we have in that church is not three different takes on Christianity – Orthodoxy, Catholicism and Oriental Orthodoxy. That would be complex enough, but it's worse than that. The territory the church occupies and all its contents are divided six ways on mostly tribal lines except for us Franciscans; we're multinational. Otherwise you've got Greeks, Armenians, Egyptians, Ethiopians and Syrians. That makes the situation in the church just like the wider issue here. My guess is that the solution to the Israel–Palestine problem will be just as tribal and territorial. Nothing will be resolved until both sides have lost so much in the kind of violence we're seeing now that they'll have to divide – just like we Christians have done in the church . . .'

We are back where we started with the Israeli professor and the

---

* In 1956 there were 360 lamps in the church: 170 Greek Orthodox, 94 Catholic Franciscan, 77 Armenian, 19 Egyptian Copt.

church as a model for conflict resolution. Father Athanasius shrugs as if in silent recognition of the absurdity of everything we have spoken about: 'For three years now,' he continues, 'I've had the job of making sure that no one infringes our Catholic rights in the holy places. I guess you can imagine what that's doing to my head, but my predecessor did it for forty-five years.'

When I laugh he suddenly turns serious. 'Look, don't get me wrong, I'm not saying my job isn't important. Guarding the Christian holy places is a great historical responsibility . . .'

To abandon the Catholic Church's claim to the holy places, to fail to live up to the proud title of *Custodia Terrae Sanctae*, would render pointless the pious munificence of Catholic kings and the centuries of sacrifice endured by generations of Franciscans from all over Catholic Europe.

~

San Salvatore's dusty library shelves are stuffed full of clues to the lives of those Holy Land Franciscans.

Seated at a long wooden table with only the shush-shushing brush of the friar librarian's habit or the strain of a chant from the church upstairs to distract me, I have been poring over French, Italian and Spanish chronicles, ancient pilgrim guides and faded photograph albums. A picture is slowly taking shape. I am beginning to suspect that the friars' lives here were not all privation and sacrifice. If martyrdom or the plague did not claim them early, many could expect to live into their seventies and eighties in the homeland of their saviour.

At the turn of the fifteenth century Venetian merchants trading in the great cities of the Middle East were their most generous benefactors. A *custos* of the time remarked that 'if it were not for the Venetian merchants of Damascus, Cairo, Alexandria, Tripoli, Amman and Aleppo, who give very big alms to the friars who go during Lent to preach and confess, the present number of friars could not live'.[xix] A Russian pilgrim of the time acknowledged

Venice's close links with the Holy Land by simply referring to the Franciscans' first headquarters on Mount Zion as the Convent of the Doge of Venice. Another noted that even the entrance fee to the Church of the Holy Sepulchre was paid in 'gold Venetian florins'.[xx]

As Venetian power waned Spain assumed much of the Catholic responsibility for the holy places. Flush with silver wealth from their New World colonies and untroubled by the rest of Europe's wars of religion, the Spanish kings and nobility were generous benefactors of the *Custodia Terrae Sanctae* throughout the seventeenth century. In 1632, for example, a Father Antonio from Granada in Andalusia brought a donation of '3,696 sequins and 6,212 pieces of eight' from King Philip IV, along with some items of church paraphernalia, frying pans, two ovens for the Franciscan house in Bethlehem, brooms and 'many trifles'.[xxi] Spain was so generous that a tradition established itself whereby the financial manager of San Salvatore was always a Spaniard.*

Every April and September the holds of the pilgrim boats arriving at Jaffa were stuffed with goods and provisions destined for the friars at San Salvatore. Barrels of sardines and tuna, wheels of cheese, brooms, cutlery, cheese-graters, scissors, razors, books, medicines, cotton underpants, censers and candlesticks, hammers, towels, nails, blankets, rope for the soles of the friars' sandals, paper, combs and tablecloths were some of the staples. Gifts for the Church of the Holy Sepulchre poured into Jerusalem from all over Catholic Europe: a clock from Spain in 1652, a church organ from Germany in 1667, a large lock from the Austrian emperor in 1675, lead for repairs to the main dome and a jewel-encrusted gilded lamp from Spain in 1696. Other items – dozens of pairs of spectacles and mirrors from Venice, another 'seventy-two pairs of spectacles, five hundred ordinary knives, and fifteen gilt candlesticks'[xxii] from Germany, a consignment of one hundred knives and an alarm clock from Vienna, and one hundred and twelve pairs of spectacles sent

---

* The *custos* was Italian, his deputy a Frenchman, his secretary an Italian or a German.

from Naples in 1697 – suggest that not everything was destined for the friars' personal use.

New-fangled goods from the thriving manufacturing centres of western Europe made ideal backhanders and sweeteners for the Ottoman authorities. In 1650 a pair of globes, 'one of the heavens and the other of the earth, with pedestals finely decorated in blue and gold' and eight pairs of 'spectacles for long sight, large and small, for the Turks'[xxiii] arrived from Rome. A consignment of 'two hundred and fifty-two little diamonds'[xxiv] from the faithful Catholics of Goa in southern India must have proved useful too, but cash was best of all. The Franciscans made a careful note of every sequin, piastre, crown or ducat they received before locking it away in a box with three keys. Five friars had to witness each donation and the bearer of the gift was obliged to make a full report of any expense – usually bribes to Ottoman customs officials – he had incurred en route for the Holy Land.

Much of the money received by San Salvatore was expended on bribes to local officials prepared to turn a blind eye to the friars' ceaseless bending of the rules governing their presence as court-eously tolerated guests on Muslim territory. Not until the limit of twelve Franciscans had been exceeded by a factor of five did the *custos* of the day find himself obliged to travel all the way to Constantinople to bribe the sultan himself. Securing annual per-mission to stage their showy Palm Sunday procession through the city, with the *custos* mounted on a donkey like Jesus himself at the head of the parade, must have been a costly operation. Arranging an ordinance forbidding Jews to cross the parvis in front of the Church of the Holy Sepulchre or to enter any of the Christians' holy places would certainly have required another considerable outlay.*

The Franciscans were not alone in resorting to these methods; their rivals, the Greek Orthodox and Armenian establishments, provided stiff competition. Unlike the always alien Franciscans, the Greeks and Armenians, whose native lands lay inside the Ottoman

---

* Jews were officially banned from the Church of the Holy Sepulchre until 1967.

empire, could prosper by lobbying from inside the system, by advertising themselves as loyal servants of the sultan and as shepherds
of vast flocks of loyal Ottoman subjects. The Greek Patriarch of
Jerusalem, who resided in Constantinople, usually enjoyed better
access to the ear of the sultan than the Franciscans did via the
various Catholic ambassadors to the Sublime Porte.* During almost
500 years of Ottoman rule all three great powers of the Church of
the Holy Sepulchre would prosper and grow far beyond the bounds
of their originally prescribed size and standing. In the mid-1830s,
almost a century before the collapse of the Ottoman empire, an
English clergyman visitor to Jerusalem disapprovingly noted the
inflated pretensions of these three religious institutions and judged
them 'most corrupting' because 'from their number, wealth and
influence, they are able to effect almost any object they please and
defeat anyone that falls under their displeasure'.[xxv]

The Ottomans usually aimed at impartiality in their dealings
with the Holy Land churches. Issuing contradictory firmans
designed to appease all parties to any dispute over the Christian
holy places was a favourite and effective delaying tactic. When
pushed very hard, after exhausting all excuses about needing time to
re-examine all documents relating to the case and accepting plentiful bribes from everyone concerned, they might finally decide the
matter by claiming that a high Ottoman official had had a dream in
which Mohammad had appeared to tell him that unless the Greeks
or the Franciscans or the Armenians were immediately granted full
rights to use and clean the Chapel of St Helena, or the Rotunda, or
Calvary, for example, the sultan would die a horrible death before
the next full moon.

Either contradictory firmans or simple avarice was responsible
for matters moving so abnormally swiftly in the 1630s that supremacy in the holy places changed hands six times. Galled by Greek
triumphalism after one Latin defeat, a friar complained that the

---

* The official name for the Ottoman government in Constantinople, derived from the
high gate leading to the building where the offices of the main departments of state
were located.

Orthodox had begun treating the Franciscans 'worse than Jews'.[xxvi] But by 1689 the Catholics were in the ascendant again and, according to a rare Greek account, taking a wicked revenge on their enemies. Greek icons, crosses and lamps were hurled out of the church and a valuable iconostasis smashed to smithereens. Greek Orthodox bishops fled to Damascus for safety while the patriarch dispatched his nephew to Orthodox Russia to plead for financial and diplomatic help from Tsar Peter the Great.

It is hard not to sympathize with the Ottomans' predicament and applaud their handling of the fractious Holy Land Christians. To the Muslim mind, the Christians had fetishized everything about the human prophet they insisted on confusing with God. And the monks' vicious battles over the positioning of candlesticks and the working of spurious miracles must have seemed to the Turks simply a faithful reflection of the incessant wars of religion Europe's Christians had been fighting among themselves instead of organizing themselves into a tolerantly multicultural empire like their own Ottoman state. The Ottomans despised the Christians but they also had more and more reason to fear and distrust them.

The library in San Salvatore has thrown up another jewel of a tale, perfect justification for that fear and distrust. In the early seventeenth century a Franciscan friar at the court of Grand Duke Ferdinand II in Florence conceived a daring scheme to punish the Turks and secure the fortunes of Tuscany for ever. Why should Florence not acquire Christendom's most valuable relic when the Savoyard court at nearby Turin had recently come by Christ's burial shroud? The Holy Sepulchre must be stolen away from Jerusalem and installed in Florence, in the lavish new Medici church of San Lorenzo. An exiled Lebanese prince named Fakhr al-Din, a friend to the Holy Land Franciscans and a man so short it was said that if an egg fell out of his pocket it would not break, struck the friar and his friends at court as the perfect accessory to the crime.*

---

* Fakhr al-Din gave the Annunciation Basilica in Nazareth to the Franciscans in 1620, a gift commemorated by a plaque there today.

Fakhr al-Din had been a thorn in the side of the Ottomans for a decade, having carved out a fiefdom comprising much of what is today Syria, Lebanon and northern Israel. In 1613 he had been gamely signalling his readiness to ally himself with the pope and Tuscany to conquer Jerusalem when a fleet of sixty Ottoman ships sailed down his coastline and forced him to seek asylum with his would-be allies in Europe. At the Florentine court of Ferdinand II of Tuscany he was fêted, flattered, given a summer palace in Pisa to live in with his family and made privy to some of the best innovations that Europe had to offer. Banks paying interest, sheep with docked tails, free health care, presses that printed in Arabic script and mixed-sex dancing all astonished and delighted him. A legend was promoted to boost his image as a faithful friend to Christendom: Fakhr al-Din and his Druze countrymen were not Arabs or Muslim followers of the mad al-Hakim who had demolished the Church of the Holy Sepulchre in 1009, but the long-lost descendants of Jerusalem's first Crusader ruler, Godfrey de Bouillon. And very soon, his hosts hoped, he would be returning home to lead a new Crusade to eject the Ottomans from the Holy Land and steal away Christ's tomb.

Five years passed and the little emir began to tire of a social life so hectic he could not find time to say his daily prayers. He was falling out of love with Italy and his hardly disinterested hosts were falling out of love with him because he was showing no signs of either converting to Christianity or wanting to embark on a Crusade. When at last he announced he was leaving for home, Duke Ferdinand was so nervous lest his guest go and sell Tuscany's commercial secrets to the sultan that he tried to deter him. Fakhr al-Din finally put to sea with a barrel of gunpowder on deck, threatening to turn suicide bomber by exploding himself, his family and the boat if he were forced 'to set his foot again on the Italian shore'.[xxvii]

The Florentine Franciscan's excited calculations about how many stonecutters should accompany Fakhr al-Din's Crusade, about how to 'detach that special part of the Holy Sepulchre from the mass of stone' around it, and how best to transport the precious booty from Jerusalem to the coast and on board a ship bound for Italy, had come to nothing.[xxviii] But while the age of Crusading lasted, the Ottomans had everything to fear, and the age of Crusading – its ideology and romance, if not its practice – lasted until well into the seventeenth century.

~

The Arab Catholic Scouts' hall up the alley is hosting a rowdy wedding party tonight. First blaring Arab dance music, then a banging Abba hit and now Madonna.

Rahme wants to show me video highlights of her nephew's engagement party. First, I must admire footage of Bishop Theophanis delivering a sermon in Arabic and then some of Nasra dancing. But the noise outside is deafening. Muttering curses under her breath, Rahme hurls herself onto her sofa to sew buttons onto a beige cardigan. I, meanwhile, pursue my investigations into the Ottomans' special relationship with Catholic France and not so special one with Protestant Holland and England.

The Franciscans' meticulous records show that in 1647 France contributed needle-worked towels and some 'fringed and lace-edged'[xxix] church vestments to the maintenance of the *Custodia Terrae Sanctae*, but the French kings had long been proving more useful in the diplomatic sphere. Firm discipline and inexhaustible funds counted for much when it came to achieving and maintaining supremacy in the holy places, but it was France that provided the Franciscans with their mightiest weapon.

In 1528 France's Renaissance king, Francis I, secured the first of what became known over succeeding centuries as the Capitulations from his friend and equal in Renaissance brilliance, Sultan Suleiman the Magnificent. This initial document awarded France an informal protectorate over Catholics trading or travelling or living within the Ottoman empire. Immune from Ottoman law, Catholics of any nation were thenceforward free to pursue their business and practise their religion in Ottoman lands without interference. In 1604 a second Capitulation included the first explicit reference to the holy places and the status of their Catholic guardians. 'It is our wish and our command,' said the Ottoman document, 'that the subjects of the Emperor of France and those of the [European]Princes who are his friends and allies may visit under his protection freely the Holy Places of Jerusalem, without any hindrance being put in their way [and] that the monks who live in Jerusalem and serve in the Church of the Holy Sepulchre of Our Lord Jesus Christ, may stay there, come and go securely without any trouble or disturbance.'[xxx]

The Ottoman Turks, a confident superpower at the beginning of the sixteenth century, had previously had little to fear from foreigners in their lands. They could afford to be generous. But that first French Capitulation was soon matched by concessions to the Venetians, Genoese, British and Dutch. Granting what was essentially privileged diplomatic status to all western Christians in the Ottoman empire, the terms of the Capitulations would be expanded and misinterpreted by Europeans and corrupt Ottoman bureaucrats. Acting like a slow cancer in the body politic of the Ottoman empire for the next four centuries, they would undermine its sovereignty and spread a poison of envy and resentment among the Sultan's subjects.

In the manner of the clergy jockeying for position around the empty tomb of Christ in the Church of the Holy Sepulchre, French kings had sought to build on their early advantage over other Christian monarchs. In 1623 a French consul, Monsieur Lempereur, was appointed to Jerusalem. The Franciscan chronicles contain two telling chapter headings about Consul Lempereur: 'XV The Christian king sent a Consul to Jerusalem to defend the friars and protect the pilgrims – a French man'; 'XVI How the Consul was thrown in prison and how they forced him to leave the Holy City'.[xxxi] The consul's coming caused uproar among the city's Muslims. More than 300 years after the collapse of the Crusader states and shortly after the abortive Tuscan plot to steal the Holy Sepulchre, a protest expressing the Muslims' abiding suspicion of the consul and all European Christians reached the sultan in Constantinople. 'Our city is a place at which infidels look with covetous eyes,' it complained, 'their schemes and plots against it never cease.' They were terrified lest the French consul 'cause others to be brought into the city, in addition to those we already have'. And the letter spelt out their main concern: 'We fear lest they occupy us.'[xxxii]

Northern Europe's Protestant powers soon grew envious of the Catholics' near-monopoly on influence inside the Ottoman Empire. When Jerusalem's Franciscans and Greek Orthodox banded together to brand all Protestant visitors to the city 'heretics' and bar them from visiting the Christian holy places, Protestant Holland retaliated by signing a Capitulation with the sultan which included a clause to the effect that 'neither the monks in the Church of the Holy Sepulchre nor anyone else' was to hinder any Dutchman's progress about the holy places nor to say, '"You are Lutherans, we do not want you to see the places!" But they must show them the places which it is customary to see without any opposition or excuse.'[xxxiii]

Shortly afterwards a Franciscan guide in the Church of the Holy Sepulchre enquired of George Sandys, a Protestant Englishman, if he was visiting the church out of simple curiosity or to gain a plenary indulgence. The former, Sandys boldly replied, and was granted a merely 'historicall relation' about the place. Sandys spent three days in the church admiring the tombs of the Crusader kings, marvelling at the sight of Catholic and Orthodox pilgrims 'prostrating themselves and tumbling up and downe' with the sort of 'overactive zeal' that pre-Reformation English pilgrims like Margery Kempe had displayed, and gleefully observing 'a faire Greek virgin' farting loudly whilst performing her devotions.[xxxiv] The 'franticke behaviours' accompanying the Holy Fire ceremony amused him, as did the news that the miracle did not work without the assistance of an Ethiopian priest.[xxxv]

The gulf separating Protestants from members of the older Christian churches was enormous by the mid-seventeenth century but Ottoman understanding of western Christendom remained trapped in the era of the Crusades. To the Turks, all European

Christians, whether Lutheran Scandinavians or Germans, Anglican English or Catholic Italian, Polish, Spanish, Portuguese, French or southern German were simply 'Franks' like the Crusaders. In Jerusalem, the Franciscan *custos*, the only highly placed representative of western Christendom resident in the city, was responsible for all of them. Although comparatively comfortable and generous, San Salvatore's hospitality was therefore compulsory. Sandys complained that the friars charged a very 'costly rate for a monastical diet' but he understood the dangers involved in refusing to lodge with them.[xxxvi]

Not everyone did. At the turn of the seventeenth century, another English merchant, Henry Timberlake, who arrived in Jerusalem determined to avoid sullying his Protestant soul by staying with the Franciscans, was immediately accused of spying and hurled into a prison 'right against the sepulchre of Christ'.[xxxvii] Once released with the assistance of a kindly Muslim, he only agreed to lodge at San Salvatore on condition he was not forced to attend mass. Timberlake learned that his horrible misfortune had befallen him because the Ottoman gatekeepers knew nothing of either the Anglican Church or England. He then had to field questions from the *custos* about why Queen Elizabeth I had not donated as generously to the upkeep of the Holy Sepulchre as her father had before he fell out with the Franciscans over his confiscation of their estates.

Although a 'heretic', Timberlake merited the formal ritual of welcome extended by the *custos* to all pilgrims: the feet-washing ceremony. While standing in the courtyard of San Salvatore he was approached by twelve 'fat-fed Fryers', all with lit candles in their hands, except for one who carried a great basin of warm water 'mingled with Roses and other Sweete Flowers'. A carpet was spread on the ground. Timberlake was given a candle and told to wait while a 'Fryer pulled off his hose'. Next, the *custos* appeared and, kneeling on the carpet in front of Timberlake, performed his unenviable task to the accompaniment of sung psalms. The entire company then processed upstairs to the church, to be edified by a sermon about 'how meritorious it was for us to visit the Holy Land and see those sanctified places where our Saviour's feete had trode'.[xxxviii]

Timberlake was more interested in practical arrangements in the Church of the Holy Sepulchre than in any Franciscan ritual. He was fascinated to see how the 300 clergy and their families who lived in the church were provisioned through a hatch in the great door and he marvelled at the primitive technology involved in a system of bells attached to ropes, which functioned as an effective intercom facility for each household. On entering the edicule he eagerly set about measuring Christ's tomb with his 'compasse': 'two foote and a halfe high from the grounde, eighte foot in lengthe and foure foote broade wanting three inches'.[xxxix]

Anglicans like Sandys and Timberlake gained little enjoyment from their visits to the Holy Land. Sceptical of all they were shown, suspected of spying by the Turks, distrusted by Catholics and Orthodox alike, fleeced by everyone, they were without even a chapel to call their own in the Church of the Holy Sepulchre. Whether English, Scottish, German, Dutch, Swiss, central European or American, Protestants would not return in any great number until the early nineteenth century. Then, like Timberlake, they would be much more interested in mapping and measuring than in gaining indulgences, witnessing Holy Fire miracles or acquiring relics. Anglicans especially – their status secured by centuries of expanded English Capitulations – would come to Jerusalem in a spirit of objective enquiry to test the historical truth of the Bible and to posit fresh scientific theories about the likely location of Christ's tomb. Guided by a more scientific and literal reading of the Old Testament some of them would reach important conclusions about the Holy Land, its rightful rulers and inhabitants and England's role in bringing about the long-awaited second coming of Christ.

Rahme and I are reaching our own conclusions about why the noise outside in the alley has suddenly intensified. The wedding guests are spilling out of the Arab Catholic Scouts' hall in a horribly violent mood. Broken bottles . . . angry shouts, louder and louder . . . thudding body blows . . . more shouting and smashing glass . . .

more thuds. Leaping up from her sofa, Rahme runs to the window to screech something at them in Arabic. But the fighting continues, with more shrieking and blows. She screams down at them again. Now we hear a different voice, calm and firm.

'It's a Franciscan,' she reports over her shoulder to me. 'One of the Italians, not your American friend, is asking them to remember they're Christians. Pah! What kind of Christians? They're Latins!' she says, ever the faithful Orthodox.

Throwing herself back onto her sofa, she gives the now completed beige cardigan a good shake before hurling it across the room at me.

'Finish now with your book!' she commands.

'For me?'

'*Ahlan wa sahlan!* – You're welcome!'

~

A polite letter that Father Athanasius recommended I write from London has borne fruit at last. The current head of the *Custodia Terrae Sanctae* Father Giovanni Battistelli is back from his summer holiday and will be pleased to receive me at 10 o'clock this morning.

Quite as interesting as meeting a twenty-first-century *custos*, whom I may also refer to as *Il Reverendissimo* if I like, will be the opportunity for a good look around San Salvatore. I cannot range freely there as I do around the Greek patriarchate, calling in on Father Athanasius as I do on Bishop Theophanis for coffee and a chat. If I want to see Father Athanasius I call him on his mobile phone or catch him at his office in the Christian Information Centre at Jaffa Gate. The Franciscans here seem busier than the Greek Orthodox, running their schools and orphanages, printing their books, coming and going between their various houses in Nazareth, Bethlehem, Ein Kerem.

Leaving Arkhangelos to climb the few steps up the alley to San Salvatore I recall that I did once penetrate through the frosted-glass doors – during my first meeting with Father Athanasius. We had been walking back from his office and were about to reach San Salvatore when he veered off to the left suddenly through a low wooden door into what he called the monastery's laundromat. A roomful of whirring washing machines opened onto a narrow courtyard where a single pair of tobacco-brown nylon shorts was drying on a washing line. From this humble back entrance to the great establishment, I had followed him into the tailors' workshop to watch a young friar being fitted for a new habit, and inspected an old wooden door scratched with the names of some seventeenth- and eighteenth-century English pilgrims. From there he had shepherded me up a flight of marble steps to the second floor to see the church, and then straight on up again to the rooftop for a view over all the Christian Quarter and beyond.

Following him around the great expanse of roof, up and down little flights of metal steps, searching for the best vantage points from which to see the city, I had felt as if I were on the deck of a gigantic battlecruiser and the city a white sea of limestone below. Athanasius had donned some Polaroid sunglasses and pulled the droopy hood of his habit up over his head. 'I don't need any more sunspots,' he said, before pointing out some flotsam for me: the buff blur of Arkhangelos down the way, the black slit of the alley, the sooty dome of the Church of the Holy Sepulchre, and the golden Dome of the Rock, just a few hundred metres away as the crow flies. Further to the east the Mount of Olives was a green haze and the Russian church's onion domes a golden shimmer in the pulsing heat. Pointing down to a patch of scrubland directly below us, Athanasius had said, 'See that plot? We used to have a school there until '48. It got destroyed in the fighting. That metal stairway leading down to it is there to remind the Israelis that it's still our land.'

We had returned inside and descended a wide flight of stone stairs to the front entrance again. Today a Filipino friar arrives to lead me through those frosted-glass doors once more. We climb the same wide stairs and walk along an even wider polished corridor whose whitewashed walls are hung with nineteenth-century scenes from the life of St Francis – the saint rolling his eyes towards a dazzling heaven, the saint consorting with a friendly wolf, the saint languishing on his deathbed. Through the open door of the friars' common room I glimpse tidy clusters of armchairs, a draughtboard, some plastic ashtrays and, in pride of place, a life-size depiction of the saint's meeting with Sultan al-Kamil.

Il Reverendissimo's manner and appearance are surprising. The sleeves of his habit are rolled up in workmanlike style to reveal the strong forearms of an Italian peasant, and when he sits down on a small sofa adjacent to my chair he hitches up his brown skirts to spread his knees. We agree to communicate in French and, since neither of us is fluent in the language, manage quite well.

In all his four years as *custos*, he tells me, he has not faced anything as traumatically testing as last spring's siege of the Church of the Nativity. Thirty-one of his friars found themselves caught up in the month-long stalemate between Israeli troops and the mix of Palestinian militants and civilians who had taken refuge inside the church. With dramatic accompanying gestures he shows me how one friar was brushing his teeth by a window when the handbasin he was using was shot to shards by an Israeli sniper. Some of the friars are still plagued by nightmares, some of them addicted to tranquillizers. Most difficult of all, he confides, he faced angry Israeli accusations that by giving the Palestinians sanctuary in the church he and his friars had taken sides in the conflict.

'I told them, I told them very clearly,' he tells me now, a fat forefinger pointed at me, 'that they should not dare start accusing me of anti-Semitism because I come from Umbria where our local hero, a man named Niccacci, did everything in his power to save Jews during the Second World War. They should remember that, I told them. *Voilà, Madame!*'

Gesturing and exclaiming in dramatic Latin style, the *custos* is enjoying himself, but the longer he speaks the clearer it becomes that he has about as many grievances against the Israelis as any of his predecessors had against the Ottomans.

Perhaps the matter of Israeli–*Custodia Terrae Sanctae* relations is uppermost in his mind because, since returning from Umbria yesterday, he has been plunged into another crisis. One of his youngest friars had been brutally harassed at an Israeli checkpoint while travelling between the Franciscan houses in Nazareth and Ein Kerem. Dragged from his car by Israeli soldiers, the youth had been ordered to prove he was not a suicide bomber with a deadly device tucked under his skirts. When he politely refused to strip off the robe of his holy calling, they had forced him to lie face down on the ground and aimed their guns at his neck. Secret-service cars and army jeeps with flashing lights and sirens had converged on the spot and stopped the traffic in both directions.

I venture to wonder if perhaps the unlucky lad was an Arab friar.

'Arab? *Pas de tout, Madame!* Look, here he comes now with our coffee. You're from Naples, aren't you?' he says to the youth, who blushes as his superior reaches up a large hand to administer something between a cuff over his ear and a fatherly ruffle of his hair.

As soon as we are alone the *custos* hitches up his skirts again, drains his little coffee cup in one gulp and looses off another volley of complaint.

'I have to tell you something, *Madame*,' he says. 'About thirty years ago Moshe Dayan* promised one of my predecessors that we friars have nothing to fear, that we are respected, that these brown robes of ours are our best protection. *Et voilà!*'

What a decline in power and influence since the days when all the Catholic courts of Europe funnelled treasure to San Salvatore, when every Catholic ambassador to the Porte spent much of his time battling to secure and expand the rights of the Franciscans in the holy places! I ask the *custos* what real leverage the Franciscans have these days, with no Capitulations to fall back on and no chance of bribing the Israelis as they used to bribe the Ottomans.

Chuckling, he says, 'As soon as you leave I will be writing letters of complaint about this checkpoint incident to the Italian, Spanish

* Israel's defence minister 1967–74.

and French consuls. These days everything for us depends on how Catholic the Catholic countries are.'

His sigh and hint of a shrug suggest that, although he does not expect much help from any of those quarters, he is not down-hearted.

'I must tell you, *chère Madame*, that the Israelis want our land here in Jerusalem but we are determined not to sell it to them, and for this reason they resent us. But these are not the hardest times we have had to suffer here while we guard the holy places. In the past eight hundred years 2,800 of us have been witnesses to our faith, martyrs here in the Holy Land!'

The *Custodia Terrae Sanctae* has kept as careful a tally of its martyrs as it has of its income and properties through the centuries, it appears. Father Athanasius once told me that an important aspect of a *custos*'s job was keeping a detailed diary, an exact record of injustices, complaints, victories and defeats. I imagine that Father Giovanni Battistelli's entry about the persecution of the Neapolitan boy-friar at the Israeli checkpoint will make as lively reading as some of his predecessors' entries.

Only yesterday I was glancing through some headings for a run of incidents recorded by a *custos* in 1633 which included multiple bribes, refused and accepted, to various Ottoman officials, interventions by the Austrian, French and Venetian ambassadors, false promises, contretemps involving the Greek patriarch, more false promises, and various petitions accepted or refused.[xl] The same *custos* also wrote at some length about the 'ridiculous ceremony that the schismatics hold on Holy Saturday to make the holy light come'.[xli] In his day it seems to have involved an Ethiopian priest entering the edicule with a pre-lit lantern hooked to his underpants and concealed under his robe.

One more question for the *custos*: 'Father, you must have heard about the fracas over the Holy Fire at Easter. Is the *Custodia Terrae Sanctae* supporting the Armenians or the Greeks in this dispute'?

'Frankly, we are having some problems with the Greeks because they changed the locks on the door of the Church of the Nativity after the siege and are now claiming an exclusive right to the key.* But in the matter of the Holy Fire, I have to say that I think they have a better case than the Armenians. I must be careful what I say now . . . *Madame*, please tell me, when will your book be published?'

'In about two years time, I think.'

'Two years? *Bon!* I will be back home in Umbria by then with nothing to fear. *Au revoir!*'

~

If the Israelis are coveting the Franciscans' real estate, how much more greedily must they be eyeing the Armenians'?

Although Jerusalem's Armenian community is now only 2,000 strong and shrinking fast, the secretively high-walled Armenian Quarter, built around the vast Armenian monastery of St James, still accounts for a whole sixth of the Old City.

I head towards the Church of the Holy Sepulchre in search of Armenian Artin, passing the Arab Catholic Scouts' hall, Arkhangelos, and the bakery Rahme has forbidden me to patronize. Turning right into the eerily deserted Christian Quarter Road with its locked-up shops I am dismayed to see that even the Internet cafe is closing down. There are boxes of computers stacked up outside. Inside, Tariq, the young Muslim proprietor, is aiming an electric drill at a bared wall. No, he explains, politely climbing down from his ladder, he is not closing, only switching to selling souvenirs and leather sandals.

'Souvenirs? When there are no tourists?'

'We must live in hope,' he replies with a patient smile.

Artin is exactly where I expected to find him, patrolling the church's shady threshold, hopefully scanning the deserted parvis for attractive quarry.

* The dispute erupted in August 2003 when the Armenians and Franciscans protested their right to own a key to the church. All three communities are entitled to a key according to the Status Quo but only the Greeks may use it.

'What's the news?' I ask him as a polite preamble to my enquiries about his Armenian community and their landholdings.

'You want news? What kind of news? The Franciscans are having a service in memory of St Francis's bleeding stigmata this afternoon. Other news? Today is the second anniversary of this intifada. Almost two thousand Palestinians have died and more than six hundred Israelis. More? The Israelis are making Arafat into an animal in Ramallah. He has no water, electricity air-conditioning now . . . Tanks . . . Gaza Strip . . . Nablus . . .'

Artin's recitation of the facts is as monotone as a Byzantine church chant, rendered dull by the repetitive horror of the past two years. It matches the deep weariness I have observed in my acquaintances on this visit. Bishop Theophanis is quieter. Nothing has changed for him but the seating arrangements in his kitchen, these days a pair of church pews upholstered in red velvet. 'What can I do? I have to do something,' he said, when I admired them yesterday. Solomon is busy trying to get a sick Ethiopian monk into hospital and Athanasius is desperate for his annual leave. Refusing to follow the news at all herself, Nasra believes Rahme is slowly losing her mind, tuning in to every television and radio bulletin, gasping and crying and expecting the end of the world.

A man of about fifty carrying a pile of books under one arm is approaching us now. 'Of course you know this man,' says Artin. 'Everyone knows this man.'

I am wondering what to say and guessing I might recognize him if he removes his sunglasses, when he comes to my rescue.

'No, we haven't met, but I think we know people in common. My name is George Hintlian.'

I have not only heard of him from friends who work or interest themselves in the region but I have read his book on the history of the Armenian community in Jerusalem. He is precisely the person I need to help me now but when I tell him the gist of my project he frowns.

'So, you're interested in the Holy Fire. You should know that the incident this Easter has developed into a very serious dispute. Only the other day when I ran into Bishop Theophanis at Jaffa Gate I warned him there would be trouble. I told him, "If you Greeks are going to stick to your version of what happened, there'll be war."'

I wonder what gives George Hintlian – neither the Armenian patriarch nor even a priest – the right to threaten the Greeks with war, but he is walking me out of the courtyard now and into the crowded souk, to a confectioner's whose pyramids of sweets on gigantic tin platters drip with honey and sparkle with poppy seeds. Without so much as a glance at the mouth-watering display, he leads me straight to the back of the shop, to an area furnished with tiled walls, strip lighting and Formica-topped tables. So much light and cool space are luxuries in the Old City.

George is a pillar of Jerusalem's Armenian community, a high church dignitary, secretary to the Armenian patriarch for a quarter of a century, mediator in the community's dealings with the Israelis and diplomats, and vast repository of lore about historical precedent in the holy places. Master of at least five languages, he has written countless learned papers on Armenian Jerusalem. Author of five books to date, he is working on eight more.

'But you must be tremendously busy!'

He dismisses this with a wave of his hand and a shake of his head. 'Now there is something I don't understand about your project. You say that you are exploring the important role that Christian powers have been playing here, right up to the present day, but haven't you noticed that we Christians have no power here any more? We're only two per cent of the population in Jerusalem today! We're beside the point, out of the picture! We're history! The struggle here now is between the Arabs and Jews.'

I explain that the final part of my story will be about American Christian Zionists.

'OK,' he says, after a pause. 'Those people are powerful and becoming more important. Of course, I find it impossible to think of them as Christians. Once I met a young American woman in a cafe who asked me, "Do you know Satan?" I told her that I did because he was inside me. After that she wouldn't leave me alone. When I told her to go away she said, "But how can I when you are in such danger? I have to help you to fight Satan." There are plenty like that these days. Only last week a man I know a little asked me how long I'd had my sunglasses. I was surprised but I told him, "Three years." He begged me to stop wearing them because I was delaying the coming of the messiah! Can you believe that? What kind of Christians can such people be?'

The memory of these encounters pains him too much to laugh. 'What concerns me most is that the majority of them are utterly ignorant about the situation here. They don't know the history; they don't even know that there are Arab Christians – Catholic, Orthodox and Protestant – in the Holy Land today, let alone Armenians, Egyptians, Ethiopians and Syrians. They arrive here with their Old Testaments in their hands, reading black and white simplicity everywhere they look, waiting and hoping for the end of the world. I'm afraid I cannot help you with this aspect of your project, so please don't ask me!'

I quickly reassure him that I was hoping he might help me with my current preoccupation, eighteenth-century Jerusalem.

'With great pleasure,' he replies. 'And now, would you care to accompany me to an Ethiopian ceremony in honour of the Empress Helena's discovery of the True Cross? I imagine that the Ethiopians will be putting on a good show to let the Egyptians see they are not discouraged by their defeat in battle.'

We climb the stairs opposite the confectioner's and reach the Ethiopians' roof terrace by way of the Coptic monastery. To judge by a low rhythmic drumming the ceremony has already begun. One corner of the roof terrace, near the spot where I first saw the old Copt on his chair, is crowded with Ethiopians in their holiday best. The monks are dancing – hopping slowly from foot to foot, then faster and faster, lurching from left to right and back – playing a medley of percussion instruments and singing ancient elemental harmonies. Their dozens of triumphantly raised croziers look like an entire forest of miraculously uncovered crosses. Their singing grows louder, their dancing faster and faster, and pure recalled joy at the unearthing of the holy relic more and more palpable. A courteous Ethiopian diplomat murmurs a translation into my ear: 'They are singing, "Your cross is singing throughout the world to save us from our sins" . . .'

The scene is illuminated by a naked light bulb dangling from the great eucalyptus tree. Directly beneath it, resplendent and seated on a throne set in a rich sea of carpets, is the Ethiopian Archbishop of Jerusalem. His face is impassive but his dark eyes, swivelling left and right, are all-seeing. In front of him, an Ethiopian toddler lurches and stomps along in time to the music, glugging at a plastic bottle like a happy drunk. Behind him, respectfully holding over his head a pearl-spangled parasol such as aristocratic Edwardian ladies affected for a summer's day at the races, stands Solomon. I try to snatch a word with my friend when the formal part of the service ends and the dancing in circles begins, but the helpful consul interrupts our exchange: Solomon's place is with his umbrella behind the archbishop, who is leading the dance.

~

George and I meet every morning now, midway between Arkhangelos and the Armenian Quarter, at Jaffa Gate, where the underemployed taxi drivers squat in the shade behind their white Mercedes. After greeting me with a businesslike 'What's new?' he marches me straight down into the souk, to the cool of the confectioner's shop.

Three or four times he stops abruptly in the middle of the alley to clarify a disputed point about an Armenian patriarch or an Ottoman sultan, oblivious to the crocodile of uniformed schoolchildren piling up behind him or a boy with a heavy carpet on his shoulders jostling to pass. More often he pauses, in mid-flow about eighteenth-century Ottoman firmans, to greet friends: 'Mr Friday', the Muslim greengrocer who wants to find him a wife and broadly hints that I might do, the Greek Orthodox newsagent who is also writing a book about Christians in the Holy Land, an American academic who lives in an old Orthodox monastery like Arkhangelos and teaches history in a Palestinian university or the friendly German woman pastor of the Lutheran Church of the Redeemer. Yesterday we encountered Tamila, sunburnt from her archaeological exertions and deliriously happy at having uncovered another Georgian inscription in a village near Bethlehem.

By the time we arrive at our destination, the tutorial has begun. My question, 'How is it that the Armenians have a sixth of the old city and are a great power in the Church of the Holy Sepulchre?' has been met with a lively survey of Armenian activities in the Holy Land since their conversion to Christianity, which was effected in 301 before even the Emperor Constantine espoused the faith and about twenty years before he gave the order for work to begin excavating Christ's tomb.

'Now, you remember that it was Bishop Makarios who first thought of looking for the tomb and mentioned the idea to Constantine at the Council of Nicaea in 325? Well, that Makarios was in friendly contact with an Armenian bishop. We have some letters they wrote to each other – very kind and intimate . . .'

I must always, George commands me, remember that Armenians were not just the first nation in the world to declare themselves Christian, but also the keenest of pilgrims. Long before the Byzantines officially designated the holy places Armenians were streaming along the old Roman roads towards their saviour's homeland. Caliph Omar recognized their rights as pilgrims to the city in the seventh century and by the time the Crusaders arrived at the end of the eleventh century they boasted their own quarter in Jerusalem.

The Crusaders had treated them well, better than other eastern Christian communities, and had even intermarried with them. Crusader Jerusalem's first two queens, Arda and Melisende, were Armenians. In the field of military fortifications and communications Armenians were unrivalled, and their loyalty to the Crusader cause was never in doubt. But Saladin showed himself equally benevolent towards them by exempting them from paying taxes or ransoms and granting them permission to buy back access to the Church of the Holy Sepulchre. To their possession of a couple of chapels in the church they added exclusive rights to the altars on Calvary. Armenian pilgrim numbers soared. By 1280, a French monk was marvelling at the sight of Armenians roaming 'in troops of one or two hundred', seeing and kissing everywhere 'sweet Jesus sat, stood, or wrought any work'.[xlii]

The Armenians had suffered as a result of the ascendancy of their Georgian neighbours and rivals in the distant Caucasus during the Mamluk era, but they seem to have liked and been liked in return by the Franciscans and Western pilgrims. A fifteenth-century *custos* declared them to be 'the most beautiful men and women in Jerusalem', as well as 'bold and generous'.[xliii] As widely dispersed but also as closely knit and industrious a people as the Jews, the Armenians would thrive under Ottoman rule,* attaining sufficiently influential positions – first at the Mamluk court in Cairo, then at the Porte in Ottoman Constantinople – to, as George puts it, 'maintain and enhance' their situation in Jerusalem.

'But how exactly did you Armenians accumulate so much real estate here?'

'*Habibi!*' George protests. 'Patience! That is the subject of tomorrow's talk. Tomorrow we will be examining what happened to the Armenians here in the eighteenth century. We will meet at 3 o'clock and go straight to the Armenian Quarter. *Ça va, Madame?*' he says in the French he learned at a school run by Catholic monks. 'Now, your homework.' And he hands me a sheaf of photocopies with his name, as translator, on the first. 'This eighteenth-century Armenian priest's account of a pilgrimage here will stimulate your appetite, I think.'

On my return to Arkhangelos this evening I laud George to the skies. Rahme, on her sofa knitting, with one eye trained on the television news, lays down her handiwork to clasp her hands to her

---

* The Armenian genocide of 1915–16 was, in part, a result of Turkish envy at Armenia's prosperity and influence. More than one million Armenians died.

bosom and say, '*Hamdulillah!* Thank God you have found a person to help you!' But Nasra, after a tiresome day spent idling in her car at Israeli checkpoints, is not so trusting. 'Who is he, this George? He is helping you? Fantastic! But an Armenian who does something for nothing? Impossible! It has never happened, not since the beginning of the world! I will try to find out what he wants.' I cannot resist telling her that George has already made enquiries about her and Rahme and learned that the Dahdal sisters are renowned as 'very strong women – no one wants to argue with them'. Nasra looks neither flattered nor amused. Lighting up the narghile, she resumes her perusal of a stack of glossy brochures.

'Shall I buy a Ford, or a Mitsubishi or a Volkswagen Passat?' she muses aloud to me now.

'You're going to buy a new car, Nasra? At this time?'

'A Passat, I think . . . Yes, this terrible time is exactly when I need something to make me happy. Don't I deserve a nice mobile home with tinted windows and a sunroof and special wheels to impress the soldiers at the checkpoints?'

'Naturally! What colour?'

'Metallic blue is very elegant, don't you think so?' she says, exhaling a long plume of apple-sweet smoke. 'You know, I'm serious. I want to have my dignity when those boy soldiers give me trouble and make me feel like an insect. Today I asked one if he would dare to treat his mother like he was treating me.'

We sit in companionable silence awhile, passing the narghile hose back and forth, each of us, in our own way, escaping the intifada blasting out of Rahme's television. Nasra reads about wheel specifications, and I about an Armenian named Zvar Jiyerji who came on pilgrimage to the Holy Land in 1721.

Jiyerji and his fellow pilgrims arrived by boat at Jaffa but had to wait until midnight before enough camels could be found for the final leg of the journey to Jerusalem. It was night again before they had paid the various tolls at Jaffa Gate and been welcomed by the entire brotherhood of Armenian monks, and the small hours of another morning when they were roused from their slumbers, provided with two candles each and led through the sleeping city to the Church of the Holy Sepulchre. The Franciscans were in the ascendant at the time; a friar was supervising traffic in and out of the edicule.

On a subsequent daytime visit to the church Jiyerji found the parvis – an empty space now in this third year of intifada – teeming with noisy traders, a 'big bazaar where everything is sold – lemons, figs, raisins, bracelets, bottles, soaps, halva, rosaries, candles, belts, pictures, cloths, dishes, carpets', and so crowded 'that there is no space to drop a needle'. Observing hordes of money changers, he warned his readers against pickpockets who would 'steal even the pupil of your eye'. The sight of a raised divan placed in front of the main door of the church, where Muslim doorkeepers lolled, smoking a narghile while collecting entrance fees, dismayed him. Like most pilgrims he was shamed to discover that the Muslim troops who patrolled Christendom's holiest shrine were not protecting the church's contents from thieves and vandals but preventing feuds among its Christian guardians. As fascinated as the English merchant Henry Timberlake by the domestic arrangements in the church, Jiyerji described an upper-storey window through which the Armenian monks living in the church routinely pulled up their provisions. In the chapel under Calvary he observed pilgrims rubbing up against the stone sarcophagi of the Crusader kings in the belief that the contact could cure stomach pain. In the Franciscans' living quarters he spied 'a partridge in a cage'.

Jiyerji visited Bethlehem and the Church of the Nativity, next door to which he noticed a Franciscan school for Arab boys of the 'Frank' religion. The wealth of the friars there – their 'four chests containing beautiful vestments' and 'very sunny and newly built' cells with glass windows and maps on the walls – impressed him. But the great monastery where he stayed in Jerusalem, still known as the Armenian Convent, was its equal in every way. Behind its high walls was not only the famously beautiful church of St James but also plentiful, comfortable accommodation for the thousands of Armenian pilgrims who arrived in the city every Easter. Large stables, a long refectory, a dairy, a courtyard filled with chickens, a building devoted to winemaking and a carpenter's shop were only a few of its excellent amenities. 'As you enter through the main gate,' Jiyerji noted, 'there are big cauldrons for washing linen. Whoever desires goes to the garden and washes their clothes. The cauldrons are kept in an iron-grilled room, which is where they also imprison people.'[xliv]

~

The mighty iron doors of the monastery are still there, but there is no sign of the laundry prison, and no time to look for it because George leads me straight past the porter's lodge and across a shady courtyard to the church of St James.*

'We Armenians are more devoted to this fifth-century church of ours than we are to the Church of the Holy Sepulchre,' he confides, tugging aside the heavy curtain in front of the door. 'I think you will see why.'

From the high light ceiling of the church hang hundreds of silver lamps and decorated porcelain eggs, some higher, some lower, their ropes and chains almost invisible. It is as if God, raining down his richest and kindest blessings on this Armenian place, had engineered a mid-air petrifaction of each one of them, to bear eternal witness to his bounty. The effect is miraculously beautiful and more conducive to the contemplation of eternity than anything I have seen in the Church of the Holy Sepulchre. St James is a hallway to heaven, and its dangling delights render me blind to the service in progress at the altar and deaf to whatever has preceded George's '. . . a very fine mixture of Byzantine, Armenian and Crusader architectural styles.'

'But all these lamps and eggs, George!'

'The eggs symbolize eternity, of course, but the lamps are more

* James was Jerusalem's first bishop and possibly Jesus' brother (Mark 6:3) who died in AD 62.

interesting. There are three hundred and fifty of them, each the gift of an Armenian pilgrim, inscribed with his name and the year he made his pilgrimage here. Now, you see that priest over there, filling lamps with oil?'

I do. I have been watching him manipulating an elaborate system of ropes and pulleys to bring to earth, one by one, entire strings of lamps for refuelling.

'He's written a book about the inscriptions on the lamps so he knows each as if it was his own child. On an important feast day it takes him three or four hours to light them all.'

Centuries of Armenian wealth and piety are concentrated in this church: finest woods inlaid with mother of pearl, tortoiseshell and ivory, rich blue tiling and icons encased in gold and silver.

'Most of this decoration was done in the eighteenth century, in the time of our greatest patriarch, Gregory the Chain-bearer. We have a wonderful account by a monk who worked on the restoration as a plasterer and tiler. Starting with the church of St James in 1726, he helped to plaster and tile the various churches of the convent, the refectory, the wine cellar, two hundred and sixty rooms, even the Armenian properties in the Church of the Nativity in Bethlehem. Now I must tell you all about this famous Patriarch Gregory the Chain-bearer. Here are his chains!'

I have followed George through a doorway in the left-hand side of the church into a gloomy sacristy. In the far corner, next to an ancient marble baptismal font, behind a red plush curtain, is a glass cabinet containing a chain thick enough to pull a lorry, with a great rusty lock.

'For many years Gregory – who already wore a hair shirt studded with nails next to his skin – also wore this chain around his neck. Now, the question is, why did he force himself to suffer like this? Patience please, while I give you the background.'

The first decade of the eighteenth century had marked a shame-ful trough in the convent's fortunes; the Armenian patriarch in Constantinople was administering it long distance, using two agents – one cleric, one layman – to attend to his affairs in Jerusalem.

These men shamelessly abused their short postings to make as much money as they could for themselves. Introducing economies such as closing the monks' refectory, they sold off the church's treasures and fleeced visitors so savagely that pilgrim traffic slowed to a trickle. Worse still, they made free with the monastery's seal to borrow large sums from Muslims at ruinous rates of interest. By around 1710 the creditors were demanding repayment in full and turning to the Ottoman authorities for help with getting it. Bailiffs backed by troops invaded the monastery. 'Sometimes,' according to one witness, the creditors 'shut up the church and refused to allow the services to take place. Sometimes, even while the priest was celebrating mass they entered and dared to snatch the chalice from the hands of the celebrant.'[xlv] Many monks fled in terror.

At last, in 1713, a priest of 'good moral behaviour' was found and sent to Jerusalem to rescue the patriarchate and redeem the Armenians' silver lamps which belonged inside the edicule in the Church of the Holy Sepulchre. But his best efforts were wasted when a change of patriarch in Constantinople heralded the advent of yet another set of thieving agents. Now the creditors were demanding the sale of the entire convent. Backed by pathetically weeping monks, the good priest eventually managed to win a period of four years grace in which to repay all the monastery's debts. Immediately he destroyed the seal of the monastery which had been so wickedly abused and, returning to Constantinople, informed the community there that their countrymen in Jerusalem were in urgent need of a resident patriarch. His listeners were so impressed by the man's acute analysis of the situation that they set him on the patriarchal throne of Constantinople and invited him to appoint whomever he pleased to that of Jerusalem.

'. . . and the person who pleased him was his, and our, friend Gregory the Chain-bearer,' says George. 'Now Gregory had no ambitions in this direction but, *habibi*, for the good of the nation, what could he do? He was consecrated in 1717, when the monastery was still eight hundred purses in debt.'

An effective publicity campaign to draw attention to the plight of Jerusalem's Armenian Convent was needed and Gregory had an idea. Draping those heavy chains about his neck, he spent the next eight years loitering outside rich Armenian churches in Constantinople, begging for funds to save the Armenian properties in the Holy Land. 'My house is in bond and my children are taken from me, and I have entered captivity and sit in bitter mourning,' he lamented to passers-by. 'I was the throne of the Apostle James and now I am a throne of debts and there is no one to help me.' Donations poured in, but his departure for Jerusalem was delayed by the news that the Greek Orthodox and Franciscans had recently won permission to renovate their sections of the Church of the Holy Sepulchre. Gregory had to increase his target sum and continue begging if the Armenians were not to be left behind in the pious contest to honour Christ's tomb.

In 1721, still hung with his chains, Gregory arrived in Jerusalem at last, so famous that 'even the Moslems, who had heard about him, wanted to see him'.[xlvi] He was lucky they did not rob him because he must have been carrying a stupendous sum of money. No sooner had he funded works in the Armenian section of the Church of the Holy Sepulchre and repaid the convent's debts, than he embarked on his gigantic programme of lavish redecoration and expansion. It was Gregory who encircled the Armenian Quarter with its high wall and Gregory who reorganized two thirds of the quarter into twenty great courtyards named after the main centres of Armenian settlement in Ottoman Anatolia.

George continues my tutorial in the monks' old refectory, which Gregory the Chain-bearer lavishly refurbished with new tiled walls and marble tables. I wonder if Gregory did not collect rather too much money from the generous Armenians of Constantinople. 'Did the monks really need marble tables?' I ask George, but he is too busy opening a small door in a cupboard behind one of the benches to attend to me. 'Come and see this,' he commands. 'The creditors always came looking for payment at mealtimes because they knew the monks would be here, so this was built. The monks could escape out of here and down a rope as soon as they heard they were on their way. There's a drop of about two metres down to the courtyard below.'

We descend to ground level by a flight of stairs and George continues: 'So every year the pilgrims came from the big towns in Anatolia – Erzurum and Smyrna and Adana and so on – and found lodgings around the courtyard named after their home town. We are in Smyrna now, for example. The rich ones donated money for the construction of rooms and had their names and the date of their pilgrimages inscribed. Come!'

Armenian inscriptions as curly and decorative but as impenetrable to me as the Georgian one Tamila and her team are replacing on the back wall of the church near Bishop Theophanis' bungalow grace almost every lintel and archway we pass on our stroll from courtyard to courtyard.

'Look, this one is from 1720.' George translates for me: 'Pilgrim Sergius, a banker, is asking for his grandson and all his family's dead to be remembered. I have to emphasize that this pilgrim business was extremely well organized. Just imagine, there was a monk stationed in Jaffa as a sort of permanent spy for the patriarchate. It was his job to collect intelligence about any Armenian pilgrims on their way here. For example, he might send word that an Austrian boat carrying a group of rich Armenian merchants was about to arrive. Well, the preparations would begin right away because the wealthier the pilgrim and the larger his likely donation the more lavish the welcome had to be.'

George and I wander on, into a sunny courtyard that must be double the size of the Church of the Holy Sepulchre's parvis. In a shady corner on the far side three little girls are playing with dolls and a toy pram. In another corner two boys in flashy trainers are bouncing a football, in a third a pair of old men are sitting chatting. None of them pays the slightest attention to the ordinarily bizarre figure of an Armenian monk in his black robe and trapezoidal headgear strolling by.

It is not too hard now to picture the tumultuous arrival of a caravan of rich Armenian pilgrims. I can see and smell their horses, the lines of donkeys heavily laden with packages of goods to trade but also silverware for the churches of St James and the Holy Sepulchre. I can easily imagine the noise and excitement, the monks scurrying to and fro about their guests' business, the chickens, the beggars . . . But I can also imagine how the money and treasure pouring into the great Christian establishments – the Armenian Convent, the Franciscans' San Salvatore and the Greek Orthodox patriarchate – from all corners of Christendom excited both the envy and the avarice of the local Ottoman officials far from Constantinople, here on the fringes of the empire. And, after wandering around this Armenian Convent, from vast courtyard to vast courtyard, I am not in the least surprised to hear that so much space and fine architecture in the middle of the Old City has long excited the avarice and envy of the Israelis. What George has to say about Israelis purchasing houses and land in the Armenian Quarter while prohibiting new Armenian building projects echoes what I heard from *Il Reverendissimo* at San Salvatore.

But Ottoman pressure on the great Christian monasteries could be much less subtle than the Israelis' if the tale I uncovered in San Salvatore's library that morning is anything to go by. On 3 April 1766 an Ottoman *qadi* stormed the Franciscans' headquarters with a posse of soldiers. He was not acting on behalf of Muslim creditors as had been the case at the Armenian Convent before Gregory the Chain-bearer set its affairs in order. This *qadi*'s purpose was simple extortion. He claimed to be acting on information that a certain friar had drowned a little boy in the monastery's water cistern. A child was indeed lying at the bottom of the cistern but it was his father who, handsomely bribed by the *qadi*, had hurled him in there. Fortunately for the Franciscans, the Ottoman governor of the city suspected foul play and the plot was uncovered. Undeterred by this embarrassing setback, the *qadi* energetically resumed his campaign. After finding a Muslim he could bribe to bear false witness against the friar, he staged a trial, but the witness let him down by announcing to the court that he did not want to sully his faith and honour by telling lies. Even this fiasco was not enough to stifle the *qadi*'s appetite for Franciscan gold. Over and over again he dispatched his servant to San Salvatore with a warning that the still incarcerated friar would be executed unless the *custos* bailed him out with twenty bags of piastres. The intervention of the Ottoman governor, who denounced the *qadi* in a report to the Sublime Porte, was what finally secured the poor friar's release.

The story is a fine example of the tension resulting from the widening gulf between the confidently wealthy Christian establishments in Jerusalem and their fast degrading surroundings.

If the Ottomans had only known it, the Franciscans' gifts and bribes of clocks and spectacles, globes and knives – just like the proliferating Capitulations – augured grave trouble ahead. Determined to conserve what they believed to be the perfect political system as revealed by God to their prophet Mohammad, the sultans had been resisting the forces of change and enterprise without which there was no competing with Christian Europe in the long term, either economically or militarily. The glory days of the Ottoman empire were gone. In the same way as eighteenth-century sultans were no longer conferring Capitulations on European monarchs in the munificent manner of Suleiman the Magnificent, but being bullied into doing so in exchange for large bribes, Jerusalem's *qadi* was not graciously accepting gifts and sweeteners and giving generously in return, but grabbing whatever he could, by whatever means he could.

The Ottoman empire was in retreat and the great Christian monasteries of Jerusalem – wealthy, expanding, busy and influential – were a constant prickly reminder to Jerusalem's Turkish authorities and Muslim population of how fast and far Christian Europe was advancing.

CHRISTMAS 2002

*'Have you heard of this deplorable Jerusalem matter?
There is not a single Anglican at Jerusalem, but we are
to place a bishop there . . .'*

– JOHN HENRY NEWMAN

From here in bed in my cell in Arkhangelos I can smell damp and hear splashing on the pile of plastic rubbish bags outside the window. The bells of San Salvatore sound muffled, the neighbours silenced behind closed windows. If I raise my head from the pillow and crane my neck up towards the narrow window, I can see a sliver of low sky whose heavy grey light belongs in the northern Europe I left yesterday.

Rahme's radio is on at full volume, tuned to an Arabic station playing 'We Wish You a Merry Christmas'. She wants me to get up. I don the holly-berry-red waistcoat she has knitted me for Christmas and the beige cardigan she gave me on my last visit, and emerge. We giggle together grimly at her Arab newspaper cartoon of a beggarly Santa Claus being interrogated by an Israeli soldier: 'Where are your documents? Who do you know in Bethlehem?' We wonder if the Israelis will lift the curfew on Bethlehem long enough for the Latins to hold their midnight mass. Nasra has offered to take me to the Franciscans' service there and to put me up overnight in her flat, if 'the situation' permits.

Booted, bundled in scarves and armed with Rahme's umbrella, I venture out into the cold and rain. The Arab Catholic Scouts are marking the season with strings of coloured lights slung across the wet front of their headquarters and a speaker blaring 'Jingle Bells'. Rainwater streams down the middle of the alleys, bobbing with bright plastic litter. The green metal doors of the souvenir stalls along Christian Quarter Street are all closed. Only the Orthodox newsagent – swaddled in overcoat and scarves – is sitting in his shop, toasting a breakfast roll on his electric bar heater. He has made no progress on his own book about Holy Land Christianity, he tells me. Sheltering in an empty tourist cafe by Jaffa Gate I watch the owner putting the last forlorn touches to his Christmas tree decorations before I set out again for the Church of the Holy Sepulchre. First left, first left again, third right.

The parvis is puddled and deserted but for three men identically dressed in smart khaki uniforms with brass buttons and dark red fezzes. Retained by the various churches to punctuate their solemn processions through the old city with a doleful banging of their silver-headed staves on the flagstones, they are Arab ceremonial guards known as *kawass*, living relics of the nineteenth century I am about to return to. One of them is playing a carol on a small trumpet – '*Glo-o-o-o-o, o-o-o-o, o-o-o-o-ri-a! In ex-cel-sis De-o!*' – as I pass on my way to a dark entrance in the far corner of the courtyard.

Climbing the rickety stairs, I arrive up on the Ethiopians' roof terrace as the whipping wind picks up to a squall. The huts are patched with damp and the rain beating a hectic tattoo on their corrugated iron roofs. Huddled in the furthest corner of the terrace, under an umbrella, are three of Solomon's brothers. We four watch in silence as the old Copt, zipped into a black anorak with a plastic sou'wester to protect his embroidered bonnet, hobbles slowly past with his chair, on his way to the dripping eucalyptus tree. No change there.

The Church of the Holy Sepulchre is damp, chilly as a refrigerator. A sudden explosion of angry voices soon lures me away from the bright reflected warmth of a group of Nigerian pilgrims singing and swaying around the edicule, back towards the entrance. At the foot of the marble steps leading up to Calvary, a young thug is booting the backside of an elderly man cowering against the wall, whimpering, his arms up around his head for protection. A small crowd of onlookers disperses as two Israeli policemen saunter in to stop the fight, but nonchalantly, as if they perform the same chore every day of the week. Artin appears at my elbow, shaking his head. 'They are guides,' he says, as if we had spoken yesterday, 'and their god is the shekel, but now they can't get the shekel because there are no tourists, so they fight.' He looks as he did when we first met in early spring: fur-trimmed cap, overcoat and tartan scarf neatly folded over his chest. 'I have new boots,' he says, raising one foot to show me, 'only 130 shekels.'

The rain has not abated. Rahme's umbrella flips inside out and back again in the wind. Heading back to Arkhangelos by way of Jaffa Gate I encounter San Salvatore's assistant librarian, a Spanish nun, wearing outsize wellington boots under her knee-length grey habit and anorak. 'A wonderful gift from God!' she declares. 'You cannot believe how much this rain is needed here!'

~

Napoleon's Holy Land campaign began in a winter like this one, in late 1799, with his capture of Gaza.

After a year of desert drought in Egypt, during which his army had been reduced to fighting over water so brackish that even the horses refused to drink it, the Holy Land's rain was a godsend. But only momentarily; the soldiers had the wrong kit and were plagued by insects, then plague itself. The spring came, and the summer when, in a mini-rehearsal for the great retreat from Moscow twelve years later, the future conqueror of most of Europe suffered a first defeat at the hands of the Ottomans and the British. His army in tatters and his campaign a fiasco, Napoleon retreated to Egypt. Towards the end of June that year one of his top generals, an *ancien régime* God-fearing man at heart, confessed in a letter to another general: 'We have committed in the Holy Land enormous sins and great stupidities; but it is necessary to let the curtain of the tabernacle fall on all this, and let us beware of ever raising it again for fear that the Almighty, in his wrath, will punish us for our temerity.'[i]

A romantic dream of conquering Ottoman Constantinople*
and ruling over a world empire as grand as that of Alexander the
Great had been the inspiration for Napoleon's foolish foray into the
Holy Land. Christianity had nothing to do with it. Although he was
inclined to play on Crusading associations and give his battles
resounding Biblical place names, Napoleon had not cared to
liberate Jerusalem. 'Oh no! Jerusalem is not in my line of operation,'
he is reported to have said. 'I do not wish to be annoyed by mountain people in difficult roads. And besides, on the other side of the
mountains, I should be assaulted by swarms of cavalry.'[ii]

So unmoved by Christian feeling was Napoleon that he made
little effort to secure the support of the Holy Land's Christians.
Instead, he wooed the Muslims with a reminder that he was the
enemy of their enemy, the Catholic pope in Rome, and appealed to
the small and beggarly Jewish community with a proclamation,
fraudulently date-lined Jerusalem, offering them swift restoration
to their ancient homeland and capital. Neither Muslims nor Jews
believed the promises of the vainglorious young Corsican. Any
dreams Jews were daring to nourish about a national homeland
would have to wait another hundred years or so, for the sponsorship
of another European power, Britain, to be realized.

Abortive though it was, that first military return of Europe to
the East, 500 years after the fall of the last Crusader stronghold at
Acre, signalled the beginning of the end for the Ottoman empire
and Muslim rule in the Holy Land. Napoleon's Holy Land campaign
launched more than a century of struggle between the colonial
empires of Britain and France, and later Russia and Germany too,
for influence in the region. The old pious love for Christ's empty
tomb and the city that housed it would be at best harnessed to, at
worst entirely replaced by, simple greed for commercial gain and
imperial sway.

But in the shorter term the chaos caused in both Egypt and

* Although conquered by the Ottoman Turks in 1453 and renamed Istanbul four years
later, the city continued to be commonly known by its former name in Europe.

Palestine by Napoleon's failure to expand his empire in a south-easterly direction resulted in a warming of relations between East and West. Ottoman Turkish rule in Egypt was replaced for thirty years or so by that of Mehemet Ali, a rebel soldier in the Ottoman army who while fighting Napoleon's army had noted its technological advantages and begun dreaming the European dream of a nation state. Mehemet Ali and his son Ibrahim, a military genius who conquered the Holy Land for his father in 1831, began dragging their people into the nascent nineteenth century by courting Europe. Every effort was made to reinvigorate western Christian pilgrimage to the holy places. The entrance fee to the Church of the Holy Sepulchre was abolished and, for the first time, Protestant missionaries were free to come and spread their message.

These proofs of respect and interest from East to West did not go unreciprocated. Although different in quality, the attraction was mutual. The 165 scientists, archaeologists and propagandists in Napoleon's retinue on his expedition returned home to enlighten their countrymen. The age's reverence for the classical embraced pyramids and hieroglyphics and all the ruins of the ancient world, and soon awakened a nostalgic interest in old French associations with the East. France's special role as protector of the Holy Land's Catholics since the time of Francis I and Suleiman the Magnificent was recalled, romantic tales of crusades and pilgrimages recollected and refurbished.

A flamboyantly aristocratic man of letters, Viscount François-René de Chateaubriand, was among the first of the new French romantics to turn pilgrim and take ship for the Holy Land – in 1806, only five years after Napoleon's ignominious ousting. In Jerusalem Chateaubriand expended more energy on bullying the Franciscan *custos* at San Salvatore into dubbing him a Knight of the Holy Sepulchre than on worshipping at the holy places, but the vivid journal he kept of his pilgrimage was a runaway best-seller back home and his principal discovery – that despotic Ottoman rule and obscurantist Islam were 'civilization's enemy' – found a ready and appreciative audience.

British pilgrims of the period saw more to criticize in the Holy Land's brand of Christianity than in Islam. Both the Orthodox and Roman Catholic taste for tacky images, tatty drapery and encrustations of gilt and marble offended the Protestant love of the bare and spare. Edward Daniel Clarke, a young curate who accompanied the British military expedition to expel Napoleon from the East, ventured to suggest that if Muslims instead of Catholics and Orthodox had been in sole charge of the Christian holy places since their capture by the Mamluks at the end of the thirteenth century, they would have ignored them and, by default, done a much better job of preserving them. Dismayed by the cluttered squalor of the Church of the Holy Sepulchre and deeply sceptical of its claim to be the single site of both Christ's crucifixion and his burial, Clarke permitted himself an outburst of pure Protestant fervour against the old Churches of the Holy Land. Exhorting his countrymen 'to quit these degrading fallacies' he urged a 'break from our Monkish instructors and, instead of viewing Jerusalem as pilgrims, [let us] examine it by the light of History, with the Bible in our hands'.[iii]

Not French military, intellectual or romantic interest in the East so much as the reforming missionary energies of Protestant Englishmen like Clarke would fuel Christian Europe's return to its old Crusader haunts.

The simple zeal and missionary spirit of the Methodists had inspired an active evangelical mood in a large and growing section of the complacently decaying Church of England.* Evangelical Anglicans believed that if Christianity was to continue to have a voice in the new industrial age of rapid social change and scientific progress, the Church must be stripped of its fancy flummery and the religion returned to its bare essentials. Disorientated and restless in their new cities, the toiling masses must be helped to keep faith with the Gospel or they would espouse a more dangerous creed –

* The term 'evangelical' is used of the Churches of the Reformation because of their claim to base their teaching predominantly on the Gospel, (*evangel* is Greek for gospel). By the nineteenth century, evangelicals were prominent in social reform and missionary work.

Republicanism. Practical adherence to Christ's precepts and a strict belief in the literal, rather than mythic, truth of the Bible as the Word of God were the hallmarks of evangelicalism, and its proponents so loved the man in their man-god that by the start of the nineteenth century hundreds were taking ship to visit his home, Bibles and maps in hand, as thirsty as Edward Daniel Clarke for factual and scientific proof that the Scriptures were true. This fashion would culminate in 1865 in the creation of the Palestine Exploration Fund (PEF),* an excellently endowed society whose chief patron was Queen Victoria. In a spirit as officiously pious as that which had informed the Crusades, officers of the Royal Engineers who ran the fund would set about excavating and measuring and mapping the Holy Land, to test the reliability of the Bible.† One of the PEF's main objectives was to uncover traces of the wall that had marked the city's limits in Christ's day; its position would prove or disprove the old Holy Land Churches' claim that the Church of the Holy Sepulchre housed the sites of both Jesus' death and his burial.

Most British visitors to Palestine in the first half of the nineteenth century contented themselves with identifying the rivers, mountains, valleys and towns named in the Bible, but many were as satisfied as Edward Daniel Clarke had been to conclude that the chief attractions of the Church of the Holy Sepulchre were flagrant lies, put about and held to for centuries by churchmen who did not merit the name. For them Christendom's holiest site was simply a derelict den where, like the novelist William Thackeray, they observed 'priests clad in outlandish robes, snuffling and chanting incomprehensible litanies, robing, disrobing, lighting up candles or extinguishing them, advancing, retreating, bowing'. Thackeray caricatured the English visitor of the period as a man 'with his hands in his pockets', elbowing his way inside the church, where he 'flings

---

* By the end of the nineteenth century the British, the Germans, the Russians, the French and the Americans would all have archaeological missions in Palestine.
† The Royal Engineers were seconded by the War Office. The PEF's detailed maps of Palestine would prove invaluable to General Edmund Allenby's invading army in 1917.

a few scornful piastres to the Turkish doorkeeper and gazes round easily' in a place where Orthodox and Catholic worship 'in rapture or wonder'.[iv]

In the eyes of ardent evangelicals, Holy Land Christians, Orthodox and Catholic, had blackened the very name of Jesus. Furthermore, by peddling a Christianity that was repellent and ridiculous to Muslims and Jews alike, they had been denying both those peoples not just eternal salvation but also a share in the advanced European civilization that enlightened Protestant Christianity had produced. With armed Muslim guards policing the Holy Sepulchre, violently curbing the monks' daily demonstrations of disobedience to the Saviour's injunction to love one another, the evangelicals' reforming zeal seemed only sensible. And news of the bloodbath which accompanied the Holy Fire ceremony of Easter 1834 only heightened it.

Although no evangelical, the Honourable Robert Curzon was a typically appalled British witness of the Holy Fire's unfinest hour. One aristocratic Anglican among the thousands of mostly Orthodox Christian pilgrims packing Jerusalem for Easter that year, his status as the guest of Palestine's ruler – Mehemet Ali's affable son Ibrahim Pasha – spared him the discomfort of rubbing shoulders with the excited, stinking herd of Greek and Russian peasants, Armenians, Egyptians, Ethiopians and local Orthodox. Instead, his path into the church cleared by soldiers, he was ushered straight up to a gallery and onto a divan to view the spectacle. Once he and his host had settled on their cushions and refreshed themselves with sherbets served by a friar, Ibrahim Pasha discreetly signalled their readiness for the ceremony to begin.

All proceeded to plan for a while. The Greeks in their glittering finery had processed three times around the edicule and the patriarch had disappeared inside to emerge a few minutes later with his lit candles, pretending, as usual, to be faint with the spiritual strain of the occasion. But then the trouble began. Far from wondering how the miracle had been achieved or acknowledging the emotive power of the spectacle, Curzon was observing 'three unhappy wretches, overcome by heat and bad air, toppling down from the uppermost gallery' and being 'dashed to pieces on the heads of the people below'.ᵛ Ibrahim Pasha left in haste, his exit route cleared by the slicing blades of his soldiers' bayonets.

Curzon waited until he judged the mayhem to have abated and the church to have emptied a little before descending from the gallery and making for the main door. Not until then did he discover that a full-blown disaster was unfolding, the product of panic and chaos, of pilgrims fighting to leave the church while soldiers battled to enter to restore order. And not until he reached the steps up to Calvary did he understand that the bodies he was clambering over were not those of people recovering by the open door from near-suffocation by candle smoke, but corpses. Many were 'quite black with suffocation, and farther on were others all bloody and covered with the brains and entrails of those who had been trodden to pieces by the crowd'. The church walls, Curzon noted, were 'spattered with blood and brains of men who had been felled, like oxen, with the butt-ends of the soldiers' bayonets'. On deciding to retreat back inside the church, Curzon found himself wrestling an Ottoman officer 'with the energy of despair'. Only after killing the man and staggering back over the heap of corpses, did he reach safety.ᵛⁱ

On the orders of Ibrahim Pasha the hundreds of dead were removed to the courtyards of San Salvatore, the Greek patriarchate and the Armenian Convent, to be laid in neat rows for identification by wailing relatives. Curzon, an unappreciative guest of the Franciscans at San Salvatore, retired to bed early but did not sleep. In the courtyard beneath his window a stiff breeze ruffled the shrouds of the bodies of the dead, tricking him into thinking they were all alive again.

The next morning he called on his friend the pasha to recommend that the Holy Fire 'trick' be immediately outlawed. While sharing the English aristocrat's dismay at the previous day's senseless carnage and acknowledging the absurdity of a miracle timed 'for the convenience of a Mohametan prince',ᵛⁱⁱ Ibrahim Pasha gave Curzon to understand that he would be inviting the wrath of too many powerful Christian nations – not least Russia – if he banned the ceremony. Such a prohibition could too easily be interpreted as Muslim persecution of Christians and used against him.

Like the Crusader King Baldwin I, the pasha might also have been considering the giant loss to his exchequer of so many thousands of pilgrims every year. Instead of abolishing the Holy Fire, he took a leaf out of the Ottomans' old book and simply fined the Greek patriarch.

~

The Honourable Robert Curzon was not the only haughty Englishman in Jerusalem that bloodied Easter.

On this last dark Sunday afternoon before Christmas, I am sitting at a table in the warm cafe annexe of Christ Church, the first Protestant church in the Holy Land, between Jaffa Gate and the Armenian Quarter. Outside, the sky is iron grey and the wind wild and wet, but in here all is light and dry and convivial. A chance enquiry to the Australian manager of Christ Church's hostel has resulted in the production of a large, suede-bound volume of a journal penned by John Nicolayson, one of the first British missionaries to arrive in Jerusalem after Napoleon's failed Holy Land campaign and the region's subsequent opening to Western influence.

The diary's yellowing pages are freckled with damp. Nicolayson's minute and spidery copperplate hand is hard to read, especially as he does not waste a millimetre of either margin. But he has new light to shed on the 'horrid wickedness' of the Holy Fire in general and the 'tragical and shocking result' of the 1834 ceremony in particular.

A year before the catastrophe, in an entry for Holy Saturday 1833, he writes that he secured himself a good place in the Church of the Holy Sepulchre from which to view 'the farce' and have his already strong belief in the urgent need for a Protestant mission to the city richly confirmed. 'O that one had the Spirit and Power of [St] Paul to attack successfully this stronghold of bare-faced falsehood and of consecrated iniquity!' is his hand-wringing verdict on the spectacle. A few months later he has 'much conversation' about the Holy Fire with a Greek priest who 'holds to it but shows so much embarrassment on the subject . . .' I cannot make out what follows, either by squinting at the page close up, or by holding the volume at arm's length.

Scanning the remainder of Nicolayson's entries for 1833 and skipping on towards the fateful Easter of 1834, I am brought up short by the entry for 20 March. 'It is now fully determined by the patriarch,' Nicolayson wrote, 'to put a stop to the disgraceful institution of the Holy Fire.' The Greek patriarch in Jerusalem had asked the 'more enlightened part of the clergy' to pass this brave ruling on to their fellows in the various Orthodox lands, that they might spread the word to their flocks. But many pilgrims had already embarked on their voyages to the Holy Land. Nicolayson is soon irritated to discover that, after all, the farce would take place as usual, 'but that for the last time' because the patriarch had pledged to announce the discontinuation of the custom just as soon as Easter was over. The righteous missionary's long entry for the ensuing carnage of Holy Saturday 1834 concludes with a prayer that sounds more like a curse: 'O, that this divine judgment upon them [the eastern Churches] might at last open the eyes of the infatuated multitudes and strike terror into the hardened hearts of the wicked perpetrators of that abominable imposture! . . .'

I am flipping pages again, looking for an account of Easter the following year, but can find little more than daily references to Nicolayson having 'general conversation' (networking social chat) or 'serious conversation' (heated theological debate) with Muslims, Jews and Christians of every sort. Here and there my straining eyes alight on something of greater interest. In June 1835 an Ethiopian priest gave Nicolayson 'a very extraordinary account of the Jews in Abyssinia, much of which seem[ed] utterly incredible'. On 1 July he visited the most squalid Jewish quarter of the city to view progress on the building of a new synagogue, and heartily approved it as marking a change for the better 'in the situation and prospects of this nation in the land of their fathers'. Two months on he was having some 'serious conversation' with a Muslim about the Holy Trinity, but also wearily complaining that the Franciscans were 'making special efforts' to prevent local Catholics sending their children to the Protestant mission school he had opened, while the Greeks were keeping 'still more aloof'. Both Greeks and Latins were slyly sabotaging the British mission by misinforming their flocks that England was a 'Protestant' rather than a 'Christian' country.

Someone is wiping down surfaces and pushing chairs around as I transcribe a final few lines. In late May 1836 three 'very noisy and boisterous' Polish Jews came to call on Nicolayson for 'several hours of discussion'. Nicolayson reported that 'at length they admitted that it was all right for Christians to believe in Jesus as the Messiah, but not anyone born a Jew and added, only let us alone and we will let you alone, to which my reply was that Christ had commanded us to teach all nations, to convince by argument but not by force or any other means'.

Determined to force their way into the city's already over-crowded religious market place, Nicolayson and his fellow mission-aries were debating with 'all nations' in Jerusalem but it was the Jews they most wanted to convert to their evangelical Christianity. There was no hiding this fact because they were employed by a mission society called the London Society for Promoting Christianity Amongst the Jews.

Founded in London in 1809 by a German Jewish convert to Christianity and zealous English evangelicals, the London Jews' Society, as it soon became known, was one among many similar manifestations of the exalted mood galvanizing the Church of England and British society in general at the start of the nineteenth century while Napoleon was sweeping across Europe overturning thrones and hierarchies. In the utterances of the prophets and the apocalyptic revelations of St John the Divine many evan-gelicals were thrilled and comforted to discover an uncannily accurate reflection of the events they were witnessing. Here, they believed, was a clear plan to reorientate themselves by. History was not collapsing into barbarous chaos but working up to a thrilling climax. The end of this world, Christ's promised second coming and his thousand-year reign of peace were nigh. The great Protestant nations of the north – Britain and Holland, presumably – were about to set the end times in motion by confronting Napoleonic France and Catholic Europe on the battlefield at Armageddon in Palestine.

However, none of this grand drama could come to pass unless God's first chosen people, the Jews, could be persuaded to play a crucial role in its preparation. According to the prophet Isaiah, it was the duty of a maritime nation – Britannia ruled the waves at the time – to send 'ambassadors by the sea, even in vessels of bulrushes' to effect the conversion of the Jews to Christianity and the restoration of that 'scattered and peeled' people to their ancestral home. A thoroughly British sympathy with the underdog, a thoroughly insular disdain for the anti-Semitism of both Catholic and Orthodox Europe, and a thoroughly Protestant love for the Old Testament lent force and fire to these millenarian visions. They also generated plentiful funds for the London Jews' Society.

The Duke of Kent, Queen Victoria's father, was the society's first and most illustrious patron. William Wilberforce, whose evangelical energy had fuelled the campaign that abolished slavery in 1807, was its first vice-president. Seven earls, a viscount, four lords, some bishops and plenty of MPs secured its visibility and prosperity. The society was soon furnished with Palestine Place, an attractively landscaped new five-acre estate in East London's Bethnal Green.

Napoleon's defeat at Waterloo rather than Armageddon in 1815 did nothing to extinguish the evangelicals' fervour, and the matter of Britain's sacred duty to help fulfil God's promises to the Jews remained a live issue. Members of the London Jews' Society could see no reason why these poor and oppressed outcasts of society – if approached with the kindness and respect due to them as God's chosen people – should not abandon their ancient faith, convert to Christianity and remove themselves to a dry and desolate corner of the Muslim Ottoman empire. Would they not be grateful for aid in realizing the goal they prayed for at every Sabbath meal, 'Next year in Jerusalem!'? Converting the Jews already settled in Jerusalem seemed a good way to start to fulfil the prophecies.

John Nicolayson was not the first missionary to leave Palestine Place for the Holy Land. In early 1822 a German Jewish convert and accomplished polyglot named Joseph Wolff had found a kind welcome at the Armenian Convent, happily employing the son of the establishment's dragoman* to sit outside in the street distributing his evangelical tracts for him. After only a month the city's Jewish Quarter was saturated with his literature. A magnificent result, Wolff thought, until he learned that angry rabbis were burning any tracts they could find. How dared one of their own, a born Jew, come to their holiest city to tell them that the half-man half-god of their Christian persecutors was the true messiah? Wolff wrote to the rabbis threatening to make them 'pay the full price of the books and all expenses of them'[viii] if they continued to abuse his kindness. Enraged, the rabbis convened a meeting with Wolff at which some serious discussion took place about whether Christ could possibly be the Jewish messiah. The wise and witty Rabbi Mendel told Wolff that he could believe no such thing because 'if God had intended to perform a miracle, why did he not ordain that a man should bring forth Jesus Christ? – then all would have believed!'[ix]

Although Wolff was making no general headway among the Jews, he continued to evangelize a friendly Spanish Jew on a neighbouring rooftop from the terrace of his lodging in the Armenian Quarter every evening: 'I tell him, Isaac, I love Jesus my Lord. How much I feel his love in me! He is the very lion of the tribe of Judah!'[x] Wolff's favourite companions were a pair of similarly evangelical American missionaries who lodged at Arkhangelos courtesy of the Greek patriarchate. He recorded the guilelessly tactless approach one of them made to a rabbi on the subject of the Jews' return to Palestine: 'Christians in America and England are constantly pray-

* Interpreter, manager, fixer, mediator between foreign Christians and the Ottomans.

ing for your restoration; we long to have the time come when the Holy Spirit shall be poured out upon you, and when you will feel your sinfulness.'[xi] The Americans were thrown out of Arkhangelos when the Greek patriarch caught them evangelizing among his Orthodox flock. Wolff soon proved too colourfully idiosyncratic for the London Jews' Society to manage.

Wolff's successor and Nicolayson's immediate predecessor was a doctor who tried to sweeten the pill of his message to the Jews by putting his medical expertise at their service. Dr Dalton lasted less than two years at his post before falling ill and dying. Early struck by the impracticability of the task he had undertaken, he had complained to Palestine Place that the Jews were too 'prejudiced and unwilling to listen'[xii] to ever be converted to Christianity. The Jews of Jerusalem, who numbered some 700 families at the time, most of them descendants of refugees from Catholic Spain in the late fifteenth century, were generally the most faithfully religious of their race. The majority of them spent their days in prayer and Torah study, subsisting on the charity – *halukkah* – of their more worldly brothers in the diaspora. The English missionaries' excited talk of introducing them to the Christian messiah and 'restoring' them to their ancient homeland was anathema. They had been living in their ancient homeland for many centuries, and why should they be interested in the second coming of a man whose first coming had brought their people only centuries of woe? Brave missionaries who ventured into the city's impoverished and squalid Jewish Quarter to preach the Gospel could expect not just furious abuse to be hurled at them, but stones and dead cats.

Faced with such stubborn hostility and serious internal disagreements about the precise meaning and timing of the prophecies, the London Jews' Society was obliged to admit that the time was not yet ripe for a mass 'restoration' of Jews to Palestine. But the equally thankless work of trying to convert them to Christianity continued. In 1839, seventeen years after Joseph Wolff arrived in Jerusalem, Nicolayson reaped a first tiny fruit of so much labour by baptizing an entire Jewish family, 'the first Israelitish family that, in all probability, has been baptised in this city since the early Christian times,' he reported ecstatically to Palestine Place.

Although conversion to Anglicanism carried with it the advantage of British consular protection and therefore status equivalent to that of a citizen of the most powerful country in the world at the time, converts needed to be uncommonly courageous. Rabbis forced male converts to divorce their faithfully Jewish wives and they were ostracized, rendered destitute by being deprived of their share of the *halukkah*. When William Thackeray attended one of the missionaries' Sunday services in 1843 he found himself pitying the pathetic handful of them he saw leaving 'in their European dresses and shaven beards' to run the gauntlet of their 'grisly, scowling long-robed countrymen'.[xiii] A decade or so later Edward Lear was describing the London Jews' Society as a preposterous organization, as absurd as a 'society to convert all the cabbages and strawberries in Covent Garden into pigeon-pies and Turkey carpets'.[xiv]

By the end of the century, after over sixty years of missionary effort, only a few hundred Jews had volunteered to help fulfil the prophecies regarding Christ's second coming by converting to Christianity.*

~

To judge by my very 'serious conversation' with Pastor Neil Cohen of Christ Church, the grand plan of the London Society for Promoting Christianity Amongst the Jews has not yet been consigned to the rubbish bin of history.

Almost two centuries on, the Christian mission to the Jews here is not as tactlessly aggressive as the one pursued by Nicolayson, Wolff and his American friends. These days there can be no question of the London Jews' Society's modern successor, the Israel

---

* Mordecai Eliav in *Britain and the Holy Land* (1997) sets the total at 450. The Reverend W. T. Gidney in *The History of the London Society for Promoting Christianity Amongst the Jews* (1908) cites a total of 648 baptisms in Jerusalem between 1849 and 1907. Bernard Wasserstein in *Divided Jerusalem* (2001) cites 131 converts by 1852.

TOP: The Church of the Holy Sepulchre as it appears today and in a fifteenth-century French illuminated manuscript. ABOVE: The Ethiopians' terrace on the roof of the Church of the Holy Sepulchre, with the central dome of St Helena's Chapel and an Ethiopian pilgrim.

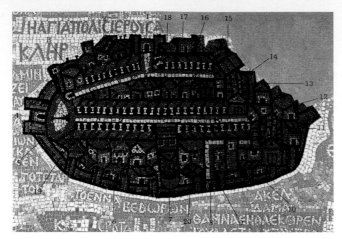

1. St Stephen's Gate
2. St Ann's Church
3. Church of St Mary Magdalene
4. Damascus Gate
5. The Column
6. Monastery of Theodorus
7. Church of the Holy Selpulchre
8. Jaffa Gate
9. The Citadel
10. Palace of the High Priest Caiphas
11. Zion Church
12. Petros Tower
13. Dung Gate
14. Nea Church
15. Western Wall
16. Temple Mount
17. Golden Gate
18. Antonia Fortress
19. The Cardo
20. Market

Sixth-century Byzantine mosaic map of Jerusalem, found in Madaba, Jordan.

The first Crusaders lay siege to Jerusalem, 1099, from a fourteenth-century French illuminated manuscript.

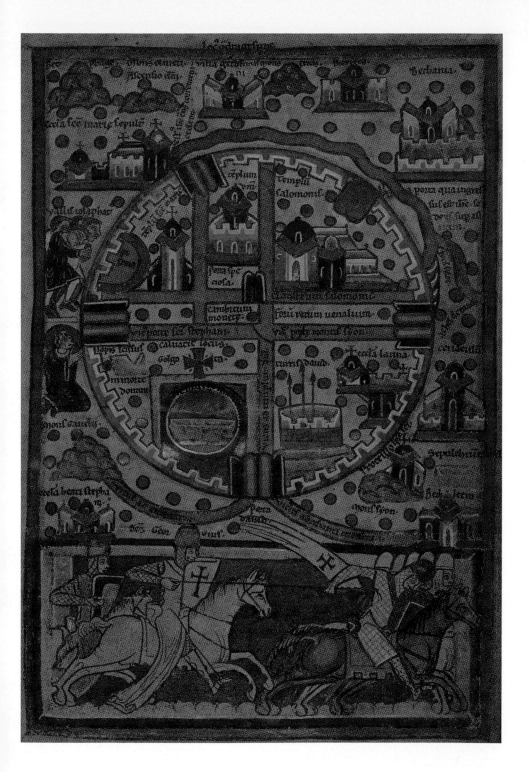

Map of Crusader Jerusalem, *c*. 1200, showing the city divided into quarters but with only Christian holy places marked.

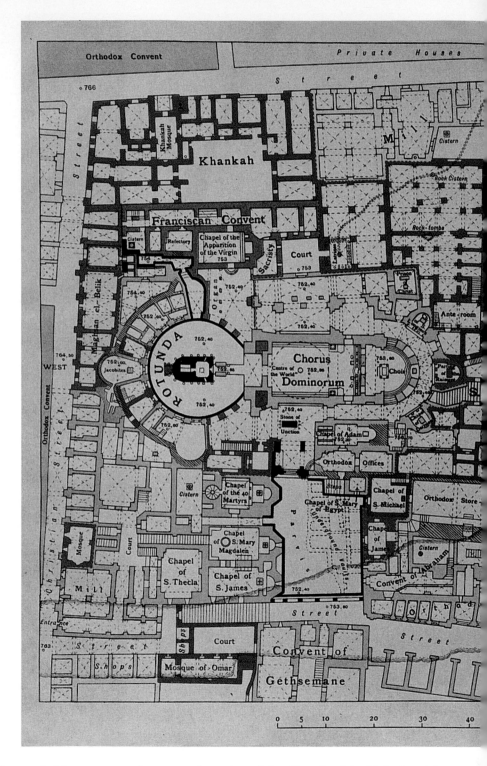

Colour-coded late nineteenth-century floor plan of the Church of the Holy Sepulchre.

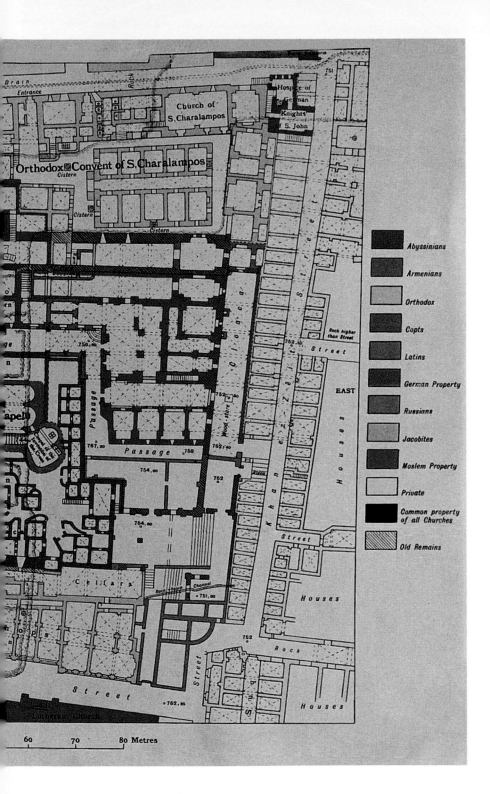

Drain

Entrance

Rock

751

Church of
S.Charalampos

Hospce of
German
Knights
S. John

Orthodox Convent of S.Charalampos

Cistern

Cistern

Cistern

Street

756,00

Passage

Rock higher
than Street

752,50

Street

EAST

apell

Cloaca

752,40

Wood store

752,40

Houses

767,20

Passage

758

752,40

754,60

752

752

754,60

Khan Ezzet Street

Houses

Street

Cellars

Rock chapel

Channel

751,60

Houses

Bishops

Street

752
.

Rock

752,85

Street

Houses

Lutheran Church

60   70   80 Metres

Abyssinians

Armenians

Orthodox

Copts

Latins

German Property

Russians

Jacobites

Moslem Property

Private

Common property
of all Churches

Old Remains

ABOVE: Mosaic in the chapel of the Austrian Hospice commemorating Emperor Franz Joseph of Austria-Hungary's pilgrimage to Jerusalem in 1869.

OPPOSITE: Russian pilgrim to Jerusalem, 1912, with a double lantern for Holy Fire.

BELOW: Kaiser Wilhelm II of Germany in Jerusalem, 1898, after a visit to the Russian Compound.

ABOVE: America's President Harry S. Truman holding a Torah presented to him by Chaim Weizmann in Washington, May 1948, two weeks before the creation of Israel.

BELOW: American members of the International Christian Embassy in Jerusalem celebrate the Jewish holiday of Sukkot, October 2003.

Patriarch Irineos of Jerusalem tumbling out of the edicule in the Church of the Holy Sepulchre following the tussle over Holy Fire, May 2002. Bishop Theophanis is the dark-bearded figure on the right of the picture.

Trust of the Anglican Church, 'converting' the Jews to 'Christianity' because both words are too irredeemably blackened by the experience of the mid-twentieth-century Holocaust. It is now a matter of 'reaching out' to the Jews with open arms, rejoicing in their chosen-ness and encouraging them to 'reconnect' with Jesus – Yeshua in Hebrew – who was their Jewish messiah long before he belonged to the Christians. Jews who make the gigantic leap of faith these days do not become Christians but Messianic Jews. Nor do they join any Christian church congregation but have their own, such as the one here at Christ Church which is a stronghold of British Christian Zionism in Jerusalem.

Pastor Neil Cohen, born a Jew and then again as an evangelical Christian, like Joseph Wolff, does not need to think before answering my first question.

'What am I up to here?' he says. 'Very simple. I'm bringing the gospel of Christ the Jew back to the Jewish people. Romans, chapter one, verse sixteen, is key.' So saying, he produces a Palm Pilot from the pocket of his windcheater and, with a few deft taps on its keyboard, summons the relevant passage on its mini-screen: 'the gospel: it is the power of God for salvation for everyone who has faith, to the Jew first, and also to the Greek . . .' 'Now let's have a look at Isaiah fifty-six' – tap, tap, tap – 'the text I used for the first sermon I preached here.'

Palm Pilot in hand, he races me through a long list of 'key' texts. One after another, quick as a flash, he calls up the same fragments of scripture the early nineteenth-century evangelicals used to prove their points about the approaching apocalypse and Christ's second coming.

'You want the key text about the restoration of the Jews? We'll start with Ezekiel, chapter thirty-seven to the end. Here we are: "and I will bring you home into the land of Israel". Verses twenty-one and -two are the crucial ones. "I will take the people of Israel from the nations among which they have gone and will gather them from all sides and bring them to their own land and I will make them one nation in the land, upon the mountains of Israel." You see? There's your restoration of the Jews to Israel, which has been happening for the past hundred years. In fact, right now my wife is with a group somewhere in the former Soviet Union helping more Jews to emigrate here. You see how the prophecy is being fulfilled!'

I cannot share his enthusiasm. Israel's defiant planting of new settlements for such immigrants in the Palestinians' West Bank and Gaza Strip has long been doing an excellent job of tarnishing the dream of a safe homeland for the Jews. Nowhere in the world are Jews in more danger than in those settlements, surrounded by implacably hostile Palestinian Arabs who have the moral authority of countless United Nations resolutions, if not Bible prophecies, on their side.

Pastor Cohen is hurrying on – tap, tap, tapping – in search of Daniel, chapter nine. 'You want an end days prophecy,' he says slowly, peering at his scrolling screen. 'Here we are! "Seventy weeks of years are decreed concerning your people and your holy city . . . and at the end there shall be war; desolations are decreed." That'll be the battle of Armageddon – Megiddo as it's known now – just up the road. People are calculating that we're already in the sixty-ninth week of years, which means we've only got about seven years to go until that showdown. Zechariah, chapter twelve's all about the Battle of Armageddon. Then there's what happens when God finds that only a small part of his chosen people has recognized Jesus as the messiah. Here we go – verses eight and nine – "two thirds shall be cut off and perish and one third shall be left alive".'

Pastor Cohen and his sort are assisting Jewish immigration to Israel in the belief that the majority of Jews who then fail to recognize Jesus as their messiah will perish – along with secular agnostics, Muslims, Buddhists and Hindus and all other non-Christians. I wonder if Israelis are aware that an energetic section of the Christian Church has cast them as expendable extras in a second great Holo-caust aimed at hastening Jesus' return to earth.

Pastor Cohen seems oblivious to my unease at his eager contemplation of the approaching apocalypse. Feeling secure among the automatically saved, I imagine, he races on – tap, tap, tap –

'Now here's a more direct reference to Christ's second coming: "On that day his feet shall stand on the Mount of Olives . . . and the Mount of Olives shall be split in two from east to west." There's a geographical fault line there already, so that's got to happen.'

'But what if what we've got here,' I interject, 'is not a foolproof forecast but some tribal history mixed with myth and ancient propaganda?'

Switching off his Palm Pilot at last and leaning back in his chair he pauses. A practised pastor, he slows his tempo and softens his tone. 'Look, I don't claim to understand 99 per cent of what's in the Bible. That's not the point. The point is that I believe every single word of it's the true word of God.'

The effort of tempering his enthusiasm proves too great to sustain and, with a flick of his Palm Pilot's ON switch, he is off tap-tapping again. I am reminded of an early nineteenth-century German evangelical's polite reservations about the Christ Church missionaries. Frederika Bremer could not help wishing that they 'saw more clearly the essential in Christianity, the one thing needful; that they had less zeal for the letter, more for the spirit'.[xv] Pastor Cohen is burning with zeal for the letter, unstoppable now. 'Some of it's pretty strong stuff, very clear! Take Genesis, fifteen, for example. You've got God giving Abraham and his Jewish descendants most of the Middle East. "On that day the Lord made a covenant with Abram, saying from the river of Egypt to the great River, the River Euphrates, the land of the Kennites, the Kennizites, the Kadmonites . . ."'

'You support the creation of a Greater Israel in this region as part of the Almighty's plan?'

'As I've just told you,' he counters slowly now, eyeing me testily over the rims of his spectacles, 'I don't claim to understand everything I read in the Bible. All this sounds like a recipe for World War Three, doesn't it? But if it's written there it must be true. You see, the question of how much land the Jews should have comes up again in Joshua, thirteen. Here, you've got God saying to Joshua that there "remains very much land to be possessed", and he lists all the places – half the Sinai peninsula, half of what's now Lebanon, all modern Jordan and parts of Iran and Iraq and Saudi Arabia . . .'

'Pastor Cohen, would you call yourself a Christian fundamentalist?'

With a quick snap of his Palm Pilot's OFF switch he swivels in his chair to face me, closes his eyes, strokes his neat beard and then places the tips of his fingers together as if he were suddenly at prayer or perhaps stifling an eruption of irritation. At last he reopens his eyes to say, 'I don't like that word "fundamentalist" because it's used as an insult these days. But yes, OK, in the sense that the Bible is fundamental to my life. And I'm a fundamentalist if you're using the word properly. It was coined at the beginning of the twentieth century by American evangelicals who wanted to go back to the fundamentals of the faith. But I'd much prefer to call myself a literalist.'

I am having no trouble imagining Bishop Theophanis' response to Pastor Cohen's literal reading of the holy book: a slamming of the fridge door, a crashing of coffee cups and a volley of invective at the man's failure to grasp the spiritual essence of the faith.

Pastor Cohen glances at his watch. He seems as ready as I am to halt our electronic tour of the scriptures, but there is a good deal more I am curious to know about him. After three hours of conversation, a person with whom I share both nationality and language remains a creature more mysterious to me than Ethiopian Solomon.

'How did you make the transition from Judaism to Christianity?' I venture before he has a chance to terminate our talk.

'I didn't,' he replies and pauses dramatically, enjoying my confusion. 'I didn't even know I was a Jew until I'd been baptized a Christian. I wasn't anything at all for the first thirty years of my life, except a pretty hardened criminal!'

Relishing my surprise at this last revelation, in his busy matter-of-fact way he races me through the highlights of a prodigally misspent youth,

'I was expelled from school and got into crime, then mental hospital, then a spell in prison, next the army where I got even deeper into crime, and so on. It wasn't until a couple of years after I was born again that I learned I was a Jew by birth. I was sitting at my parents' home at the time watching *Fiddler on the Roof* on the TV with my father and found myself weeping at the story. My father suddenly said, "You know, that's how your grandparents came here to Britain, fleeing from pogroms like that in the Ukraine." We'd changed our surname to assimilate. How could I have known I was Jewish? I only changed it back to Cohen six years ago.'

Only now am I beginning to understand why Pastor Cohen is devoting his life to the same cause that the early London Jews' Society missionaries, many of them Jewish converts too, espoused and pursued out here 200 years ago. He needs to reconcile his new-found pride in his Jewish heritage with his equal pride in his rebirth as an evangelical Christian. This is the only logical way, and he exudes satisfaction with the path he has taken. I am thinking that the best description of Neil Cohen is not fundamentalist or literal-ist but Christian Zionist.*

Cohen tells me that in 1990, on his first visit to Israel, God addressed him directly. 'I think he wanted to break my Gentile superficiality, because twice – on two separate visits to the Wailing Wall – he spoke to me. "Neil," he said to me, "you're a Jew first."'

'Amazing!'

'It's really thrilling, Victoria!' he agrees. 'If even ten years ago someone had told me that an uneducated drop-out like yours truly would be where I am today, in Jerusalem, where I wake up every morning rejoicing that I'm on Mount Zion!'

'But how many Jews are responding to your offer to introduce them to the gospel?' I ask him, recalling the hostility encountered by Wolff, Dr Dalton and Nicolayson.

'Every Sabbath we get a congregation of between ninety and a hundred Messianic Jews here at Christ Church, and there must be

* Christian Zionism has been defined as 'the belief that Jews must live in a recreated Israel before Christ can return to Jerusalem'. (Grace Halsell, *Forcing God's Hand*, Washington, 1999)

a few thousand in the whole of Israel now. Little by little, with God's help . . .'

'The Israelis must love that!'

'Well, there's a law against active evangelizing, but on the other hand of course they're grateful for our support for Israel and our assistance with helping Jews to immigrate. The only trouble I get is at the airport when I have my passport checked. No one understands how someone called Cohen can be a Christian pastor!'

~

Opposite the cafe, on the far side of a neatly paved terrace strewn with dead leaves and stacks of wet plastic garden furniture, stands Christ Church.

A decent and plain example of the neo-Gothic style fashionable in northern Europe in the mid-nineteenth century, it is white Jerusalem limestone outside, light and bare inside. Only a communion table inscribed with the words of the Lord's Prayer in Hebrew and a Star of David etched on its sides and some stained-glass windows inscribed with Hebrew passages from Isaiah and Genesis testify to the high seriousness of its original mission. It would be a calm haven from the cold and rain of Jaffa Gate were it not for a young man standing in the middle of the centre aisle with his arms outstretched and face lifted heavenward, singing louder and louder, 'My *Lord, my lovely Lord! MY LORD! MY LOVELY LORD! MY LORD! MY LOVELY LORD* . . .'

John Nicolayson had soon grasped the fact that if aspiring converts were to bond with their new messiah they needed a brand new house of worship, one untainted by conventional Christian associations. Equally, he and his fellow missionaries were struggling to make their mark in a place where largesse, display and prestige were everything. Without so much as a candlestick or an altar, let alone a chapel in the Church of the Holy Sepulchre, without a rich and ancient patriarchate, without even a gorgeously robed bishop to rank alongside a patriarch or a rabbi, the new *Bordistanti* – the

Arabic rendering of 'Protestants' – commanded precious little attention or respect. A large new church built in the latest European style
would help Jews see the error of their ways, but it would also impress
the Muslims and challenge the Orthodox and Catholics.

Nicolayson set about circumventing the Ottoman law banning
foreigners from owning real estate or buildings in the city. Using an
obliging Armenian as his proxy, he succeeded in purchasing two
plots of land near Jaffa Gate, opposite what is now the Old City's
police station but was then an Ottoman barracks. The alley separating the adjacent plots was then diverted and a wall erected around
the area. Muslim protest was immediate and loud; building a church
was in flagrant breach of the rules laid down by Omar in the seventh
century and the proposed structure would dwarf a neighbouring
mosque. Only the timely intervention of the British ambassador in
Constantinople secured the project's survival. The sultan was eventually persuaded to give the go-ahead for the church to be built, but
on condition that it would function purely as the private chapel of
the newly appointed British vice-consul in Jerusalem.

The London Jews' Society had long lobbied and prayed for a
consul in Jerusalem so the appointment of William Young to the
city in 1838 was marvellous proof of God's hand at work in the
affairs of men, and his energetic engagement in the task of fulfilling
his prophecies. A British consulate and a British church represented two giant strides forward. While the church wooed the Jews, the
consulate would protect the missionaries, as well as any converts.

Ignorant of the leading role assigned to him in the drama
of implementing God's plan for the Jews, Foreign Secretary Lord
Palmerston's main motive in appointing Young to Jerusalem had
been to send an important message to two of Britain's principal foes:
Russia, which had boldly claimed a formal protectorate over the
Orthodox Christians in the Holy Land after defeating the Ottomans
in a war in 1774,* and France, which had had the care of Catholics
there since the early sixteenth century. Palmerston was boldly

* By the Treaty of Kutchuk Kainardji.

serving notice that, if and when the ailing Ottoman empire collapsed, the scramble for its vital parts would be a three- rather than
a two-way affair. But the real credit for merging the feverish
millennial expectations of the London Jews' Society with the
cooler exigencies of British foreign policy should probably go to
Lord Ashley, later better known as the great reformer, the seventh
Earl of Shaftesbury, who was involved with the society for half a
century and its president for thirty-seven years.*

Possessed of a moral rectitude to match his high collar, the Earl
of Shaftesbury was one of the colossi of the Victorian age. As long
as he avoided going 'where the Scriptures would not guide',[xvi] there
seemed to him no limit to the amount of change for the better he
could effect in the world. A passionate Christian, he described himself as being 'from deep and rooted conviction an evangelical of the
evangelicals'.[xvii] So ardent was his yearning for Christ's second coming that the Greek motto on the back of his envelopes read, 'Even
so, come, Lord Jesus!' and the words engraved on a ring he wore all
his life were, 'O pray for the peace of Jerusalem!' Intent on practising what Christ had preached, he strove to love his neighbour as
himself and laboured tirelessly on behalf of factory workers, boy
chimney sweeps, the mentally ill and Jews. But it was his privileged
access to the ear of Lord Palmerston, who happened to be his
stepfather-in-law, that counted in the delicate but urgent matter of
hastening the end of the world and Christ's second coming.

Shaftesbury's long diary entry recording the decision to open a
consulate in Jerusalem and staff it with a member of the London
Jews' Society is ecstatic. 'Took leave this morning of Young, who has
just been appointed her Majesty's Vice-Consul at Jerusalem!' he
wrote. 'If this is duly considered, what a wonderful event this is!'
With the confident humility of the Christian who seeks and finds
God's fingerprints everywhere he looks, Shaftesbury only hints at
the extent of his own part in the affair: 'If I had not aversion to writing almost insuperable, I would record here, for the benefit of my

---

* From 1848 until his death in 1885.

weak and very treacherous memory, all the steps whereby this good deed has been done,' he wrote. 'I shall always, at any rate, remember that God put it into my heart to conceive the plan for His honour, gave me influence to prevail with Palmerston, and provided a man for the situation.'[xviii]

Was it also Shaftesbury who pointed out to Palmerston that the new vice-consul might find himself at a loose end in Jerusalem with no one but a handful of missionaries, some Jewish converts and the odd passing pilgrim to protect, while the Russians and French could boast tens of thousands of Arab Orthodox and Catholics in their care? Shaftesbury seems to have pressed the London Jews' Society's case with a suggestion that, for lack of an indigenous Protestant flock, William Young should exercise a protectorate over all the Holy Land Jews, whether or not they had converted to Christ. He hinted that those Jews would doubtless feel usefully indebted to Britain for her kindness. Vice-Consul Young's Foreign Office instructions to proceed to Jerusalem included the words: 'it will be part of your duty as British vice-consul at Jerusalem to afford protection to the Jews generally'.[xix]

The following month found the indefatigable Shaftesbury grandly dreaming of spreading the Protestant faith through the Middle East and the east coast of Africa, and providing the London Jews' Society missionaries with a splendid figurehead to enhance their standing in Jerusalem. 'Could we not erect a Protestant Bishopric at Jerusalem, and give him jurisdiction over all the Levant, Malta, and whatever chaplaincies there might be on the coast of Africa?' he mused.[xx] Reviewing a book about travels in the East by a fellow aristocrat in the *Quarterly Review* a few weeks later was a fine excuse for still deeper immersion in Jewish affairs and some publicity about the London Jews' Society's erection of a church in Jerusalem: 'To anyone who reflects on this event, it must appear as one of the most striking that have occurred in modern days,' he enthused, 'perhaps in any days since the corruption began in the Church of Christ.'[xxi] But it was not until mid-1840, with Britain intervening militarily in the East again to oust the overambitious

Pasha Ibrahim from Egypt and preserve the Ottoman empire as a barrier to Russian ambitions, that Shaftesbury saw another heaven-sent chance to employ his stepfather-in-law as a tool for the working of God's design.

Sitting alone with Lord Palmerston after dinner on 1 August 1840, the earl seized the opportunity to outline an imaginative new scheme. Carefully eschewing any tell-tale tint of religious enthusiasm, he proposed that if the Ottoman empire was to survive, the undeveloped lands 'between the Euphrates and the Mediterranean Sea' must be dragged into the modern world. Obviously, he reasoned coolly, no European businessmen would be so foolhardy as to invest in the area unless they were assured of finding there the 'principles and practices of European civilisation'. Europe's persecuted Jews who, according to his information, longed for 'restoration to the soil of Palestine', were ideally suited to importing those principles and practices, in his opinion. They would be only too willing to prepare the ground for British commerce. Shaftesbury stressed the negligible cost to the British exchequer of a Jewish 'colonisation' of the region, confidently asserting that Jews 'subsist, and cheerfully, on the smallest pittance' and could be guaranteed to work hard in their beloved ancient homeland. Far from demanding ownership of it, they would gratefully rent or purchase plots and properties from the local population. No strangers to persecution, they would submit to despotic Ottoman rule for as long as was necessary.[xxii]

The earl was deeply gratified by the sympathetic hearing his ideas received: 'Palmerston has been chosen by God to be an instrument of good to this ancient people and to recognise their rights,' he noted in his diary that night, regretting only that he had felt constrained to plead his case 'politically, financially, commercially'[xxiii] because his relative, like his own wife, was very far from being an evangelical.*

* Shaftesbury's wife mocked his passion for fulfilling prophecies about the restoration of the Jews to Palestine. Lord Palmerston's wife wrote, 'the fanatical and religious elements, and you know what a following they have in this country . . . are absolutely determined that Jerusalem and the whole of Palestine shall be reserved for the Jews to return to'. (Regina Sharif, *Non-Jewish Zionism*, London, 1983)

Three weeks later he was delighted to hear that Palmerston had dispatched the British ambassador in Istanbul to lay the grand scheme before the sultan. Four days later, in the wake of a *Times* leader devoted to discussion of a government plan 'to plant the Jewish people in the land of their fathers',[xxiv] the newspapers were full of the 'Jewish Question'. The debate over whether or not the five European powers who had upheld Ottoman rule in the region with a show of force in 1840 should, or could, agree to give God's chosen people a new home in their old home, or whether Britain should simply buy Palestine for the Jews, raged in yards of column inches.

When the imaginative initiative eventually foundered on the British ambassador to Constantinople's lack of interest in the project and the sultan's adamantine opposition to it, the indomitable Shaftesbury was undeterred. He redirected his formidable energies towards the realization of that older vision he shared with the members of the London Jews' Society: the creation of a Protestant bishopric in Jerusalem.

While holidaying in Italy in the winter of 1834, Shaftesbury had dined one night with the Prussian ambassador to Rome, Chevalier de Bunsen. There, in the belly of the Roman Catholic beast, the German's ardently risqué talk about his government's plans to 'establish for the maintenance and advancement of the Protestant faith, bishops and cathedral institutions'[xxv] in various parts of the world, had thrilled and inspired him. In the Holy Land the pope's crack troops – orders of French and Italian nuns and monks – were expanding their Catholic schools and harvesting thousands of Arab souls. In Britain the evangelicals' arch foe, the new but influential Oxford Movement, was equally engaged in papal business, undermining and dividing the Church of England.* Shaftesbury and de Bunsen were agreed that evangelicals everywhere must unite forthwith to fight the Catholic menace; the German revealed himself to

---

* Founded in 1833, the intellectually attractive Oxford Movement in the Church of England was Anglo-Catholic in spirit and intent on challenging the literalism of the evangelicals. The matter of Jerusalem's Anglican bishopric was what finally convinced John Henry Newman to convert to Catholicism.

be as keen as Shaftesbury to provoke the end of the world, the second coming of Christ and his millennial reign by settling Jews in Palestine.

De Bunsen's appointment as special envoy to London by Prussia's King Frederick William IV in June 1841 created a delightful opportunity for the Chevalier and the English peer to renew their eight-year-old acquaintance. The aim of his mission – to discover 'in how far the English National Church, in possession of a parsonage on Mount Zion, and having commenced there the building of a church, would be inclined to accord to the Evangelical Church of Prussia a sisterly position in the Holy Land'[xxvi] – could not have been more interesting to Shaftesbury. 'The mission of Bunsen is a wonder,' he noted in his diary. 'God grant that its issue may be a wonder!'[xxvii]

Indeed, it was a wonder. Teaming up with Prussia to promote the conversion of the Jews in Ottoman Palestine by creating an Anglo-German Protestant bishopric struck many as an impossibly novel notion. Baron de Bunsen had to contend with the young William Gladstone MP who complained to him that the '(as yet) dimness of the scheme'[xxviii] was worrying other members of the House. A serious theological dispute – over whether such a twinning could take place while the Prussian Lutheran Church was not even in communion with the Church of England – erupted. Some MPs wondered how Parliament would respond if the Ottoman sultan demanded that a Muslim mufti be received in London and permitted to work at converting Anglicans to Islam. A few Liberal MPs sensibly protested that if something had to be done for the Jews, why not start by lifting the ban on them entering Parliament, a measure the Earl of Shaftesbury had long opposed on the simple grounds that England was a Christian country.*

John Henry Newman, chief luminary of the Oxford Movement, objected to the Jerusalem bishopric on ecclesiastical grounds but he very easily grasped the political dimension of the evangelicals' plan too, and attacked it with savage clarity: 'Have you heard of this

---

* The ban was eventually lifted in 1858.

deplorable Jerusalem matter?' he fumed in a letter to a friend. 'There is not a single Anglican at Jerusalem, but we are to place a bishop there to collect a communion of Protestants, Jews, Druses, Monophysites,* conforming under the influence of our war steamers, to counterbalance the Russian influence through Greeks and the French through the Latins.'[xxix] But no amount of scepticism could curb the influence of the evangelicals or quench their zeal for a Protestant bishopric in Jerusalem.

Within a couple of weeks of de Bunsen's arrival Shaftesbury had arranged for him to meet the new prime minister, Robert Peel. Like Lord Palmerston, Peel could see the sense in Protestant Anglo-German consolidation in the face of Russian Orthodox expansionism and French Catholic pretensions. Baron de Bunsen scented victory: 'So the beginning is made, please God, for the restoration of Israel,' he noted gleefully in his journal.[xxx] On 23 September 1841 the two Houses of Parliament passed a bill creating the Jerusalem bishopric.

Once again Shaftesbury had been too busy to record all his efforts in securing the final splendid result, and the pace of momentous, God-ordained events continued to outstrip his humble pen. No sooner was the bill passed than another 'prodigious sensation' gladdened his heart: the pastors of no fewer than twenty-four churches in Liverpool made the Jerusalem bishopric the theme of their Sabbath sermons. Next, the Archbishop of Canterbury assured him that the Jerusalem bishopric was already 'deeply rooted in the heart of England'.[xxxi] To crown his magnificent achievement, his own young sons needed little prompting to donate all their pocket money to the cherished cause.

On 18 November 1841, in the church at Palestine Place in Bethnal Green, Michael Solomon Alexander – a converted German Jew and former rabbi who had been Professor of Hebrew at King's College, London – was consecrated Jerusalem's 'first

* The pejorative term for Oriental Orthodox – Armenians, Ethiopians, Copts and Syrians.

Christian bishop of the Israelite nation since the earliest days of the church'. To Shaftesbury's exalted ears, the ceremony's accompaniment of a Jewish children's choir singing in Hebrew sounded 'like the song of the redeemed in Heaven'.[xxxii] Soon afterwards Queen Victoria gave the Jerusalem bishopric a royal nod and asked King Frederick William to stand godfather to the future Edward VII. 'There is no end to God's goodness!' wrote Shaftesbury. 'What will happen next?'[xxxiii]

What happened next only confirmed the singularity of what one of the men who accompanied Bishop Alexander to Jerusalem admitted was a 'most interesting and peculiar mission to the Holy Land'.[xxxiv] On Shaftesbury's stubborn insistence (Lord Peel had 'pettishly' baulked at the expense it entailed), the new prelate was granted special transport to his distant new diocese, but aboard a frigate named HMS *Infernal*. When the bishop protested the unsuitability of that name, another warship, the equally ominous-sounding *Devastation*, was grudgingly placed at his disposal. The forty-two-year-old Alexander, his heavily pregnant wife Deborah, their six children, a nursemaid and some missionaries departed from Gosport in December 1841.

The precariousness of the bishop's position should have struck all but the most zealous of evangelicals. First, although equipped with a fine set of vestments stitched by the good Christian women of Reading, Alexander had barely a congregation, let alone a completed church, to call his own. Second, the lack of a native Anglican community in the city meant that the Ottomans would not recognize him as the chief of a *millet* and treat him with the respect shown to the Greek and Armenian patriarchs and the *custos* of the Franciscans. While they and the Jewish rabbinate regulated the civil as well as the religious lives of their communities, Bishop Alexander's remit would be limited to the religious. Third, he was barred from making Muslim converts, and from exacerbating existing tensions between the other Christian churches by fishing for souls among their members. His only business was with the Jews therefore, but many Holy Land Jews were Russian immigrants under the protection of the Russian consul in Beirut, which left only the Ottoman Jews. This group might have yielded a tiny bounty of souls, if only the British Foreign Office had not belatedly woken up to the perils of mixing geopolitics with evangelical religion and denied the new prelate vital consular support. Shortly after Alexander's arrival in Jerusalem Vice-Consul Young was instructed to refrain from promoting 'any scheme of interference with the Jewish subjects of the Porte, in which Bishop Alexander may possibly engage'.[xxxv]

The new bishop's entrance to a cold and rainswept Jerusalem in late January 1842 was a confused and dismal affair. No pasha was there to greet him, either on account of the inclement weather or because the newcomer did not have the sultan's official sanction. Even William Young, recently promoted to full consul, was away on leave. Instead, there were a lot of gawping bystanders and a band playing music which the bishop described as sounding 'something like the beating of a tin kettle'.[xxxvi] A ragged artillery salute from the barracks opposite the new foundations of Christ Church might have been in his honour but, like the music, might have had nothing to do with him since his arrival happened to coincide with the celebration of a Muslim festival. Mrs Alexander and the children, borne by six sturdy mules in a rickety litter, were exhausted by the journey's 'awful ascents and precipices over most strangely ragged paths'[xxxvii] and rattled by the raucous din. The family lodged with John Nicolayson for a time, before moving to a house in the Muslim Quarter of the city until that proved too noisy and insanitary. Finally, they accepted the kind offer of a refuge in the Armenian Quarter from an American evangelical mission.

The temporary homelessness of his family was only one of Bishop Alexander's many worries. Catholic friars and Orthodox monks sniggered at the size of his brood and ogled the children's pretty young nursemaid. An English missionary grumbled that the bishop was overly preoccupied with outward show: 'a bishop in his full canonicals, preceded by a janissary with two silver-headed staves' – the 'janissary' an antecedent of the trumpet-playing *kawass* I encountered in the courtyard of the Church of the Holy Sepulchre

– 'does not form the best arrangement for convincing the Jews of the simplicity of Christian worship'.[xxxviii]

Within less than a month of arriving in the city, Deborah Alexander had lost the baby she was carrying and the bishop had demonstrated that he was, as Consul Young put it, 'surprisingly in the dark as to the state of affairs in this and other countries'.[xxxix] In the first sermon he preached he infuriated the Ottomans by describing their rule as 'an usurped one' and was ticked off for tactlessness by the British consul in Beirut. Although cordially received at the Greek patriarchate and the Armenian Convent, he neglected to pay a courtesy call on the Franciscans at San Salvatore. Alexander's insensitivity to local customs was about to cost him dearly. His pious zeal to advertise his presence by ceremonially laying another foundation stone for Christ Church – with a fish slice for lack of a silver trowel – only reminded the Ottoman authorities of their original objections to the entire project. With the walls already standing five feet high, all work was stopped.

Fretting about the church whose forlorn unfinished state insulted both the might of Britain and her Protestant faith wasted Bishop Alexander's time. Sparring with Consul Young about three Russian rabbis whose attempt to convert to Christianity and seek refuge in the homes of the missionaries almost sparked an international incident with Russia sapped his morale. By 1844 Consul Young was complaining to his superior in Constantinople that Alexander's habit of 'indulging in speculative theories regarding a superhuman view of the future'[xl] was irritating the Muslims and infuriating the Latins and Greeks, who were venting their spleen on the poor Jews. Was this any way to 'protect' the Jews? Young believed that the Jews should and would be returned to Palestine and converted to Christ before the end of the world, but in his view Alexander's method of obtaining these ends involved throwing 'plain and obvious duties and sound reason overboard'.[xli]

Permission to resume work on Christ Church was finally secured in 1845, a month after Bishop Alexander had died, broken by strain and overwork at the age of only forty-six.* Grieving for his protégé, the Earl of Shaftesbury confided a rare fear to his diary. 'Have we run counter to the will of God? Have we conceived a merely human project and then imagined it to be a decree of the Almighty?' No, he answered himself confidently, the tragedy was surely but 'a means to a speedier and ampler glory'.[xlii]

~

I am sheltering in Christ Church's cafe again, viewing a survey of the place's curious history attractively arranged on all the available wall space, lingering over a lithograph portrait of Bishop Alexander – high, broad forehead, sad widely spaced eyes and a cupid's-bow mouth – while pondering another baneful by-product of his appointment.

Alexander's coming to Jerusalem had launched the ecclesiastical equivalent of an arms race. Every great Christian power in Europe would now hurry to stake a claim to this choicest morsel of Ottoman land by means of the same dual strategy Britain had employed: exploitation of religion and centuries of expanded 'Capitulations'.

In the year Bishop Alexander arrived in Jerusalem the French coaxed the Vatican into dispatching a Latin patriarch to the city, the first since the Crusading era.† In 1842 the Russian Orthodox Church sent an archimandrite, whose pectoral cross contained 'twelve of the largest rubies',[xliii] to keep watch on the Greek patriarchate from lodgings in nearby Arkhangelos. The Greek Patriarch of Jerusalem himself, long resident in Constantinople for the sake of proximity to the source of Ottoman power and favour, returned to his seat in 1845, to hold court from 'a great divan of scarlet, over which was spread a leopard-skin'.[xliv]

Where the churches led, consuls followed. A Prussian consul arrived three years after Consul Young, and the following year a Frenchman took up residence, one who delighted in 'dwelling on

* Christ Church was completed in 1849.
† Monsignor Joseph Valerga arrived in Jerusalem in 1848.

the spirit of the crusades'[xlv] and caused a furious tumult among the city's Muslims by raising the French flag above his consulate. A grandly uniformed Sardinian who styled himself the envoy of the King of Jerusalem* stayed until 1849, when an Austrian Count Pizzamano, who was genial and sang very nicely at consulate soirées, joined the expatriate community. A Spaniard arrived on the eve of the Crimean War, Russian and American consuls after it, and envoys of the freshly united Germany and Italy after that.

This new cast of important personages added to the din and confusion regularly caused in Jerusalem's narrow alleyways by processions of Christian churchmen, tradesmen with camels and loads of wares and pilgrims of all three faiths. The consuls' pompous displays rivalled and even surpassed those of the Orthodox and Catholic establishments and those of the British missionaries who, the Pre-Raphaelite artist Holman Hunt remarked disapprovingly, conducted themselves 'more like consuls or political agents than priests'.[xlvi] Like each of the Churches, every consul employed his own *kawass* or two to signal his approach and clear a way ahead by banging on the paving stones. Those of the British consul were clad in gold-trimmed red jackets replaced annually on Queen Victoria's birthday, those of the Prussian consul in gold-embroidered blue jackets and wide trousers 'of tussore silk'.[xlvii] The European customs of the consuls' wives and children – their glass windowpanes, nursemaids, baths, foods and medicine – delighted and fascinated the locals, at least for a time.

Christianity's image, already besmirched by ceaseless feuding in the Church of the Holy Sepulchre, was not improved. Legitimized by an unscrupulous stretching of the old trading Capitulations, immune from prosecution by any Ottoman court, interfering and demanding, puffed up with national vanity and haughtily impatient

---

* Along with those of Cyprus, Austria, Spain and Naples, Sardinia's royal family claimed inheritance of the old Crusader title. The genealogy is very complex. The Hapsburg emperors of Austria claimed it from the 1740s until 1918. King Juan Carlos I of Spain, as successor to the royal family of Naples, is chief claimant to the title today.

of local mores, the consuls were an offensive nuisance in the eyes of the Muslim religious establishment and a bitter reminder to the Ottoman authorities that their 400-year-old empire was fatally weak.

Jerusalem became a mirror in which the intense and growing rivalry between Europe's great powers was faithfully if grotesquely reflected. The consuls' rival pretensions to occupy the place of honour at the Christmas mass in Bethlehem, to finance repairs to the great cupola of the Church of the Holy Sepulchre or to build the biggest hospice for pilgrims or school or hospital were the talk of the town and also of every chancellery in Europe. While Consul Young painstakingly reported his French counterpart's strenuous efforts to set himself above his peers on the grounds that France had secured the first Capitulation, the French consul wonderingly observed the failure of the British mission to the Jews and surmised that Britain had darker designs on the region. While the Austrian consul coveted France's title 'Protector of Christianity' for his own Hapsburg emperor and never wasted an opportunity to 'speak disparagingly of French promises, French exaggeration, and the inefficiency of French negotiations in the matter of the Holy Places',[xlviii] the French consul kept a close and suspicious watch on his Prussian counterpart and mocked some American missionaries who, while waiting for Christ's second coming, made 'excellent jam'.[xlix]

Young's successor, Consul James Finn, another fervent evangelical with his heart set firmly on the second coming of Christ, was particularly alert to the comings and goings of the Russians in the Holy Land. In the summer of 1850 Consul Finn reported back to his superiors in London 'that not only have the Greek pilgrims been unusually numerous this year, but that several Russian ships of war have landed bodies of men wearing a white uniform, with foraging caps, and polished black belts. Whether these are soldiers, sailors or marines I know not, but they always keep together in a corps, and march in step. They come ostensibly on pilgrimage, and go to the Jordan etc. like other pilgrims; but their military appearance attracts some attention.'[l]

The Church of the Holy Sepulchre was none of Consul Finn's business since the Church of England had no foothold there, but that did not prevent him championing the Ethiopians' cause against that of the Egyptians, perhaps because many of his domestic servants were Ethiopians still mourning their monks' eviction. 'I wish to inform you that the Copts have begun to beat the Abyssinians with an unequalled cruelty . . . men and women indiscriminately,' he once reported.[li] Finn suspected the Russians of scheming to gain control of the Ethiopians' roof terrace for use as a corridor from their new consulate to the Church of the Holy Sepulchre. In their turn, his fellow consuls suspected Finn of using his influence with the Ethiopians as a means of winning a foothold for Britain in the church.

The Christian Churches and consulates, rather than local Muslims or Jews, led the expansion of the city beyond its sixteenth-century walls. The Greeks bought land for cultivation while Consul Finn built a summer house and founded an agricultural enterprise for Jews in the conviction that if God's chosen people could only work the land they would one day make it theirs. Schools, clinics, orphanages and hospitals, the raiment of Christian piety in which the great powers draped their naked politicking, were turning Jerusalem into a global village; events in the city acquired the international resonance implied by the first word while retaining the poisonous, gossipy intimacy suggested by the second.

Not since before the seventh-century Arab conquest, when rich Byzantine widows had scattered their largesse on the city in the shape of gorgeously ornamented churches, monasteries and religious monuments, had Jerusalem experienced such a sudden upturn in its physical fortunes. By 1853, another British traveller, the landscape artist William Bartlett, was marvelling at how fast 'the waste, ruinous look of the place'[lii] was changing and its amenities improving. There were three European tailors to choose from, cow's milk on sale, and mail arriving from Europe thrice a month by French or Austrian steamer to Haifa. Best of all, he wrote, 'the society of the place has been enlarged and improved, so that in winter when the city is visited by numerous travellers as many as fifty or sixty invitations have been issued for an evening party at the [British] consulate'.[liii]

On the site of that old consulate I am being distracted now by the strains of a modern hymn issuing from Christ Church's guesthouse kitchen – 'Bringing you the gift of grace, to put a smile upon your face . . .' At the table behind me an elderly Welshwoman has just told a young man that the 'gift of grace' cost her her marriage. On my right a troubled young Messianic Jew from Canada is seeking advice from a motherly-sounding Englishwoman: 'I keep getting the same question from Israelis: how can I be a Jew and a Christian? What do I say to those guys?' Her answer is soothing and practised. 'You have to say that Jesus didn't come to start a new religion but to fulfil something.' She is Pastor Cohen's wife.

Pastor Cohen himself, smartly turned out in navy slacks and cardigan, is weaving his way among the tables towards me, arms outstretched in a gesture of pastorly giving.

'You must be busy preparing for Christmas,' I begin nervously.

'Christmas? Christmas doesn't mean much to people like me. It's just a pagan festival about the victory of the unconquerable sun. Of course, we have to do something because a lot of the conventional Christian congregation who use the church would complain if we didn't –' his eyes light up suddenly '– but if you've got five minutes I can prove the real date of Jesus' birth for you.'

He slaps his trouser pockets in search of his Palm Pilot but by the time he locates it and flicks its ON switch he is frowning. There is a fretful impatience about the way he throws himself into the chair beside me.

'Before I start,' he says, 'I have to have your word that you believe every word of the Bible is true. You've got to approach this without cynicism or scepticism.'

I cannot promise him that, I tell him, because the important thing as far as I am concerned is that *he* believes every word of it. My job is to try and understand how he thinks. He is already busy tap, tap, tapping.

At dizzying speed, we jump from Luke's Gospel in the New Testament back to the Old Testament and the Book of Chronicles, and back further still to Exodus to determine which ancient Israelite priest was serving his two-week stint in the Temple at what time of year, before hopping back to Luke to determine the date on which Mary must have conceived Christ.

'You see, there's been a traditional assumption that Mary must have conceived Jesus the minute the Angel Gabriel told her she would give birth to the Son of God. Just like that. Bingo!'

'Yes?'

'But conception had to happen on a very auspicious day, so these days people like me agree that she probably conceived around the important Jewish festival of Hannukah, sometime between mid-December and mid-January.'

'Which would give us an early-autumn Christmas!' I say, relieved to have been able to follow this much of his reasoning.

'That's it! You've got it!' he concludes in triumph, snapping the Palm Pilot shut.

~

Pastor Cohen has been so quick that I am a full five minutes early for my appointment with Father Athanasius next door at the Christian Information Centre.

Housed in the former Austrian post office, another great power contribution to the city's nineteenth-century transformation, the Christian Information Centre is deserted but for a French nun shuffling papers at an empty desk. Its sepulchral gloom is somehow conducive to serious thought. While waiting for my friar friend and listening to the clock's loud ticking, I ask myself why it is that I would so much rather pass my time in Jerusalem with churchmen like Bishop Theophanis or Solomon or Father Anthanasius than with Pastor Cohen and his Palm Pilot. Perhaps because religious literalists, fundamentalists of whatever creed, exude so absolute a certainty regarding their place and purpose in the universe that they rob themselves of a vital human capacity for doubt and change and learning.

Father Athanasius' spirits are even lower than mine to judge by the droop of his broad shoulders and his weary greeting. 'You know, on a normal Christmas this whole place would be packed with foreign pilgrims collecting tickets for our midnight mass in Bethlehem. This third Christmas of the intifada there's only you.'

I wonder if he suspects, as I do, that the future of Christianity here is in the hands of fundamentalists, of Christian Zionists like Cohen and the marchers I had seen in 2001 who find reasons and energy to offer unconditional support to the modern state of Israel in the words of Old Testament prophets. For his sake, I hope he does not share my growing sense that the older Churches of the Holy Land – the Orthodox, the Catholics, the Anglicans and Lutherans – whose weary sympathies are with their embattled and dwindling Christian Arab flocks, are doomed. 'There'll be at least two of us in the pews,' I say in an effort to lighten his mood. 'My friend Nasra's coming.'

'I guess I'm exaggerating,' he relents with a half-smile. Fiddling with the buttons on his mobile phone, he forces himself to continue on a more positive note. 'The Catholic consuls and their wives will be there, the French, Belgian, Spanish and Italian. They get to sit up at the front of the church.'

I am interested to hear that Israel's reoccupation of much of the West Bank is proving no obstacle to the proud assertion of traditional consular rights in the holy places. And I can think of another reason to rejoice. 'The Israelis are going to lift the curfew. That's good news, isn't it?'

'Yes,' Athanasius concedes. 'They've agreed to withdraw their tanks from Manger Square. We're just hoping they'll be pulling back a little earlier so that people have time to organize themselves to get there.'

Father Athanasius does not sound enthusiastic about the occasion but I have never been to Bethlehem or Nasra's flat there, and I need to see the Church of the Nativity in order to recall the

Orthodox monks and Franciscan friars whose dispute over a silver star ornament provided Russia, and France and Britain and the Ottoman empire with an excuse for a war of words and then of armies a thousand miles away on the Crimean peninsula.

Without the advent of Bishop Alexander and Consul Young, without the European consuls' bellicose jockeying for prestige and primacy, the Crimean War of 1854–6 might never have been. The mysterious theft of a silver star marking the spot of Christ's birth in the grotto of Bethlehem's Church of the Nativity might only have merited an entry in a *custos*'s journal instead of upsetting the peace of Europe and costing tens of thousands of lives.

~

Up ahead are inky black storm clouds. A sharp wind whips at the flags flying from the petrol station where Nasra is filling her Volkswagen saloon for the ten-minute drive down the empty motor-way to Bethlehem.

'We may be delayed at the checkpoint,' she warns. 'We'll go to Manger Square first to see what the atmosphere's like. We can pick up some takeaway chicken and chips to eat at home, I have some good brandy . . .'

Nasra's knack of banishing all the ugly facts of her life – checkpoint delays, surly boy-soldiers, suddenly imposed curfews, tanks down her street, nights disturbed by firefights and long periods of enforced cohabitation with Rahme – strikes me as heroic, and I tell her so.

'What are you talking about? Am I living like an animal in Gaza? Is there a bulldozer aiming at my house? Am I losing my olive trees or my life? No. I am a lucky Palestinian. I never forget it.'

She indicates the greyish bulk of the checkpoint and a cluster of military vehicles up ahead whose white markings and red and blue lights flash glamorously under the leaden sky. There is hardly a queue. We have our identity papers ready and are soon drawing level with an Israeli boy-soldier whose lower face is hidden by his helmet's chin strap. From the passenger seat I cannot see his eyes but Nasra smiles up at him.

'Hi, hello, how are you?' he says in American-accented English. 'Fine. And you?' she answers in her Arabic-accented English. They sound like badly rehearsed actors. 'Fine, thank you. Where are you going?' 'To the Christmas service in Bethlehem. I work for an international aid agency and this is a foreign guest,' says Nasra, but she need not have bothered with her little white lie, or with reaching into the glove compartment for the piece of paper to back it up. The young soldier is already straightening and waving us on with a 'Happy Christmas to you!'

The rain starts as we reach Bethlehem, great fat drops on the windscreen and then a downpour so heavy that the locked-up hotels, souvenir shops and neon-lit fast-food joints called Ranchero and El Mundo on either side of the potholed main road pass in a blur. Manger Square is dark and filled with police vans and four-wheel drives with TV or PRESS taped on their sides and back windows. There are a few children begging, heedless of the cold and wet, but no sign of the customary Christmas tree or Christmas market, nothing to see but a candyfloss stall and the sad reproach of a grand new 'Peace Centre'. By the entrance to the Church of the Nativity is a cluster of men peddling black and white keffiyeh scarves. 'Arafat, Arafat, Arafat,' they mutter at me.

'Oh,' breathes Nasra, gripping her umbrella with one hand and putting up her coat collar with the other, 'the saddest Christmas we've ever had. There should be people everywhere and all the restaurants open, families and friends enjoying themselves. Let's go.'

Nasra's modern apartment building on the edge of town is as dark as the street and the waste lot opposite, abandoned by its inhabitants since the Israelis began their West Bank 'incursions' in the spring and took up sniper positions in the buildings all around. She tells me that before the firefights between the refugee camp opposite and Gilo, a western suburb of Jerusalem, grew too frequent and forced her to seek refuge at Arkhangelos, she had grown used to the way the Israelis' searchlights blinded her if she happened to stray onto her balcony at night.

'I love it here because I can be independent and people respect me,' she explains while arranging our takeaways tidily on plates and finding fresh napkins. 'Such things are not so easy for a single woman to arrange here. It was worth working hard, wasn't it?' she says, indicating the plush sofa and armchairs, the deep-pile rug and slimline television. I toast her good health in Greek brandy.

By the time we have to leave for midnight mass at the Church of the Nativity we are both warmed and sleepy. 'You want to stay and watch it on television?' jokes Nasra, surfing the channels. CNN is hosting a phone-in on whether religion is a good or a bad thing, Al-Jazeera is showing footage of an Israeli bulldozer ploughing into the West Bank home of a headscarfed wailing woman. A BBC World reporter is standing in rainy Manger Square saying '. . . a sub-dued Christmas here in Bethlehem'.

At a few minutes to midnight Manger Square is jammed with more police vans and press cars. The great basilica church is entered through the lowest of narrow doorways in its mighty stone walls. Tonight, the echoing expanse with its gigantic rows of pillars and dark mosaics, restored to its bare splendour since its desecration dur-ing last spring's siege, is acting as a thoroughfare for Catholics on their way to the cloisters where they turn left into the adjacent Catholic church of St Catherine.* Nasra and I nudge our way into St Catherine's, manoeuvring ourselves into a tight standing space near some colleagues of hers from the university. Father Athanasius need not have worried; the place is almost as packed as the Church of the Holy Sepulchre for a Holy Fire ceremony.

The arrival of the consuls is heralded at last by a rhythmic bang-ing on the cloister flagstones. Nearer and nearer it comes. The first *kawass* to appear is gorgeously arrayed in red fez, gold-embroidered black waistcoat and baggy Turkish trousers, with an ornate dagger in his cummerbund. Four disappointingly sober-suited consuls and

* St Catherine is part of the Church of the Nativity complex.

their equally drab wives, heads humbly lowered, hurry up the nave behind him to the front pews where, Nasra has just discovered, there is an empty seat draped in a black and white keffiyeh to honour Yasser Arafat, who has been imprisoned in his half-demolished head-quarters in Ramallah since the summer.

As the service begins I watch some sweet-faced young friars hoisting Palestinian toddlers on their shoulders for a distant glimpse of the concentration of white and gold at the front of the church – robed churchmen, flowers, candles, linen. The Franciscans' Latin chanting almost fills the church, but there is lively competition from the back, where restlessly muttering local youths are eyeing up girls with hot stares. Some Norwegian peace activists in bright anoraks and knapsacks are already bored and threading their way towards the exit. 'Nasra, I'll be back soon,' I whisper, and follow them out, back along the cloister, to the Church of the Nativity. I am in search of the Grotto of the Nativity, the place where, in the early fourth century, the Emperor Constantine's mother Helena decreed that Jesus had been born.

The purposeful domestic bustle of two Orthodox monks near the front of the basilica church is the clue to its location, down a steep and creaky flight of wooden stairs to a low and airless space like a bomb shelter, lit by a few low-watt overhead lights.

Alone there, I inspect its two chief attractions. The first, a neat little candlelit alcove, is labelled as the site of the manger in which Christ was laid. But the second, the more important to judge by the seventeen silver lamps hanging around it, is a little cave the size of a pizza oven, framed in embroidered white linen cloths and hung with holy pictures. The silver star it contains is about a foot in diameter and securely fixed to a marble slab with no fewer than twenty-six heavy bolts. I read its Latin inscription – *Hic de Virgine Maria Jesus Christus natus est** – and the date, 1717.

In one of the countless shifts of power effected through a combination of bribery and influence the Catholics had secured this

---

* Here Christ was born of the Virgin Mary.

holy place and affixed the silver star. When the tables turned again in 1757, the Greeks gained the upper hand and substituted a more relaxed regime. The Church of the Nativity became a place for locals to 'idle, smoke and converse about their affairs', a place where tradesmen set up their stalls and Bedouin tethered their horses to 'the abandoned columns of the nave'.[liv] The Franciscans' fury at these casual insults to Christ's birthplace reached such a pitch that when the Orthodox obstructed their entrance to the grotto one day in late October 1847 the friars resorted to cudgels. Unnoticed in the ensuing battle, the silver star disappeared.

The friars blamed the Orthodox of course, who hotly denied any responsibility. Each party appealed to the consul of its protecting power – the friars to the French, the Greeks to the Russians. The French consul was so slow to act that the irate Franciscans threatened to appeal to the sultan as their protector in his stead. Before long heated dispatches were flying back to Paris and Moscow, but it would be another six years before the silver star affair escalated to involve first Emperor Napoleon III of France and Tsar Nicholas I of Russia, then the Ottoman sultan and the British ambassador to Istanbul and finally all the great powers of Europe in the carnage of the Crimean War.

From the start Napoleon III, the first Napoleon's nephew, knew the uproar over the silver star was *'une affaire sotte'*,*[lv] but he had just crowned himself emperor and he was hungry for respect and recognition abroad. Anxious to put his republican past behind him, he planned to reacquaint France with her imperial history by embarking on a foreign adventure as grand and glamorous as those of his uncle's glory days. To do so he needed the support of France's clergy; a noisy championing of Catholic rights in and around the Holy Places was guaranteed to endear him to them.

The motives of Tsar Nicholas I of Russia were marginally purer, if only because he was a pious Orthodox Christian who sincerely cared for the holy places. But, just like all Russian monarchs since

* A ridiculous business.

Catherine the Great in the mid-eighteenth century, he was eyeing the declining Ottoman empire and dreaming of regaining its capital – Byzantine Constantinople until 1453 – for Christendom. The matter of the silver star and the Ottomans' treatment of twelve million Orthodox Christian Slavs as second-class citizens were perfect pretexts. Nicholas' devoutly Orthodox subjects, their always deep attachment to the land of their saviour reinforced by an upsurge in pilgrimages to the Holy Land and their hearts bleeding for the sufferings of their fellow Orthodox in the Ottoman Balkans and Middle East, eagerly espoused the cause.

France moved first, demanding that the sultan remedy all affronts to Catholic dignity in the holy places. The Bethlehem friars must be permitted to own a key to the front door of the Church of the Nativity as well as to the grotto itself, where a new Latin-inscribed silver star and a wall hanging must be installed. In Jerusalem urgent repairs to the dome of the Church of the Holy Sepulchre must likewise be an exclusively Catholic responsibility. Most of Catholic Europe – Spain, Portugal, Piedmont, Naples and finally Belgium, whose ambassador to the Porte took the opportunity to demand the restoration of the tombs of the Crusader kings who had founded the Belgian royal dynasty – lined up in support of France.

The sultan's response arrived in February 1852. At his own expense, he promised, he would have a copy of the lost silver star made and affixed, and the Latins could have the keys they requested, to the church and to the doors of the grotto. The crisis seemed safely past until the Franciscans discovered that none of the new keys fitted the locks. From Istanbul the furious French chargé d'affaires wrote to a colleague in Munich: 'I don't see what we have got, the victory is reduced to ridiculous proportions,' he railed, 'the Greeks and the Russians are rubbing their hands with glee'![lvi] The French were to lose still more when retaliatory Orthodox pressure applied to the Porte succeeded in getting even that '*demi-succès*' reversed. Jerusalem's Catholic consuls were mortified, outraged.

Although careful to keep his distance from a dispute that did not directly concern Britain, Consul Finn marvelled greatly at 'what schemings, what heart palpitations, what reservations, what guessings at motives, what scanning of words'[lvii] the silver-star crisis was provoking among his fellow consuls. Jerusalem swirled with anxious rumours of war. News that there would be no war after all was 'supposed to have originated, as much spurious information is said to do, at the Austrian consulate'.[lviii] The Franciscans were said to be stockpiling weapons in the cellars of San Salvatore. A panicky report that the Turks were massacring Christians in Jaffa so terrified the wife of the French doctor that she jumped out of a window and broke a leg.

Napoleon III signalled his grave displeasure at France's humiliation by sending the ninety-gun battleship *Charlemagne* through the Dardanelles. By the end of 1852 the Sublime Porte had swung back in favour of the Latins; a new silver star graced the Nativity grotto and the friars were in possession of working keys to the church. In the Church of the Holy Sepulchre they were granted more salubrious apartments for their resident clergy and the Latins triumphed over both the Greeks and the Armenians in the church at Gethsemane. Russian passions over the birthplace of Christ and the oppression of their fellow Orthodox were duly reignited. Tsar Nicholas dispatched a battleship named *The Thunderer* to Istanbul. Aboard was his envoy Admiral Menshikov with a small army of military and naval personnel. Rapturously received by a phalanx of the city's Greek and Russian clergy, who hailed him as 'The Liberator', Menshikov instantly offended his Ottoman hosts. His manner was discourteous, his clothes disrespectfully scruffy and his new demands exorbitant. The Tsar of all the Russias was now insisting on absolute Orthodox supremacy in the Holy Places, on a protectorate over all the Ottoman empire's Orthodox Christians, on the appointment of all the Ottoman empire's senior Orthodox clergy, on building a pilgrims' hostel and a Russian church next door to the Church of the Holy Sepulchre and on repairing that church's crumbling dome.

Rattled but still defiant, Napoleon III confided to one of his ambassadors: 'I don't know the details of the Holy Places affair; I'm sorry to have made such a fuss out of it and even more for the exaggerated importance it has assumed, but we can't give back any of the little we've got.'[lix]

The trusty old stratagems – bribes, prevarication, or claims to have seen Mohammad in a dream – had outlived their usefulness to the Porte. The sultan was doubtless regretting that, on capturing Jerusalem from the Mamluks in 1517, Sultan Selim the Grim had not simply banished all Christians and razed their idolatrous shrines. The Christian holy places were now a matter of life and death for his failing empire and he saw nothing for it but to turn to the one Christian power disposed to conserve it, Britain.

Britain's interest in answering the sultan's cry for help was motivated by the old fear of Russia expanding south-west towards the British-controlled Mediterranean and south-east towards British possessions in India. A former British ambassador to the Porte, Sir Stratford Canning, arrived in Istanbul on the navy steamship *Fury* to mediate the quarrel and defuse the deepening crisis. As shocked as the sultan to learn of Russia's demands, he advised the sultan to reject them all. In a report back to London Canning reasoned, 'What if her Majesty's Government were to interfere in a similar way on behalf of the Protestants in France? . . . What would be thought in Europe if France or Austria were to demand a guarantee from Great Britain for the protection and good treatment of the Roman Catholic priesthood in Ireland'?[lx]

Tsar Nicholas for his part believed that since the great powers of Europe were agreed that the Ottoman empire was moribund, there could surely be no serious objection to his plan to hurry death along a little. At a ball in St Petersburg in early 1853 he had uttered his blackly humorous words to the British ambassador: 'We have on our hands a sick man – a very sick man; it will be a great misfortune if one of these days he should slip away from us, especially before all the necessary arrangements are made.'[lxi] The tsar would fail to recognize Britain as his enemy until his experimental invasion of the then Ottoman provinces of Moldavia and Wallachia* provoked furious alarm and bellicose noises not only in London, but also Paris, Vienna and Berlin. Still, the peace of Europe might have been kept, if the Europeans had exerted themselves to enforce on the Ottomans the useful results of an eleventh-hour Vienna peace conference. As it was, all interested parties now rather favoured a showdown. Confident of British support, the Sublime Porte declared war on Russia in October 1853. Six months later Britain and France followed suit.

Attending the Holy Fire ceremony that year, the French man of letters Melchior de Voguë disdainfully observed the usual ecstatically chaotic scenes from the safety of an upper gallery and wondered 'if Europe was ready to take an interest in such a people and if Russia was to shed its blood for a church which allowed the faith of its followers to go astray to such an extent'.[lxii] But in the Cathedral of Notre Dame the Archbishop of Paris gleefully sounded the old Crusader call to arms *'Dieu le veut! Dieu le veut!'* and in England's House of Lords the Earl of Shaftesbury struggled to justify war against a fellow Christian power and prayed to God for 'a speedy peace, in this just and inevitable quarrel'.[lxiii] Away to the east, in St Petersburg, the cosmopolitan Baltic Russian Princess Lieven penned a note to an English aristocrat friend recalling the origins of the conflict with a wryly wondering aphorism: 'Tout, pour un few Grik priests.'[lxiv]

'Un few Grik priests', two Greek Orthodox monks to be precise, have joined me down in the grotto. They are filling the oil lamps and buffing the silver star, muttering at each other through their bushy beards.

* Today, with Transylvania, Romania.

EASTER 2003

*'We believed, and I still believe, that there was
in the world no aspiration more nobly idealistic than the return
of the Jews to the land immortalised by the spirit of Israel.
Which nation has not wrought them infinite harm?'*

– COLONEL RONALD STORRS,
BRITISH GOVERNOR OF JERUSALEM 1917–20

Easter again, but George Hintlian is not celebrating Christ's victory over the grave, or even the natural world's over winter. All the way from Jaffa Gate to the confectioner's, past the locked-up souvenir stalls and through the twilit bustle of the souk, he bombards me with bad tidings.

For the time being, Jerusalem's history has lost its power to console my friend. The present is too big to ignore. First comes talk of the war in nearby Iraq, 'America's new Vietnam', and its implications for the entire Middle East. Next he tells me how the Israelis' 'security fence'* is slicing through orchards and olive groves, severing Palestinians from relatives, hospitals and livelihoods. I want to tell him what Nasra told me the moment I arrived in Jerusalem this morning, that a section of the barrier in front of her apartment block in Bethlehem will prevent her crossing the street, but his attention has already shifted. A dear friend of his, a Greek bishop, stands accused of trying to hire a Palestinian hit man to assassinate Patriarch Irineos.† 'Scandal like this is shaming,' he says, 'not just for the Greeks, but for all Christians here.' I would like to know

---

* In June 2002 Israel began erecting a 450-mile partly concrete barrier to deter incursions by Palestinian suicide bombers from the West Bank but also to take in a large part of the Palestinian West Bank.

† In May 2003 an Athenian court formally charged Bishop Timotheos of Vostra under a new counter-terrorism law with offering Yussuf Naim al Mufti $500,000 to assassinate Patriarch Irineos.

171

more, but his focus has narrowed again, to the threat of war breaking out at Saturday's Holy Fire ceremony.

A whole year has slipped by without a settlement of last Easter's dispute. The question of whether both the Greek patriarch and the Armenian priest, or only the patriarch, is entitled to take his Holy Fire directly from the oil lamp has not been resolved. The Greeks are refusing to give an inch and a large majority of Armenian bishops has persuaded their old patriarch that history will never forgive him if he compromises. For the past three weeks the Israeli Department of Religious Affairs and Jerusalem's police chief have been trying to broker a truce, but without result. George is deeply offended by their interventions: 'The Israelis have inspected all the documents and interrogated both sides, so of course they know now exactly how the miracle is managed, the role of the oil lamp and everything! We all look like fools!'

With less than forty-eight hours to go before the ceremony, the situation is horribly dangerous. A cross word, an angry shove or a stray spark of Holy Fire is all it would take, says George, to reignite the conflict. But I have arrived too recently from another world to begin imagining scenes such as Curzon witnessed in 1834. I have to assume that the toxic fumes of regional turbulence, combined with what Edward Lear called Jerusalem's 'squabblepoison', are impairing George's judgement, but listen with mounting alarm as he declares, 'We Armenians don't want a fight, but we can have people ready to take up strategic positions around the church . . .'

I suggest that one person hurt, let alone killed, because Armenians and Greeks can't agree on how to perform the Holy Fire miracle would be a heinous iniquity. My advice to the Armenians is if Patriarch Irineos wants to make a fool of himself over this nonsense, let him.

'You think the Holy Sepulchre is a nonsense, *habibi*?' George fires back. 'We can't turn the other cheek in such an important matter.'

'But where better to practise what Christ preached than over the shrine of his empty tomb?'

'Look, we Armenians believe that, as one of the great powers in the Church, we have a duty to uphold the tradition.'

'Didn't Christ rebel against tradition?'

'But we're not the ones provoking all this—'

'What does that matter? If the probability of violence is as high as you say it is . . .'

'If our patriarch turns the other cheek now there'll be no end to this. Irineos will go on violating the Status Quo – in the Church of the Nativity, at Gethsemane, on and on. We Armenians are suffering now but it will be the turn of the Franciscans next. Where will it end? With the Orthodox in total control of every holy place in the Holy Land, that's where!'

I start to ask him how he would feel if someone got hurt or killed on Saturday, but he interrupts: 'No, listen, the point is that we are seeing here a mustering of diplomatic clout by the Russians in the old nineteenth-century style. The Russians are bringing out their big guns.'

'What "big guns"?' I ask, bewildered.

'The Mayor of Moscow is in town for the ceremony, with a delegation of fifty or so . . .'

But what does Russia really count for now?

~

Time was – during the sixty years separating the end of the Crimean War from the middle of the First World War, to be precise – when imperial Russia counted for a very great deal, when experts on the region would willingly have staked their reputations on the tsar ruling Palestine after the demise of the Ottoman empire.

Holy Russia had lost the Crimean War but the peace treaty signed in Paris did not cost Orthodox Christendom its supremacy in the holy places; the pre-war Status Quo of 1852 was confirmed and remains in force to this day. Russia's Black Sea misadventure only deepened her passionate attachment to the Holy Land.

In the latter half of the nineteenth century no western Christian product of the Age of Reason and Enlightenment, whether Roman Catholic or Protestant, could boast as profound a reverence for the holy places as the Russian Orthodox peasant whose conception of the Holy Land remained one any western Christian would have regarded as medieval.* This small, parched slice of a foreign and frequently hostile empire represented the gateway to eternity for tens of millions of illiterate and recently liberated serfs, the rightful inheritance of all good Orthodox Christians, a spiritual home. The pilgrimage to Jerusalem – often undertaken in old age or in the hope of dying in the Holy Land – was at once the Russians' passport to, and preview of, heaven. The holy places and all their rich adornments were as beloved to him as the icon corner in his log-built *izba*.† When a fire in the Church of the Holy Sepulchre laid waste the edicule and much of the cupola in 1808, ordinary Russians had collected the stupendous sum of four million roubles for repairs and a new, Ottoman Baroque edicule, and suffered more than half of that sum to be wasted on bribes to the Ottoman authorities.

The Crimean War only intensified great power interest in the body parts of the terminally sick Ottoman empire. It also forced the Turks to make generous new concessions to the natives of those countries that had come to its assistance against Russia. In 1854 the Anglican bishop of Jerusalem was recognized as chief of a new Protestant *millet* composed of converts to the Church of England from Judaism and Orthodox Christianity. The following year the Franciscans were allowed to mark the promulgation of a papal dogma concerning the immaculate conception of the Virgin Mary with fireworks, let off 'in abundance and with childish glee' from the roof of San Salvatore.[i] When Sevastopol fell to Turkey and its allies in the autumn of 1855 the European consuls managed to raise their national flags over their consulates without provoking a Muslim riot and the entire city partied together amicably for three days and nights. God performed his Holy Fire miracle two hours earlier than

* Russian peasant – the word connotes simplicity, hardiness and 'salt-of-the-earth'-ness.
† Peasant's cottage.

usual the following Easter simply because a courteous pasha offered to escort the German Duke and Duchess of Brabant around the Dome of the Rock and Al-Aqsa mosques. The last Christian infidels to penetrate that holy precinct in European dress instead of Muslim disguise had been Crusaders.

Christian Europeans were freer to purchase land and expand their building programmes. New churches, monasteries, convents, schools, orphanages and hospitals – each reflecting the native style of its founders and most too madly grandiose for such a tiny and dilapidated place – sprang up all over and around the Old City.

A far-sighted and businesslike Armenian patriarch invested in land outside the city walls, land that would become Jerusalem's modern commercial heart in a few decades. The Greeks, who were reported by then to own a third of the Old City as well as a ring of land around it, extended their patriarchate in honour of a visiting Russian grand duke. Austria began erecting a gigantic hospice near Damascus Gate, employing 600 muleteers equipped with a type of wheelbarrow pioneered in the Crimean War to level a low hill. The Austrians would more or less monopolize shipping and postal services between Western Europe and the Holy Land until the First World War and no consulate could compare with theirs in showy expenditure. The French, rewarded for their support in the Crimean War with the Crusader church of St Anne in the Muslim Quarter of the city, turned its outbuildings into a school for well-born Catholic Arab girls. By the end of the century France would boast some twenty large religious institutions in the city, including a hostel with room for 600 pilgrims and a life-size statue of the Virgin Mary on its roof. French influence over one local pasha infuriated Britain's Consul Finn, especially when it succeeded in getting a brand new gate cut in the city walls.* Vying for Catholic supremacy with both France and Austria, Italy entered the fray in the decade before the Great War, erecting a large hospital whose tower resembled that of the Palazzo Vecchio in Florence and whose gates were studded

---

* New Gate, conveniently near the Franciscans' San Salvatore.

with Italian municipal coats of arms. German Protestants ran the city's biggest orphanage. Members of a southern German evangelical sect, the Templars, arrived to await the second coming of Christ and begin assembling a German colony of solid stone houses set in tidy gardens to the west of the Old City. They would soon be running the first efficient horse and coach service between Jaffa and Jerusalem.*

The London Jews' Society spread its influence by way of schools, workshops for the training of converts cut off by their Jewish community and a hospital, one of whose pavilions was named after a generous donor, the Cadbury family.† Construction of a new, emphatically non-evangelical Church of England stronghold – St George's Close, with its cathedral, schools, theological college and pilgrims' hostel – began in the 1890s. The tower, added in 1910 and named after King Edward VII, resembles that of Magdalen College, Oxford, while the rest of the close is modelled on New College.

But Turkey's old enemy Russia also benefited from Ottoman glasnost, not least because swelling numbers of Russian pilgrims were stimulating the city's trade in cheap souvenirs. When the Russian government purchased five plots of land – a former Ottoman military parade ground only 300 metres outside Jaffa Gate – the Ottoman authorities made Tsar Alexander II a gift of a sixth plot. Naturally, Russia's pilgrim numbers and land acquisitions alarmed the other Europeans. Jittery Franciscans believed the tsar was planning a gigantic barracks for his troops on the site, in readiness for when he conquered Palestine. Unrepentant, unbowed by defeat in the Crimea, the great Orthodox power of the East was apparently staking as bold a claim to a post-Ottoman Holy Land as France and Britain.

The tsar's brother Grand Duke Konstantin Alexandrovich had

---

* By the time a British army captured Jerusalem in 1917 the German colony was over 2,000 strong.

† Now a Church of England school, an inscription over its main entrance still reads, 'The London Society for Promoting Christianity Amongst the Jews – Mission Hospital for the Jews. Founded 1843. Erected 1896'.

made a pilgrimage to Jerusalem in 1859 and recognized a painful anomaly: in the matter of pilgrim numbers and true Christian piety there was no great power to compare with Russia, but what had she to show for her devotion to Christ's homeland? No ancient patri-archate, no chapel in the Church of the Holy Sepulchre, no monastery, no pilgrims' hostel, not even a church where the liturgy was performed in old Church Slavonic instead of Greek. The grand duke could not fail to see how fat the Greek patriarchate was wax-ing on the donations of thousands of Russian pilgrims, and how Greek monks tricked the tsar's humblest subjects into buying relics like sawdust from the coffin of Christ while fleecing them for squalid lodgings in Greek monasteries like Arkhangelos.*

Russia would not break ancient Church law by creating a Russian patriarchate of Jerusalem in the way Britain had manufac-tured an Anglican bishopric but she could shield her pilgrims from the worst Greek abuses. She could also ensure that Austrian steamship companies did not monopolize transport to the Holy Land. The grand duke redeployed the vessels of his own steamship company to ferry Russian pilgrims from the Black Sea port of Odessa to Jaffa and instructed his agent in Jerusalem to start building on the old parade ground. An entire Russian town was planned, complete with high stone walls and gates that would be locked at night for the safety and convenience of pilgrims. Mismanagement and periodic shortages of funds meant that over twenty years would elapse before 2,000 pilgrims could be herded into two-storey blocks named after members of the Russian imperial family and grouped around a giant new cathedral with ten green domes; before what became known as the Russian Compound boasted the best water supply in Jerusalem, fine sewers, a hospital, a bathhouse, a smithy, a carpentry shop, a laundry, a library, a post office, a consulate, gardens, a bishop's palace and even stalls selling duty-free imported Russian food.

Today, the Russian Compound is a shabby patch of West

---

* Arkhangelos accommodated 200 pilgrims. Today there are around forty people living in its flats.

Jerusalem, earmarked for a combination of redevelopment and con-
servation at some unspecified point in the future. The walls of the
infamous police jail, once those of the Tsarina Elizabeth Men's
Hostel, are shabby and crowned with curling barbed wire. A grander
two-storey hostel, in which a wealthier class of pilgrim and clergy
was lodged, houses Israel's Society for the Protection of Nature. The
old hospital building retains its Russian inscription but the once
startling green domes of Trinity Cathedral are a dull grey. A few
stone gateposts carved with the symbol of the Imperial Russian
Orthodox Palestine Society survive to mark the entrances to the
compound that Russians loved to call their Novaya Ierusalim.*
Nothing else in Jerusalem so eloquently recalls and indicts an era
when Christian faith and imperial aggrandizement were one and the
same; not the German replica of Aachen cathedral near Zion Gate
or the grandiose French Notre Dame hostel with its hundreds of
rooms, not the Austrian hospice whose cafe still serves Viennese
Sachertorte or the Latin patriarchate with its shady courtyard and
feel of a Roman palazzo, or even the scaled-down Oxford college of
St George's cathedral close.

Generously patronized by the Romanovs, the Imperial Russian
Orthodox Society more or less efficiently combined the functions of
church, consulate, travel agency and college, as well as patronizing
an archaeological institute to rival Britain's Palestine Exploration
Fund. Visiting royal patrons boosted its profile and fortunes. Grand
Duke Sergei Alexandrovich, a brother of Tsar Alexander III who
arrived on pilgrimage in 1881, persuaded the Greek patriarch to
allow a Russian priest to perform one service a week for Russian
pilgrims in the Church of the Holy Sepulchre. In memory of his
mother he also arranged the purchase of a large plot of land in the
Garden of Gethsemane on which to build the Church of St Mary
Magdalen, whose seven gilded onion domes remain the most
memorably Russian landmark in Jerusalem.

* New Jerusalem, inspired by what St John the Divine saw and recorded in his Book of
Revelation.

The number of Russian pilgrims arriving in the city climbed more or less steadily every year between the Crimean and First World Wars. Elderly peasants bundled in sheepskin coats and heavy woollens, sucking on Jaffa oranges and munching on dry crusts they had brought from home or Cornish salt cod they had bought in the souk, hymn-singing like angels in the city's narrow alleys, camping in the Church of the Holy Sepulchre or toiling barefoot over the dusty rock-strewn hills towards the River Jordan, swamped the Holy Land.

Jerusalem's sellers of the burial shrouds that Russians liked to rinse in the River Jordan, purveyors of false relics, of candles and of olive-oil soap stamped with an outline of the Church of the Holy Sepulchre, icon-painters and the tattooists who sat outside the Armenian monastery pricking 'Jerusalem' and the year onto arm after arm, all welcomed the Russian pilgrims. Everyone accepted the rouble and almost everybody in Bethlehem spoke Russian. The Franciscans regarded the Russian pilgrimage season as an annual invasion but could not help envying their rivals' force of numbers and faith. The French Catholic Church did manage to muster a competing army of a thousand pilgrims for the great Penitential Pilgrimage of 1882, but the Catholics could not regularly compete with an Orthodox phenomenon as natural as the spring greening of the hills around the city.

'Dark-coloured and sad, in the midst of this bright Orient' was how the Russian pilgrims struck one eloquent French tourist, 'jostling everything and seeing nothing, like somnambulists, their hypnotised eyes wide open in a celestial dream'.[ii] For the city's rising population of Russian Jews the hordes of peasants must have awakened nightmare memories of the pogroms that had forced them to flee their homeland.* Executed by Cossacks but abetted by the peasantry, those terrifying bursts of persecution were condoned by

* In 1840 when the British consulate opened, there were approximately 5,000 Jews in Jerusalem. British consular protection, pogroms in Russia and improved transport meant that by 1914 there were 45,000 – most of them Ashkenazim. (Yehoshua Ben-Arieh, *Jerusalem in the 19th Century*, Jerusalem, 1984, Vol. I p. 279, Vol. II p. 241)

the state and blessed by an Orthodox Church as anti-Semitic as that of early Byzantium.

No longer in the grip of evangelical millennial expectation, Britain was more concerned about Russia's military strength than her mistreatment of Jews. Counting the packed Russian pilgrim boats putting in at Istanbul after sailing across the Black Sea in 1899, the British ambassador to the Porte grimly forecast a replay of the Crimean War: 'After some time the whole rural population of Russia will have made the pilgrimage, and by it their naturally deep devotion will be inflamed to such an extent that they will gladly die for any cause having any connection with the Holy Land.'[iii] By 1909 almost two thirds of Jerusalem's 15,000 Christian pilgrims were Russians.

Grigory Rasputin, the Siberian peasant whose apparent ability to ease the bleeding of Nicholas II's haemophiliac son and heir had secured him fateful influence at the Russian court and evil fame outside it, visited Jerusalem in 1911. Revelations about his licentious private life had embarrassed his imperial protectors and obliged him to absent himself from St Petersburg until the fuss died down but, for Rasputin, a keen and experienced pilgrim, temporary exile was no hardship. His account of his pilgrimage of penance is a pungent mix of vivid actuality and conventional piety. Christ's tomb, he claimed, filled him with love for everyone and he rejoiced in his Orthodoxy after sampling both the Catholic and the Orthodox Easter celebrations, but he noted the high incidence of drunkenness among Orthodox monks and blamed the cheap local wine.* Bethlehem's 'monkish intrigues'[iv] and the town's dismal lack of facilities for Russian pilgrims irritated him. He took the Imperial Russian Orthodox Society to task for not serving pilgrims their meals at regular times and for transporting them along the new railway from Jaffa in trucks 'like cattle, sometimes seven hundred together'.[v]†

* On the night of his murder in St Petersburg five years later, Rasputin was drunkenly reminiscing about Jerusalem and how he had bribed someone to secure a place at the Holy Fire ceremony.
† The French-built line was opened in 1892.

When the intrepid British journalist and author Stephen Graham disguised himself as a simple Russian *muzhik* to travel to Jerusalem the following year he used the same simile to evoke the passive masses of Russian faithful on the move. After fifteen days spent crammed with over 500 others in the stinking hold of a boat called the *Lazarus* and an arduous trek up to Jerusalem from the coast, they were herded around the city 'like cattle that have been driven too far'[vi] by a mounted Montenegrin *kawass* arrayed in the 'scarlet and cream cloak and riding knickers'[vii] of the Imperial Russian Orthodox Society.

For all the stench and discomfort of his straw mattress in a dormitory block accommodating 300, for all the pickpockets and charlatan monks infesting the Russian Compound, Graham did not envy the handful of French-speaking upper-class Russians and fastidious English tourists in their modern hotels. He thought the Church of the Holy Sepulchre 'vast and strange, ruined, dirty beyond words, with verminous walls all cracked and chipped'[viii] but he was not interested in the prettily appointed Garden Tomb, the pristine alternative empty grave of Christ that General Gordon had located just outside Damascus Gate to the north of the present-day city wall shortly before he left for the Sudan to die a hero in the defence of Khartoum.* With the Russians Graham felt 'equalled and made a family'.[ix] He joined with them in their worship of their lowly born God and was profoundly moved. Deep in the seething crowd in the Church of the Holy Sepulchre he observed their exaltation and doubt while waiting for the Holy Fire to appear. When all the candles about him were lit, dripping hot wax and singeing his ears, he watched them extinguishing their Holy Fire in the black 'death-caps' filled with perfumed cotton wool that they would wear in their graves with the shrouds they had dipped in the Jordan. Other Russian pilgrims were lighting their double lanterns decorated with crosses, for safe transport of the light back to their homes and

* The Garden Tomb remains a favourite holy site for both English and American evangelicals, although the Anglican Church no longer endorses its authenticity as the site of Christ's grave.

churches. A small army of Turkish police could barely keep order in the church and surrounding streets. Graham was pushed outside and borne along on a tide of pilgrims greeting each other ecstatically, '*Khristos Voskrese! Vo Istine voskrese!*' (Christ is risen! Indeed, he is risen!)

He left Jerusalem the following day, Easter Sunday 1912. The Ottomans, battling to maintain their dominion over the restive peoples of the Balkans, were at war again and he needed to catch a last boat passing through the Dardanelles into the Black Sea. Graham could not have known that he had witnessed a phenomenon at its height but with only two years left to run. By 1914 Russia owned more territory in and around Jerusalem than any other great European power, but a world war, a Bolshevik revolution, a civil war and an atheist totalitarian state were about to sever the Russians' physical and spiritual links to the Holy Land and demolish any chance of her replacing Turkey as the ruling power in the region.

The transformation of the Russian empire into the Union of Soviet Socialist Republics ruined the Russian Orthodox Church. Churchmen who baulked at coexisting with a regime intent on replacing faith in God with faith in socialism either perished in prison camps or fled to regroup in exile. Known as the Russian Orthodox Church Abroad or as the 'White' Church, it retained properties in East Jerusalem, on the Mount of Olives and at Gethsemane. Properties in West Jerusalem remained with the 'Red' or Moscow Church. In 1967 Russia's impoverished communist leadership struck a deal with Israel: the entire Russian Compound except for the cathedral was bartered for seven million dollars' worth of Jaffa oranges. Two shiploads of rotten fruit eventually reached Odessa.

~

Rahme remembers:

'My grandfather certainly spoke Russian . . . My father too, but he forgot it when the Russians stopped coming here after the First

World War. Now, for the last ten years, so many Russians are coming for Easter! I hear from the window people passing in the street, '*Gospode . . . Gospode . . . Bozhe . . . Bozhe . . .*'*

The collapse of Soviet communism in 1991 and the ensuing economic turmoil has brought around a million Russian immigrants to Israel, by no means all of them Jews.† It has also sent millions of other Russians reeling back to Russia's imperial past in search of an older, safer identity. The Jerusalem pilgrimage is back in vogue, the holy old connection with God's homeland being lovingly restored. At Easter 2002 I spotted dozens of Russian monks with their straggling beards, long hair in ponytails and dusty cassocks in the courtyard of the Church of the Holy Sepulchre. In the alleys of the Christian Quarter pale young Russian women in headscarves and long skirts asked me directions to 'Christ's grave'. There are far fewer Russian pilgrims this third Easter of the intifada, but enough for the souvenir-sellers to open their shops, enough for the city's police to be worrying about whether to let dozens of them spend the night before the Holy Fire ceremony in the Church of the Holy Sepulchre.

Rahme is driving us up to the Mount of Olives, high above the golden-domed Cathedral of St Mary Magdalen, to the Russian Convent of the Ascension, another active vestige of Russia's pre-revolutionary past in the city. It is not our first visit; we have made this journey on each of my previous trips. I always have something to bring a relative of Rahme's, an elderly Arab nun named Mother Athanasiya. At our first meeting she requested a hundred lengths of the whalebone she uses as stiffening in the high velvet hats she makes for her sisters. During my second visit she begged me for four sets of thermal underwear. Her heart's desire in the autumn was a white plastic short-wave radio on which to listen to Radio Moscow. At Christmas it was more haberdashery and enough black organza to make three veils. I have the haberdashery but not the black organza . . .

* 'Lord . . . Lord . . . God . . . God . . .'
† Some 300,000 Russian immigrants are Orthodox Christians, whose presence causes many right-wing Israelis to fear for the future of the Jewish state.

Visibly enlivened by this jaunt out of the old city, Rahme has stopped the car in the middle of the road for the third time – to greet a greengrocer she knew as a baby. The Mount of Olives is an Arab village and Rahme, who spent her childhood summers up here in a caretaker's house in the grounds of the Greek patriarch's summer residence, knows everyone, Christian and Muslim. When at last she drives on again, hurling her cigarette end and a cheerful farewell out of the window, she tells me we must visit her father's dentist and a butcher whose father and grandfather were family friends.

More than two hours have passed and the afternoon sun is setting behind the hills to the west of the city when at last we veer sharply off the busy main road into a narrow alleyway between two shops and come to a halt before a pair of high green metal gates crowned with a Cyrillic inscription. 'Abu Is-*sa*! Abu Is-*sa*!' shrieks Rahme. The convent gates creak open to reveal first a wizened and toothless Arab gatekeeper, then a long nineteenth-century stone building and, beyond, a vast expanse of pink-gold sky. From here on the top of the Mount of Olives the view of all Jerusalem far below is as breathtakingly clear as it was on my first visit a year ago. In summer and early autumn the city had shimmered translucently in the white heat like St John the Divine's New Jerusalem. At Christmas a low-slung curtain of rain clouds had obscured the city. It looks like a giant's handful of black-flecked pearls today.

Disobeying the instruction to respect the peace and quiet of the convent by not driving into the grounds, Rahme races up the tree-lined path and round the little church to come to a stop directly outside Mother Athanasiya's bungalow. While she hurries in to greet her relative, I follow the soul-stirring strains of Russian Orthodox singing back to the church.

Inside, the perfume of incense is dizzying. The hanging lamps, the icons and the faces of the black-clad nuns grouped around the walls like shadows are gilded by glowing candlelight. In this tiny corner of old Holy Russia, fixed and unchanging, the war for this land, with its tanks and ambulances and graffiti and bombs and bull-dozers, shrinks and recedes to a senseless restlessness far away. I would happily linger here a while, sampling a Russian eternity, but a monk – his eyes two dots of fury above his hollow cheeks and straggling grey beard – is approaching fast. Hissing in Russian and pointing at my trousered legs, he shoos me out of the church.

As I stroll back towards Mother Athanasiya's bungalow, listening to the breeze in the cypress trees and enjoying the mountain's cooler air, it strikes me that I have carelessly flouted the convent's no-trousers rule for the third time. The first occasion was the most shaming.

Rahme and I accepted an invitation to join the community for a formal reception in the abbess's parlour on Easter Monday last year. At the head of a long table spread like an altar with a linen tablecloth and laden with bowls of cakes, sweets, soft drinks and wines, sat the sturdy young abbess flanked by bearded bishops and monks. Arranged stiffly around the edges of the room on straight-backed chairs were some fifty silent nuns. A few of them, Rahme whispered to me, were of second- or third-generation émigré Russian stock from France, Belgium or Germany, some were Russian or Ukrainian, but most were Romanian or Arab Orthodox. On the walls above their heads hung icons and sepia-tinted photographs of grandly whiskered nineteenth-century Russians wearing military uniforms ablaze with medals. The Arab nun sitting on the other side of me kindly pointed out the last tsar of Holy Russia Nicholas II, his eternally sailor-suited son Alexei, a couple of grand dukes and a modern photograph of an ancient and bespectacled former abbess, a niece of Tsar Alexander III. A clock set to Orthodox holy time ticked loudly,* glasses clinked against plates and Rahme dropped a biscuit on the carpet. I was uneasily tackling a hard-boiled egg dyed a festive violet while sipping carefully at a flute of dessert wine when the Arab nun pointed to the far end of the room. One of the bishops was signalling a furious request that I immediately uncross my legs. 'Trousers are not really allowed here,' said the nun.

---

* Russian Orthodox time in Jerusalem's White Russian convents is an hour behind Jerusalem time.

The second time, I caused offence to Mother Kseniya, an elderly and highly cultured Australian nun of Estonian extraction, who greeted me grumpily with, 'I can't talk with you because you're wearing pants, which I find quite abhorrent. You bring the world in here and disturb us.' When I apologized she kindly relented, and though her venerable seniority forbade her from engaging in 'any small talk whatsoever' permitted me to quiz her on the history of the convent.

She told me that when an uncommonly energetic Russian priest called Father Antoninus Kapustin arrived in Jerusalem in the 1870s he had been shocked to discover only mosques on the Mount of Olives, where in happier, Byzantine times there had been dozens of churches. By learning Arabic and spending hours on his haunches drinking coffee with the locals – forebears of Rahme's greengrocer and butcher friends perhaps – he had managed to acquire a plot of land, after seeing off competition from a French countess planning to erect a Catholic convent on the mountain. Work on a church and bell tower had proceeded apace, assisted by bribes of the finest Russian tea. Decorative, six-storeyed and fifty metres tall, the tower would be visible for hundreds of miles around and a source of great wonder to the people of Jerusalem. A Christian Arab schoolchild attempting to answer the question 'Where is the Mount of Olives and what took place on it?' overlooked the fact that Christ had ascended into heaven from the spot and confidently replied, 'It's to the east of Jerusalem, and the Russian tower took place on it.'

The Russian tower struck terror into the hearts of the consuls in the city below. From its great height, they imagined, Russian agents disguised as monks and nuns would be spying on all movements in the city, signalling to Russian naval traffic on the Mediterranean and monitoring Turkish troop movements to the east. But the Russians confounded all expectations by simply fitting the new landmark with the biggest bell in Jerusalem. Mother Kseniya told me that it had taken 150 hymn-singing Russian women pilgrims three weeks to drag the four-ton gift of the merchants of Perm all the way up from the coast to Jerusalem on wooden rollers. 'Never underestimate the strength of a woman!' she added with a rare smile, before concluding her account. 'We're on the road from Jerusalem to the Jordan here. There were thousands of pilgrims passing by. A few nuns came to serve them refreshments. It was something like a motorway cafe,' she observed, 'and soon a house was built for them and soon that house grew into a convent, and that building there,' she pointed back towards the gate and the long building near it, 'was a hostel built in 1906. It's out of use but now we're planning to renovate it for pilgrims. So many Russians are coming here these days and we've nowhere to put them all.'

As I reach Mother Athanasiya's bungalow a last shaft of afternoon sunlight is painting the three upper storeys of the famous bell tower an old-icon gold, but closer to hand is a less uplifting sight. About twenty feet from me among the trees the convent's famously ferocious Alsatian is barking madly, leaping and straining at his chain, jaws gaping. During one of my previous visits another nun had dropped by to see Mother Athanasiya and hoisted her habit to reveal a crescent of purple weals extending more than halfway up her muscular calf.

Mother Athanasiya has to stand on tiptoe to hug me. She giggles like a girl and greets me in Russian, the lingua franca of the convent that she speaks more fluently than her native Arabic. A woollen Russian shawl tied tightly around her hips is keeping the chill off her kidneys, she informs me. Her plastic-covered kitchen table, under a gaudy holographic poster of a crucified but sporadically winking Christ, is spread with bowls of sweets and cake. Her electric samovar is bubbling and Rahme is helping to make tea in the old Russian way: a half-glass of strongly stewed leaves, heavily sugared and topped up with boiling water. Rahme's story, a rumour from the patriarchate about a Greek bishop who was blackmailed, kidnapped and abandoned in a cave outside Jericho to make his way back to Jerusalem on foot, causes Mother Athanasiya to tut-tut and roll her eyes. She is out of touch with the affairs of the Greek patriarchate but has her own strange tale to tell. During last night's storm a bolt of lightning struck the little church I have just been ejected from. One of the sisters, woken by the howling wind, dashed out onto her balcony to watch in terror as flames sprouted out of its dome and then see them suddenly and unaccountably extinguished. This morning the community declared a miracle.

I interrupt this exchange of gossip and marvels to question Mother Athanasiya about her life, a subject with which she is not nearly as comfortable. 'Oh, the tears I have cried could fill a whole bottle!' she sighs, consoling herself with a chocolate.

Mother Athanasiya's Via Dolorosa began in the early 1930s when Britain ruled Palestine and her Palestinian Orthodox parents, too poor to provide for their three-year-old daughter and the rest of their growing brood, deposited her in a White Russian convent in today's West Bank. 'Every day for three days I cried for my mother,' she recalls, 'and then I decided I never wanted to see her again.' Two White Russian nuns cared for her, one harshly with spanks and threats, the other with tender sweetness. Mourning the demise of old Holy Russia they nostalgically taught her the gentle manners and elegant accomplishments of a Russian aristocrat and all they knew of the delicate art of embroidery and sewing seed pearls onto bishops' capes. Relocated here in East Jerusalem in 1948 she put her skills to good use fashioning the community's velvet hats with their whalebone stiffening and satin linings, painting icons and leading the choir.

'She was as beautiful as an angel and she sang like a bird! She has golden hands,' interjects Rahme, waving her own hands in my face. 'Unbelievable!'

More unbelievable in my view is the fact that Mother Athanasiya has lived all her life in a world that ceased to exist before she was even born. Her account of the reburial of the Grand Duchess Elizabeth – sister-in-law of the last tsar and saintly last patroness of the Imperial Russian Orthodox Society – in the golden-domed Convent of Mary Magdalen at the foot of the Mount of Olives in 1921 is as touchingly vivid as if she had been an eyewitness to the procession of weeping churchmen wending its way across the city.

Rising heavily from her chair and disappearing into her workroom she says she has something to show me: a brand new and beautifully reproduced Russian coffee-table book of photographs of the haemophiliac tsarevich, Tsar Nicholas II's only son. Together we pore over image after image of the doomed child. There is Alexei dressed as a soldier, saluting the camera. Mother Athanasiya giggles fondly. 'You know that when he was three he stood before the Duma, asking them if they knew how to shoot guns?' Here he is as a toddler, playing with the ropes of pearls around his doting mother's neck, and here with his cat in the gardens of Tsarskoe Selo. In the next he is larking about with his four older sisters, all of them in long white dresses, and here he is standing alone up to his waist in water with a cross around his neck, an icon of holy baptism. But most touching of all are the last few pages, of his childish artwork.

With tears in her eyes Mother Athanasiya says, 'Thanks to this new book I know that Russia loves God and the tsar again – at last!'

Her parting gift to me is a wooden Easter egg, as delicately decorated as a Fabergé treasure with hand-painted pink and gold flowers, an appliqué remnant of gold braiding from a bishop's cope she has been making, some pearl beading of the kind used to adorn Orthodox mitres and a pink ribbon.

~

The city is a glitter of orange lights below us now, the hills all around black velvet. Descending from the Mount of Olives, we pass a grand entrance I have failed to notice on any of my previous visits. 'It's the Augusta Victoria,' Rahme informs me. 'Nasra teaches Arabic to Lutheran aid workers from Iceland and Denmark there on Wednesday afternoons.'

Doughty Father Antoninus had seen off the French countess and her Carmelite convent but the Russians did not retain their mono-poly on the high ground to the east of the Old City for long. During their pilgrimage to the Holy Land in 1898 Augusta Victoria, the wife of Kaiser Wilhelm II, ordained that a copy of a medieval German Crusader castle be built on neighbouring Mount Scopus, as a retirement home and haven of German culture for missionaries of the Second Reich in Palestine.

Vast, imposing and lavishly appointed with heavy neo-medieval furniture, the Kaiserin Augusta Victoria Stiftung boasted the most modern amenities in Jerusalem at the time of its completion, including running water for baths and lavatories, and electricity. Life-size statues of Wilhelm II and Augusta Victoria in Crusader garb graced its inner courtyard, and its tower, ten metres higher than the Russian one, was equipped with the biggest, loudest bells in the city and a powerful searchlight. No one could fail to recognize the Second Reich as the latest and hungriest vulture to alight in the region. The British Foreign Office surmised that the Kaiser would be installing a German governor in the Kaiserin Augusta Victoria Stiftung just as soon as Germany had conquered Palestine; France, still smarting from her defeat in the Franco-Prussian War of 1870 to 1871, was equally alarmed.

Germany, only unified in 1871, was making her mark, and not only physically. First came the withdrawal from Christ Church's Anglo-Prussian bishopric; Lutheran Germans had long resented that idealistic but irritatingly unequal alliance. Second, Germany relieved the British of their increasingly cumbersome protectorate over the Holy Land Jews. From a purely political point of view it was hardly the moment for Britain to be abandoning God's chosen people, if only because Jews fleeing the Russian pogroms of the 1880s already outnumbered Christians and Muslims by almost two to one in Jerusalem and the first socialist Jewish settlements were appearing in the countryside. But evangelicalism was out of fashion. For the time being, the mission to convert the Jews and restore them to their homeland before Christ's second coming had lost its urgency.

That unseasonably hot autumn of 1898, when Wilhelm (mounted on a white charger and sporting a white silk dust cloak) and Augusta Victoria (enervated from too strict a diet) toured Jerusalem together, marked the zenith of German influence in the East. Small wonder that Theodor Herzl, the Jewish journalist father of the fledgling Zionist movement, identified Germany as the great power most suited to realizing his dream of a Jewish national homeland and seized the occasion of the imperial visit to present his petition to the Kaiser.

Queen Victoria's eldest son Edward and the Austro-Hungarian Emperor Franz Joseph had already enhanced and advanced their countries' interests in the region by beating a path to Christ's empty grave, but Wilhelm II's tour was of another order entirely – more parade than pilgrimage. His retinue of over 2,000, including a forty-two-man orchestra, camped in orderly fashion on German-owned land to the north of the city, in row upon row of 300 white tents transported from Germany and furnished with iron bedsteads and Turkish carpets. Over a hundred carriages and carts, 800 muleteers, 1,500 horses and dozens of camels were pressed into service. The British travel agent Thomas Cook, which had been running tours to the Holy Land since the 1860s, oversaw all arrangements with a military attention to detail, and won a sneering accolade from *Punch* magazine. The caption beneath a cartoon of the kaiser dressed up as a Crusader read 'Cook's Last Crusade'.

The Ottoman authorities played their part too. Nothing was too much trouble for the sultan's new friend, who would act as the ideal counterweight to what he was beginning to regard as excessive British, Russian and French influence in Palestine. Jerusalem gained new roads, street lighting and splashes of the German imperial colours – flags and yellow and black painted walls. All stray dogs were poisoned. Since the kaiser insisted on entering the city on horseback, the Ottoman authorities circumvented the ancient ban on any mounted foreigner passing through the gates by demolishing a section of the old walls by Jaffa Gate. A prime plot of land by Zion Gate was set aside as a gift for the German emperor, who would ordain the construction of a Benedictine abbey on the site, in the Romanesque style of Aachen cathedral.*

* Catholic Germans were favoured in this way because Wilhelm wanted to advertise his protection over all Germans, whether Catholic or Protestant. German Catholics had hitherto been protected by Austria.

An artillery salute and a carpeted path leading all the way to the Church of the Holy Sepulchre greeted Wilhelm on his arrival inside the Old City. After paying his respects to Christ's tomb, he demonstrated Germany's intense devotion to the holy places by presiding over the consecration of the egregiously tall new German Lutheran Church of the Redeemer built directly opposite the Holy Sepulchre on the ruins of the headquarters of the Crusader Knights of the Hospital of St John. Next, he rode north-west out of the Old City to the Russian Compound's Holy Trinity cathedral, and then north to admire the new Anglican Cathedral of St George and Queen Victoria's gift to it. 'I must telegraph Grandmamma and tell her that I have seen her font,' he observed. His conversation with Bishop Blyth there would have dismayed Theodor Herzl. 'Do you believe in a future for the Jews?' he asked and, when the bishop replied in the affirmative, answered, 'I don't agree with you at all! What future can there be for the people who crucified Our Lord?'[x]

Although the visit had to be cut short on account of the heat and the intolerable discomforts of travel, it was pronounced a grand success. The sultan had been properly dazzled by the youngest and most blatantly ambitious of Europe's rulers, and the Young Turks who supplanted him in 1908 would continue to pin all their hope for great power protection on the kaiser. On 1 August 1914, just as the web of alliances across Europe began ensnaring one after another power in the Great War, Germany and Turkey concluded an alli-ance. Two months later the Young Turks doomed their empire to final disintegration by entering the Europeans' war on what would be the losing side.

At last, the end of the Ottoman empire was in sight. In the hearts of those who never doubted that Britain, France and Russia would triumph over Germany and her allies in the Great War, the old dream of England playing her part in the restoration of the Jews to their ancient homeland was reborn. 'What is to prevent the Jews having Palestine and restoring a real Judaea?' asked the author H.G. Wells in an open letter to a newspaper as soon as Turkey entered the war.[xi] Within months, the only Jewish member of the British cabinet, the Zionist Herbert Samuel, was suggesting that Britain establish a protectorate in Palestine and oversee wholesale Jewish resettlement there. But the war would not be won and the Ottoman empire dismantled for another four years. It was still too early to plan for an enlargement of the British empire and Prime Minister Herbert Asquith pronounced himself firmly opposed to any such 'addition to our responsibilities'.[xii]

In the Jerusalem of late 1914 the Turks celebrated their entry into the war by taking a merry revenge on the local British, French and Russians. The Christians' legal and commercial immunities, the invaluable product of 300 years of Capitulation agreements, were abruptly cancelled and a postage stamp emblazoned with 'Suppression of the Privileges of Foreigners' issued. A general jihad against the British, French and Russian empires in their various Muslim colonies was declared. Only Germany and Austria-Hungary were exempt from the war against the European infidel with the kaiser claimed as a distant relative of the sultan. Half Palestine's Jews, about 30,000 – those who remained subjects of the tsar in spite of having fled Russian pogroms to build socialist communes in the Promised Land – were declared enemy aliens and faced expulsion until Germany stepped in to reverse the order. In December 1914 all but the most ancient and infirm among Jerusalem's Catholic, Anglican and Orthodox religious were more successfully designated enemy aliens and expelled. A residue of neutrals, notably the Spanish consul and some American missionaries, suffered frightening isolation after the closing down of the various European postal services.

The Kaiserin Augusta Victoria Stiftung with its commanding view of the city became the Turks' military headquarters. Notre Dame, the grand hostel built for French pilgrims in the early 1880s to rival the barrack blocks of the Russian Compound, was commandeered as the Turkish army's medical headquarters, and Christ Church's outbuildings turned into a disinfecting station. After a former pupil of St George's Anglican school confused the words 'canon' and 'cannon' the Turks dug up the floor of the cathedral in search of hidden weaponry. Scrupulously neutral American missionaries dispensed free soup from cauldrons borrowed from the Armenian Convent and tended the Ottoman wounded even after America entered the war on the opposing side in April 1917. Later that year, as the Bolsheviks staged their revolution, murdered Tsar Nicholas and his family and withdrew from the Allied war effort by signing a peace with Germany, a few young Russian novices at the Convent of the Ascension on the Mount of Olives continued praying for protection to a miraculous icon of the Mother of God. Back down in the city an Armenian bishop recorded the Turkish army's requisitioning of a hundred carpets from his community for use in the trenches. How could he refuse? Meanwhile, the Turks' genocidal campaign against the ancient Armenian communities of Anatolia was bringing tens of thousands of refugees to Jerusalem, George Hintlian's parents among them, to seek refuge in the Armenian Convent. The Turks requisitioned valuables, furniture and even cutlery from all the Christian foundations.

In 1916 David Lloyd George succeeded Asquith as British prime minister. The first most Jerusalemites knew of his redirection of the war effort from the muddy stalemate of the Western Front to the Middle Eastern theatre was the early morning of 26 June 1917 when ten British aeroplanes buzzed over the Mount of Olives to drop a few bombs on the Turkish high command in the Kaiserin Augusta Victoria Stiftung. Only the church with its portraits of the kaiser and his wife suffered any damage so a German general was able to make himself at home in the castle when he assumed emergency command of the embattled sector a few months later. Although the Turks were keen to defend the city against the Allied advance, Berlin piously decided that the holy city must not become a battleground, and commanded a retreat. With France almost exhausted, Russia out of the war and Germany and its ally Turkey close to beaten, Britain was about to triumph in the Christian powers' most recent and century-long contest for control of the Holy Land.

A few days before Christmas, on 13 December 1917, General

Edmund Allenby strode through Jaffa Gate like a simple pilgrim to take formal possession of Jerusalem. The contrast with the kaiser's vainglorious entrance on horseback in 1898 was intentional and appreciated, as was his swift undertaking – relayed in eight languages including Russian, Hebrew and Italian – to protect 'every sacred building, monument, holy spot, shrine, traditional site, endowment, pious bequest or customary place of prayer of whatever form of the three religions'.[xiii] British, French and Italian soldiers were deployed to guard the Church of the Holy Sepulchre and, on the Haram al-Sharif, Muslim troops of the Raj watched over the Dome of the Rock and the Al-Aqsa mosque.

Allenby was adamant; there would be no showy crowing over the conquest of the Christian holy places, no trampling of Islam and Judaism in the manner of the medieval Crusaders, no bombastic flag-waving. A devout Christian, he often lectured his troops on the biblical significance of the places they passed in the Holy Land with the aid of a copy of George Adam Smith's *The Historical Geography of the Holy Land** given to him by Lloyd George, but he was no Earl of Shaftesbury. Although he read the Bible, he cherished no romantic illusions about his role in the fulfilment of any biblical prophecy concerning the end of the world and Christ's second coming. Anyone who dared refer to the campaign as a Crusade was sharply reminded that there were plenty of Muslims in the army – the Egyptian Camel and Labour Corps, for example. His account of his formal entry into Jerusalem in a letter to his wife was characteristically matter of fact: 'Great enthusiasm – real or feigned – was shown. Then I received the notables and heads of the Church, of which there are many, including Abyssinian. After this, we reformed our procession and returned to our horses which we had left outside the walls.'[xiv]

But for many western Christians the moment's grand symmetry was too powerful to ignore. Not since 1244, when the truce the

---

* The book expressed the opinion that the Ottoman Turkish rule over Palestine must be replaced by rule by Jews, 'who have given to Palestine everything it has ever had of value to the world'.

German Emperor Frederick II had negotiated with his friend Sultan al-Kamil expired, had a Christian power ruled the holy city. Back in London Lloyd George rejoiced at Britain having conquered the 'most famous city in the world' and recovered possession of Christendom's 'sacred shrines'.[xv] The Franciscans immediately spied their chance of regaining sole possession of all the holy places from the Greek Orthodox: 'It is now seven centuries since Christian Jerusalem, Latin Jerusalem, fell into the power of the followers of Islam,' wrote a friar. 'Today the warrior descendants of the Crusaders of the XII century have re-occupied the Holy City. They therefore retake what belongs to them.'[xvi] An American missionary in the city received from her husband a commemorative gold ring engraved with a cross and the date of Allenby's entry into Jerusalem. 'We thought we were witnessing the triumph of the last crusade. A Christian nation had conquered Palestine!' she later recalled.[xvii] A fellow American, an evangelical Christian aid worker with whom Allenby liked to spend evenings perusing the Old Testament, felt moved to pen a hymn of praise set to the tune of 'O Tannenbaum': 'And God has led thee on, O Knight, Allenby, O Allenby! / In thy great battle for the Right, Allenby, O Allenby! / The Earth's free nations now will bring / Their genius to its glorying / And they who sat in darkness sing, / For e'er of thee, O Allenby!'[xviii] Evangelicals at Christ Church were especially thrilled to learn that Allenby was a descendant of Oliver Cromwell, the man who had allowed Jews to re-enter England after an exile of some 400 years. Arabs, relieved to be rid of Ottoman Turkish misrule, were entranced to find that to their ears the name Allenby sounded extraordinarily like *Allah-nebi* – prophet of God.

But the city's winter cold and wet soon dampened the highest Christian spirits. 'The only tolerable places in Jerusalem are bath and bed,' grumbled one British general.[xix] Allenby's Australian troops tore the wooden shutters off the buildings in Christ Church's compound for fires to warm themselves by. The new British governor Colonel Ronald Storrs spent his first month in the city seated at his desk in his overcoat, with a paraffin stove between his knees.

Storrs hardly mentions that first Christmas of British rule in his memoirs except to say that the French seized the occasion of midnight mass in Bethlehem's Church of the Nativity to reassert their country's claim to a protectorate of the Holy Land's Catholics; a Franciscan friar presented the French representative with a two-inch-thick candle while Britain's had to make do with one half the size.

The Holy Fire ceremony of 1918 was a miracle of orderly calm. Governor Storrs followed the Ottomans' example, cautiously deploying 600 soldiers to police the event, and positioned himself with six British officers at the doors of the church. He was only forced to intervene with an outstretched arm when some Armenians aimed 'a few but fairly hard blows' at the archbishop who was standing in for the absent Greek patriarch. Later, he recalled how instantly the 'medieval tumult dwindled to boulevard prose' as the prelate gasped into his ear, '*Mon cher, vous m'avez sauvé la vie!*'xx

Storrs preferred the Orthodox to the Catholic establishment in Jerusalem. In his Anglican mind the Latin patriarch and the Franciscans were identified with papal power and sinister French pretensions to a protectorate of the Holy Land, whereas – in spite of what he diagnosed as 'defects of indifference, supineness and corruption' – he respected Greek Orthodoxy as 'the national Christianity of Palestine, an eastern church in an eastern country'.xxi He loved the 'blare and flare' of the Holy Fire ceremony too, enough to witness it seven years running. 'There is in it a Dionysiac mysticism,' he later rapturously recalled, 'heightened by the memory of what has happened there in the past, which seems in Jerusalem but a backward continuum of the throbbing present.'xxii

~

Events are moving as fast and confusingly as on a battlefield this Holy Saturday morning in 2003.

Bishop Theophanis calls round to Arkhangelos at eight because a painful leg has rendered Rahme more than usually sofa-bound and she has begged him to bring her Easter holy communion. While emptying a Marlboro carrier bag containing his stole and some bread and wine onto her sofa, he mutters about Israeli police having banned pilgrims from spending the night in the Church of the Holy Sepulchre.

'We have to face facts. The Holy Fire ceremony may be cancelled,' he warns me.

An hour later, up at St George's theological college, George Hintlian is urgently addressing a party of visiting Anglicans.

'What we will see here today is the Orthodox rekindling the spirits and quarrels of the nineteenth century. Russia has sent the Moscow mayor. Athens has contributed commandos dressed as ceremonial guards or boy scouts to defend their patriarch. Early this morning the Israelis cordoned off the Old City and deployed around two thousand police. They are checking that no Armenian under the age of forty can get near the Church of the Holy Sepulchre. The situation is very serious. Believe me, I have seen how trouble can erupt suddenly, waves of fighting flowing up and down the church, and the Holy Fire is an extra hazard. It's your decision to go to the ceremony or not, but you will be taking your lives in your hands. At least find places in the galleries. If there is trouble it will start at ground level.'

The visiting Anglicans' faces register a mixture of shock and disbelief. One or two emit nervous giggles. 'Can anybody respond to what George is saying?' says their group leader. No one can.

George belatedly informs me that I need a pass to attend the ceremony but he cannot procure me one because the Israelis have strictly limited the Armenians' quota. There is no time to lose.

Back down at Jaffa Gate I go in search of Father Athanasius, and find him alone in his office on the second floor of the empty Christian Information Centre. 'I know, you need a pass to the Holy Fire,' he says, flipping open his wallet and handing me a laminated ticket before I can stutter out a breathless request. He is out of sorts, annoyed. 'The Greeks and Armenians have totally lost their grip on this show! Have you seen the Israeli police strength out there?

They've taken the Old City; we Christians should never, *ever*, give them the excuse to do this!'

I hear fear. Every time the old Christian Churches disgrace themselves, every time they give the Israelis an excuse to play the patient mediator and peacekeeper, they believe they surrender a little of their autonomy, a little of their right to be taken seriously or even into account, a little of their hold on the holy places.

A police cordon bars my entrance to the souk. Taking the long way round past San Salvatore and Arkhangelos, I run into another checkpoint by the Internet cafe and the corner of Greek Patriarchate Road. Behind the metal barrier is a crowd of about a hundred pilgrims from Ukraine, from Romania, from Russia and Cyprus, grumbling at having travelled all this way only to find themselves barred from attending the climax of their Easter celebrations. A young Israeli policeman, eyes shaded by his visor and holster bulging at his hip, does not know when or even if the barriers will be lifted. His radio crackles urgently. A flash of my laminated pass enables me to slip through.

The courtyard of the Church of the Holy Sepulchre, packed tight with pilgrims last Easter, is empty of all but police this year. Inside, there are the makings of a crowd around the edicule but the rest of the great church is empty and the atmosphere calm. Following George's instructions nonetheless, I make straight for the safety of an already crowded upper gallery in the Armenian section of the church and settle on the floor for the three-hour wait for the ceremony to start.

As the hour approaches and the crowd around the edicule – brightly flecked with the red and gold of church robes and the blue of police flak jackets – thickens and expands, the tension mounts. An argument has erupted; two deacons frogmarch a man away from the shrine. There are angry scuffles over places. Someone causes a fracas by becoming entangled in TV light cables after climbing too high into one of the niches opposite the edicule. Another eruption of pushing and shoving near the shrine indicates that George's imagined worst may be about to happen. Police reinforcements arrive. The mood calms again.

The customary cheering and whooping begins as the churchmen start processing around the shrine, banners waving, voices raised in a lusty anthem. Once, twice and three times, they pass. Patriarch Irineos has arrived but this year he is so tightly ringed by a cordon of tall guards dressed in the short skirts, tasselled caps and pom-pom shoes of Greek national dress that only the glitter of his mitre is visible. The Armenian left side of the edicule is growing restive again. A hasty exchange of blows results in another swift march away from the scene.

The throng around the shrine is now too tight and the light too dim for me to see when Irineos and the Armenian enter the edicule but the Armenians' porthole is suddenly blazing with Holy Fire and the area around the edicule is a circle of raging orange light, spreading fast, from bundle of candles to bundle of candles, to single candle and up to this gallery, to the elderly woman seated on a folding stool in front of me who is making the sign of the cross with it over her face and chest. I light my own candle from hers as the stink of singed hair attacks my nostrils and the church bells begin clanging like a fire alarm. My vision is blurred with tears and my heart beating too fast. The involuntary overflow of emotion, the din and the smoke and heat are at least as disorientating as they were last year.

But all is well. Awed by the mysterious emotive power of the Holy Fire, I am also flooded with relief that there are no mounds of corpses by the door at the foot of Calvary, or screaming ambulance sirens. The barriers were lifted in time to allow the pilgrims in to see their miracle, so the sunlit parvis is filled with people brandishing their Holy Fire and shouting Easter greetings. I wave to Nasra standing high above me on the wall of one of the Greek monasteries and head back to Arkhangelos and Rahme.

Rubbing at her bad leg, Rahme is on the phone to her nun friend in Illinois. On the coffee table beside her is a candle lit with Holy Fire. No sooner has she hung up than George calls.

'We were lucky!' he begins.

'Was there a last-minute agreement?'

'No, in the end we Armenians compromised a little. We did not send the priest who did the ceremony last year but someone Irineos gets on well with. They had a friendly little chat when they arrived inside the edicule and agreed that Irineos should go into the inner chamber first to get the Holy Fire. The main point is, we did not allow the patriarch to be the one to give our Armenian the fire!'

I point out that surely the 'main point' is that no one has been hurt and that the pilgrims have not come all this way for nothing. But George is not listening.

'*Habibi,* there is something else you should know but it's not safe to talk about it on the telephone. Let's meet at the Ethiopians' celebration tonight.'

By the time we meet on the Ethiopians' rooftop I have spoken to the genial old Greek bishop who deals with Status Quo questions for the patriarchate and learned that despite the decent compromise Irineos does not consider the matter permanently resolved. While Solomon and his countrymen dance around the dome of St Helena's chapel with their lit candles, banging their drums and ululating with joy at the resurrection of Christ, I share this bad news with George and he imparts his own.

'I have it on excellent authority that the Israelis barred pilgrims from sleeping in the church last night because they needed to enter the edicule secretly to fix a hidden camera above the tomb. Very clever of course!' he says bitterly. 'When there is a problem next year they will simply produce the recorded evidence of what happened today and say, "Look, here's the precedent! You perform the ceremony like this. No room for more argument." *Voilà!*'

'I suppose, ultimately, the Israelis are responsible for security,' is my insensitive reply. I am weary of the paranoia and the melodrama, but I know perfectly well that George is as sure as Father Athanasius that every upset in the Christian holy places only gives the Israelis an excuse to mock, that every unholy scuffle represents another opportunity for them to portray the old Churches as doomed to convenient extinction and the abandonment of their prime real estate.

Trudging back towards Arkhangelos through empty alleys strewn with the day's litter of plastic bottles and newspapers, I feel suffocated by an Old City filled with hearts breaking and minds fearful of forfeiting places of worship, homes and lands and pasts. Tonight, the dimpled effect of the limestone walls and paving stones in the ghostly glow of the street lights reminds me of the interior of a padded cell.

~

Citizens of Jerusalem have that first British governor of the city, Ronald Storrs, to thank for the usually pleasing effect of Jerusalem's ubiquitous limestone.

A good friend to George Hintlian's bibliophile father and an erudite orientalist who spoke fluent Arabic and some Hebrew, Storrs ruled Jerusalem as a benevolent despot, with what he believed was 'sympathy, energy and imagination'.[xxiii] It was his to enhance and improve as he saw fit and he began with an ordinance requiring building in limestone and new street names, many of them recalling the Crusader era – Coeur de Lion Street, Saladin Street, Godfrey de Bouillon Street and St Francis Road. Better water supplies and sewerage were secured by a Department of Public Works housed in the Russian Compound's old pilgrims' hostels. Finding that his 'ear and nose were violently assaulted at every corner', Storrs had seven sanitary teams of British soldiers keep the area around the Church of the Holy Sepulchre 'free from offence'.[xxiv] Cruelty to beasts of burden was frowned upon.

Storrs devoted much of his three years as governor to mediating in the quarrels of the various religious communities. These multiplied when religious Jews entered the arena, demanding their own protected holy places and resorting to the sort of devious antics the Christians had been practising in their holy places for centuries.*

* Judaism had hitherto designated the whole city as holy, not any particular place within it.

After Storrs's failure to broker the Jews' purchase from the Muslims of the Wailing Wall (the ruined western wall of the second Temple destroyed by the Romans in AD 70 which had become the western flank of the Haram al-Sharif), the Jews set out to improve their situation by stealthy invasion. Benches, a screen and other religious items appeared by the Wailing Wall in 1922. Removed by order of Storrs after protests from the mufti, they soon reappeared, were removed again, and reappeared, and so on. A Christian commission of inquiry into the matter eventually upheld the Muslim case. The Jews would not win the freedom to do as they wanted with their most precious holy place until twenty years after the end of British rule in Palestine, when Israeli troops conquered East Jerusalem and the Haram al-Sharif in 1967.*

Equally troublesome for Storrs was the Greek patriarchate's bankruptcy, a side effect of the Russian revolution and the collapse of the Russian pilgrim trade. An abrasive Latin patriarch's inability to comprehend how a Christian power could recapture the Holy Land and then fail to favour Christians above Jews and Muslims was another serious inconvenience, but there was routine holy house-keeping to see to as well. Storrs and the French consul exchanged stiff letters on the subject of the Church of the Nativity's silver star, one of whose bolts had worked loose due to 'excessive cleaning'. He also dampened down trouble when a dispute between the Latins and the Copts over a right of way past the edicule escalated to the point where Egyptian monks were gleefully emptying buckets of slops over friars' heads as they processed along the Via Dolorosa.

Storrs tried to convene a committee to codify the terms of the Status Quo but failed because the Vatican demanded that its head be a Catholic. The news that the edicule was collapsing from the weight of the lamps hung inside it on feast days must have dismayed him, but another eight years would pass without any repairs because the six communities could not agree on what should be

* After the war the homes of 650 Muslims in the city's North African district were demolished to create a space by the Wailing Wall. Much larger than the parvis of the Church of the Holy Sepulchre, it is not as large as the Haram al-Sharif.

done and by whom. An earthquake inflicted more structural damage to the shrine in 1927 but it would be twenty years before the ailing edifice gained the cage of Bengali steel girders that still supports it today.

The orientalist in Storrs loved the Byzantine flavour of life in the city – what Father Athanasius would later call its 'toxicity' – but he formed a special attachment to the Armenians' Church of St James with its dangling eggs, and to the White Russian convent on the Mount of Olives, where he taught the nuns how to sing Wagner's *Die Meistersinger* in four parts using his walking stick as a conductor's baton. His chief and most pious delight however was one the Earl of Shaftesbury would have applauded: facilitating the return of the Jews to their ancestral homeland. 'We [the British] believed, and I still believe,' he wrote in his memoirs, 'that there was in the world no aspiration more nobly idealistic than the return of the Jews to the land immortalised by the spirit of Israel. Which nation has not wrought them infinite harm?'[xxv]

If the early nineteenth-century evangelical vision of restoring the Jews to their homeland to hasten the second coming of Christ had faded somewhat, many still believed that Britain had a pious duty to compensate God's chosen people for two millennia of suffering at Christian hands. Two powerful works of fiction, Benjamin Disraeli's novel *Tancred*, in which a Jerusalem Jew opines, 'The English will take this city; they will keep it,' and George Eliot's magisterial saga *Daniel Deronda*, in which the eponymous hero dreams of 'restoring a political existence to my people, making them a nation again', had been colouring the Jewish issue with romance and urgency since the last quarter of the nineteenth century. More significantly, a series of brutal pogroms in eastern Europe in the 1880s had forced thousands of impoverished Jews to flee west. By the turn of the century many Jews had recognized the shocking truth that they were hardly more welcome in western Europe than they were in the backward, agrarian east. Some, like George Eliot but more notably Theodor Herzl, had identified the path to Jewish survival as linked with western Europe's new ideology of the nation state.* After a first successful congress in Basel in 1897, Herzl's Zionist movement was growing. The search for a great power sponsor for an independent Jewish homeland had begun.

After failing to interest Kaiser Wilhelm in the project during the emperor's pilgrimage to the Holy Land in 1898 Herzl fastened his hopes on Britain, where he engaged a young Welsh Member of Parliament, David Lloyd George, as the Zionist Federation's lawyer. Together, the passionate Viennese journalist and the eloquent Welsh MP succeeded in attracting the attention of the British government of the time. In 1903, the offer of 6,000 square miles of British East Africa, in what is today Uganda, was made. Herzl's personal preference was for either Palestine or Argentina but he was perfectly prepared to consider East Africa.† The majority of his Zionist followers were not; the biblical poetry of Jews returning to their ancient Zion after almost 2,000 years of exile was far too inspiring to waste, they believed. A national home without Jerusalem was out of the question, they argued. And rightly; that insistence on a homeland in Palestine would prove crucial to the recruitment of key British politicians to the cause.

Lloyd George's chance involvement with Zionism lapsed but did not end. In 1916, while he was minister for munitions in Asquith's war cabinet, his friend the ardently pro-Zionist editor of the *Manchester Guardian* C. P. Scott introduced him to a Russian-born Jewish chemist, Dr Chaim Weizmann, who happened to be a leader of the British Zionist movement. Dr Weizmann wasted no time in obliging the minister by inventing a substitute for the acetone needed to produce the cordite that kept British guns firing in France. Years later Lloyd George would breezily boast of discharging his debt to Weizmann the chemist with the gift of a homeland to Weizmann

* The Dreyfus Affair – the case of an immigrant Jew unjustly sentenced for treason – divided French high society into philo- and anti-Semites in the 1890s. It also laid bare the depths of anti-Semitism all over western Europe and prompted Theodor Herzl to despair of assimilation and write *Der Judenstaat*, a proposal that Jews be granted a nation state.
† Baron Maurice de Hirsch, a millionaire philanthropist, had founded agricultural colonies for 6,000 Jews in Argentina, as Lord Rothschild had been doing in Palestine.

the Zionist, but his true motives for conquering Palestine and granting the Jews a homeland were many, and a great deal more complex.

By early 1917 the Allied war effort was stalling on the Western Front and Russia was close to collapse in the east. Freshly elevated to the premiership, Lloyd George confidently calculated that switching resources to the Middle East and backing the establishment of a Jewish homeland in Palestine made excellent military, political and moral sense. He would be buying Britain the support and friendship of Jews everywhere, he reasoned, but especially in enemy Germany and Austria-Hungary. Moreover, the goodwill of Russian Zionist Jews would be an invaluable counterweight to the godless Bolshevism that was threatening to remove Russia from the war, leaving Britain and France to fight on alone. In addition, powerful American Jews would almost certainly want to express their gratitude to Britain by coaxing the United States into finally entering the war on the Allied side. Lloyd George was taking no chances; if there did happen to be such a thing as an international Jewish conspiracy, and he suspected there was, he would do everything in his power to keep Britain on the right side of it.

He was also thinking ahead to the post-war world order. Unlike those so appalled by the casualty lists from the Western Front that they favoured suing for peace at any price, Lloyd George dreamed of scoring first a decisive victory over the 'Hun' and then booty in the form of a new colony in the Middle East. British control of Palestine through Jewish proxies would further secure the Suez Canal and so the route to India, he reasoned, and he relished the prospect of gaining an advantage over the French in the region. He would later confide to Chaim Weizmann that, as far as he was concerned, Palestine was 'the one really interesting part of the war'.[xxvi]

Most members of the cabinet either did not guess the prime minister's other, religious, motive for switching so much of the war effort to the Middle East or they shared his deep emotional attachment to the Holy Land. The South African Boer, General Jan Christian Smuts, was a particularly close friend and ally of the prime minister but no fewer than seven of the ten members of the war cabinet shared Lloyd George's Nonconformist familiarity with the Old Testament – the drama of God, his chosen people and their land.[xxvii] Lloyd George himself had been reared by a revered uncle, a Welsh Nonconformist lay preacher who interspersed hours of psalm reading every Sunday with compulsory attendance at three church services. Profound immersion in the world and mores of the ancient Israelites and their Jehovah had left him, as he was apt to boast, more familiar with the Old Testament and the names of Jewish kings and places in Palestine than with those of Welsh and English monarchs or of battles on the Western Front. Lloyd George was quite capable of referring to Palestine by its Old Testament name, Canaan.

Foreign Secretary Arthur Balfour fully shared Lloyd George's pro-Zionist and anti-Bolshevik stance. He knew Dr Weizmann too. Once, in a meeting scheduled for fifteen minutes that lasted over an hour, he asked Weizmann why the Zionists had turned down the offer of a homeland in East Africa. The chemist had replied with another question: would he, Balfour, be content with Paris for his capital instead of London? When Balfour answered that the issue did not arise since the English already had London, the chemist reminded him that the Jews had had Jerusalem while 'London was still a marsh'.[xxviii] Balfour's ear thrilled as readily as Lloyd George's to names and places and kings he had lisped at the knee of his Scots Presbyterian nanny.

Much like Governor Storrs, Balfour rationalized the case for Britain creating a Jewish home in the Holy Land in three different ways. First, Britain would be proudly discharging all Christendom's debt to the people who had given the world monotheism and produced Christ. Second, she would be helping to compensate the Jews for almost two millennia of persecution by Christians. Third, he believed that a Jewish state would 'mitigate the age-long miseries created for western civilisation by the presence in its midst of a Body which it too long regarded as alien and even hostile' – Europe would be rid of its Jews.[xxix] In Englishmen like Balfour anti-Semitic leanings like these were perfectly compatible with a sincere belief that the Jews were God's chosen people and so deserved a home in the land once promised to Abraham. Recognizing this ugly ambivalence, Theodor Herzl had once wisely prophesied to his fellow Zionists, 'The anti-Semites will be our most dependable friends, the anti-Semitic countries our allies.'[xxx]

Lloyd George's Palestine strategy did have its opponents, however, the most cogent of whom was Lord Edwin Montagu, an assimilated British Jew. Denouncing Zionism as a 'mischievous political creed', Montagu reasoned that making religion the criterion for citizenship of a new Jewish state would mean recalling a single, short era of Palestine's history and claiming 'for the Jews a position to which they are not entitled'.[xxxi] He was disregarded, and so – much more significantly – was the existence of a recent British pledge to help establish a nation state for the area's Arabs in exchange for their support in the war against the Ottomans.* There was to be no consultation with Palestine's Arabs about who they wanted to rule them and how, no semblance of a democratic process in the region. Although Arabs outnumbered Jews in Palestine by more than seven to one at the time, Balfour unhesitatingly judged Zionism to be of 'far profounder import than the desires and prejudices of the 700,000 Arabs'.[xxxii]

Barely more than a month before General Allenby walked into Jerusalem, on 2 November 1917, the most prominent member of Britain's Jewish community received the following letter from the Foreign Secretary.

> Dear Lord Rothschild,
> I have much pleasure in conveying to you, on behalf of His
> Majesty's Government, the following declaration of sympathy
> with Jewish Zionist aspirations which has been submitted, and
> approved by, the Cabinet: 'His Majesty's Government view with
> favour the establishment in Palestine of a national home for the
> Jewish people, and will use their best endeavours to facilitate the

---

* In 1915, Sir Henry McMahon, the British high commissioner in Egypt, had bought Arab support in the war against Turkey with a letter to the Sharif of Mecca promising independence for Arabs after the war. The wording was vague but Arabs understood the offer to include Palestinian Arabs.

achievement of this object, it being clearly understood that nothing shall be done which may prejudice the civil and religious rights of existing non-Jewish communities in Palestine, or the rights and political status enjoyed by Jews in any other country.' I should be grateful if you would bring this declaration to the knowledge of the Zionist Federation.[xxxiii]

What was 'clearly understood' about the Balfour Declaration by Zionist Jews and Arabs alike – the former with incredulous relief and joy, the latter with equally incredulous pain and fury – was that it constituted a promise by Britain to create, maintain and defend a primarily European Jewish nation state on land inhabited by Arabs since the middle of the seventh century.*

~

As early as 1919 a twenty-three-year-old mistress of needlework and painting at Jerusalem's British High School for Girls was correctly assessing the dangerous implications of the Balfour Declaration.

'It is queer,' wrote Susanna Emery in one of her weekly letters home to Kent, '– one hears of people at home talk of the return of the Jews to Palestine, but it wouldn't be any good, one sees, for they are hated by both Christians and Moslems,' and her political analysis continued reliably, '– and the Moslems hate the Christians but they will join forces against the Jews.'[xxxiv] Christian Arabs, their minds filled with ideas of freedom and democracy they had learned at European mission schools, were more implacably opposed to Britain's imposing a Jewish state on Palestine than their Muslim brothers at the time.

The Eastertide Arab riots of 1920, the first mass violence Governor Storrs faced, forced a British military policeman named Richard Adamson to the same unhappy conclusion. Britain's attempt to make Arabs and Jews live together was 'futile', he wrote

---

* Britain never openly or formally presented the Balfour Declaration to the Arabs. It was clumsily leaked.

in his account of the crisis.[xxxv] While policing the Holy Fire ceremony in the Church of the Holy Sepulchre, Adamson had found
himself only a few steps away from the edicule, shooting an Arab
who was on the point of striking the Greek patriarch. Adamson
believed that only the astonishing ignition of the Holy Fire had
deterred another Arab from turning arsonist and burning down the
entire church. Arabs were venting their spleen against a Christian
holy place instead of a Jewish synagogue because a Christian power,
Britain, was the cause of all their woe. Most of the British military,
poisoned by anti-Semitism, were as sceptical as Adamson about
their political masters' airy scheme to return the Jews to their biblical home.*

But the misgivings of schoolmistresses, military policemen and
soldiers counted for nothing when Lloyd George and Balfour,
General Allenby, Governor Storrs and several of his senior deputies,
including two powerful heads of British intelligence in Palestine,
were all fervent believers in the plan to settle large numbers of Jews
in Palestine. However, the policy proved far harder to implement
on the ground than any of its supporters had imagined; its high-
mindedness was easily sullied. Richard Meinertzhagen, one of the
chiefs of intelligence, heartily wished 'Zionism could be divorced
from Jewish nationality' because he found defending Jews against
his fellow Christians in the British army and administration 'most
distasteful' and confessed to being 'imbued with anti-Semitic
feelings'.[xxxvi]

Nothing daunted by the difficulty of the task he had undertaken, Lloyd George attacked any obstacle in his way. To consoli-
date Britain's hold over her new colony he demolished France's
reactivated claim to a Catholic protectorate over the holy places.

---

* Translations of an early 1890s forgery made by the Tsarist secret police, *The Protocols
of the Elders of Zion*, were popular reading in the British army in Palestine. Viciously
anti-Semitic, it purported to be proof that Jews planned to rule the world. Even the
anti-Semitic Tsar Nicholas II recognized it as a forgery but it is still printed today,
especially in the Arab world. A nineteenth-century Arabic edition of the work was
withdrawn from display in Egypt's Alexandria Library, at the request of the United
Nations, in December 2003.

All it took was a single question: could republican France truthfully recommend herself as a Catholic country? When an American survey of Arab public opinion in Syria and Palestine discovered that, if they were not to be allowed their independence immediately, most Arabs wanted America rather than either Britain or France to administer them, its results were conveniently ignored.* President Woodrow Wilson was in favour of self-determination but as a devout Protestant he also believed in the restoration of the Jews to their ancient home. More importantly he would not risk besmirching America's shining self-image by burdening her with more colonial possessions. The year 1920 saw the replacement of Storrs's military administration with a civilian high commissioner, the Jewish politician Herbert Samuel. Up at British Government House in the old Kaiserin Augusta Victoria Stiftung an English major privately agreed with the Italian *custos* of the time that the appointment of 'a son of Abraham' to referee the increasingly bitter contest between Jews and Arabs was a '*bestialità*'.[xxxvii] In the event, although a passionate Zionist, Samuel took great pains to deal fairly with Jews and Arabs, and ended by disappointing both.

In July 1922, just as both peoples were turning against an administration that was manifestly failing to reconcile their contradictory aspirations and Winston Churchill had to ride to the government's rescue with a rousing Commons speech about Britain's duty to finish what she had begun in Palestine, Lloyd George accepted the League of Nations mandate to govern the Holy Land 'in trust' for both its peoples.

Little changed. The Balfour undertaking still held good and in Palestine a pattern had already been set: Arab wrath was appeased by fresh restrictions on the quota of Jewish immigrants and the appointment of implacably anti-Zionist Arab community leaders, while Jewish anger was mitigated by the freedom to set up their own administrative structures, defence force and secret service in preparation for the day when they would proclaim their own state.

* The King–Crane Commission to conduct the survey was set up in 1919.

The Zionist leaders, all of them European Jews, knew the language of negotiation, how to make concessions, how to bargain and bide their time and think ahead. The Arabs did not, and remained adamantly opposed to the imposition of a Jewish homeland on their land. They could not understand how the no-nonsense British had swallowed the Zionists' propaganda about their long-lost 3,000-year-old ancestral home, nor could they begin to imagine how the Protestant love of the Old Testament, a vast overestimation of Jewish influence in the world, the fear of Bolshevism and a mistaken appraisal of Britain's strategic interests in the Middle East had all combined to bring about their calamity.

The exasperated wife of a British intelligence officer confessed to feeling like 'banging every silly head in Jerusalem on the ubiquitous stones' by the time the Arab rebellion erupted in 1936.[xxxviii] A campaign of strikes and terrorism, it was aimed at both the British and the Jews, and it engendered an atmosphere of desperate madness. Armed skirmishes, riots, massacres of Jews, attacks on Jewish settlements, sabotage of electricity and telephone lines, ambushes and bombs were its salient characteristics.* As the unrest escalated the British police and military resorted to torture to relieve their fear and frustration. Entire Arab villages were punished for collaboration with the rebels, whether proven or not. Women, children and the elderly were starved and baked for days in open-air 'cages' while weapons searches were conducted. Muslim women were shamed, forced to bare their breasts to prove they were not male rebels in disguise. Orde Wingate, a British intelligence officer charged with protecting oil pipelines from Arab sabotage, led members of the Zionists' fledgeling army, the Haganah, on vicious night raids on Arab settlements. Moshe Dayan recalls Wingate in his memoirs as a lovable eccentric sitting around stark naked after forays, reading the Bible and snacking on raw onions: 'Before going on an action, he would read the passage in the Bible relating to the

* In the decade leading to the outbreak of the Second World War around 2,000 died in the unrest, more than half of them Arabs, but also over 400 Jews and 150 British. (Tom Segev, *One Palestine, Complete*, Abacus, 2001, p. 367)

places where we would be operating and find testimony to our victory – the victory of God and the Jews.'[xxxix] Arabs who fell foul of Wingate and his Jewish teams could expect a beating or, in at least one case, summary execution.

Shamed by ever more atrocious news from the Holy Land and concerned by the Depression and warning rumblings of another war with Germany, Britain was looking for a way out of Palestine. A more illustrious commission of inquiry than ever before was dispatched to study the viability of an exit strategy involving the division of the country into separate Jewish and Arab states. Lord Peel and his team suggested that Britain retain control only of Jerusalem and its holy places, and a narrow corridor to the coast. But the Arabs, as implacably maximalist as ever, were not about to consent to such a compromise and many Zionists did not want to forfeit their chance of winning Jerusalem. In the end, the plan's suggestion that any Arabs be forcibly transferred out of a new Jewish state was too controversially brutal for Britain to contemplate and the document was quietly shelved.

While the Arab rebellion raged, the British and the Zionists bonded in a spirit of shared adversity. But not for long; first, Zionist gangs exacerbated the mayhem with unauthorized revenge attacks on Arabs and then, in mid-1939, they began targeting the British too. In May that year Neville Chamberlain's government had produced a White Paper that left the Zionists in no doubt they would have to turn on their great power sponsor if they wanted a nation state to themselves. At the end of a decade during which Jewish immigration to Palestine had rapidly metamorphosed from a Zionist bargain-ing chip to a vital escape route for Jews fleeing the latest orgy of European anti-Semitism, when the airy dream of a Jewish homeland was starting to prove a necessity, the British government was proposing that Jewish immigration be limited to 75,000 over the following five years with any increase on that figure subject to Arab consent.*

* In 1927 there were 2,713 Jewish immigrants to Palestine. In 1934 the number was 40,000, in 1935 62,000. (Paul Johnson, A History of the Jews, London, Orion, 1994, p. 445)

For all the money and might Britain had thrown at Palestine during the past twenty years, by the eve of the Second World War she had lost the trust of both Arabs and Jews. She had quelled the Arab rebellion with ugly brutality and, with her last White Paper, effectively reneged on the promise made in the Balfour Declaration.

Britain declared war on Nazi Germany later that year, but Palestine continued to tax her energies. In early 1940 two fascist Italian architects aroused suspicion by arriving in Jerusalem to draw up plans for a new Church of the Holy Sepulchre entailing the demolition of the old Crusader church and the razing of a gigantic area of the Old City to make way for a piazza measuring eighteen and a half hectares.* Much more importantly, towards the end of 1941 the leader of the Arabs, the mufti of Jerusalem Haj Amin al-Husseini, alarmed Britain by sneaking out of Palestine disguised in a veil and a dress to lay his people's case before Hitler in Berlin. Germany and the Palestinian Arabs had enemies in common, al-Husseini told the Führer, namely the English and the Jews. In 1942 the headline tragedy of the sinking of the *Struma*, a rickety old vessel crammed with 800 illegal would-be immigrants to Israel, only highlighted Britain's clumsy mismanagement of affairs in her youngest colony. Zionists intensified their campaign to hound the British from Palestine. Soon even Winston Churchill, who revered Dr Weizmann and had long favoured Zionism as a healthy counterweight to communism, was furiously and helplessly describing Zionist militants as 'new gangsters worthy of Nazi Germany'.

The Zionists had abandoned the old vague talk of a Jewish homeland in a shared Palestine since news of the wholesale slaughter of European Jews in the Nazi concentration camps began trickling out in 1942. Dr Weizmann was demanding a 'Jewish Commonwealth'; only an independent Jewish state could begin to compensate his people for the hideous injustices visited on them by Christian Europe. Long before the Holocaust Balfour and Storrs had

---

* Publication of the plans was delayed until after the end of both the war and the British mandate. The strident opposition of the Greeks and Armenians was a foregone conclusion.

cited their guilty Christian consciences as motivations for backing the Zionists; there were many more and much guiltier Christian consciences after the war.

In July 1946 Jewish insurgents struck their most theatrical blow: cans of milk filled with explosives blew up a stronghold of the mandate power, Jerusalem's magnificent new King David Hotel. Ninety-one people, mostly British and Arabs, were killed. A young British officer who had been drinking in the hotel bar at the time of the explosion in a letter home to his father echoed the Earl of Shaftesbury's shadowing doubts after the untimely demise of Bishop Alexander: 'Through charity of heart coupled with woolly thinking (a fatal combination!) we have made a most tragic mistake – with untold consequences for the Middle East.'[xl] Unlike Shaftesbury, he could take no comfort in the hope that the calamity would prove 'merely a means to a speedier and ampler glory'. The biblical place names – Jerusalem, Bethlehem, Nazareth, Jericho, Hebron – that had resonated so richly in the hearts of Lloyd George and Balfour and General Smuts by then evoked nothing but chaos, terror and Britain's shame.

Britain's abject attempts to stop tens of thousands of concentration camp survivors fleeing Europe to a new life in Palestine on the grounds that neither the Arabs nor the resources of the country could tolerate such an influx provoked international outrage, which reached a peak in 1947. The *Exodus*, a ship loaded with 4,500 Holocaust survivors, was boarded by British troops when already in sight of Haifa, and forced to turn back to Europe. A new surge of Zionist terror began in Palestine. Viscount Montgomery, 'Monty' of the war in the desert, was charged with the resulting clampdown. In his judgement, the mandate administration needed to react to Jewish terror with precisely the same firmness as it had to Arab terror or get out of Palestine immediately. Clement Atlee's Labour government was not about to finish Hitler's job for him or even be perceived to be doing so; the Zionist press was already referring to 'Nazi Britain'. The question was how to leave Palestine without appearing to be conceding defeat.

The mandate army cultivated an air of business as usual and tried hard to keep the word 'terror' out of the press, but a lavishly cheerful street parade in honour of George VI's birthday in June 1947 fooled no one. The decision to surrender the Palestine mandate to the new United Nations organization had been made five months earlier. A United Nations commission of inquiry arrived in Jerusalem and proposed yet another partition. This plan allocated the Arabs still less land than Lord Peel's 1937 commission and their refusal was a foregone conclusion, but the Zionists decided that its provision of a small independent Jewish state would do very well, as a start.

In November 1947 energetic Zionist lobbying strongly backed by American Jewish finance and wider American sympathy for survivors of the Nazi Holocaust swung the United Nations vote thirty-three to thirteen in their favour, with ten abstentions. Zionists everywhere were delirious at gaining their independent state at last but an important bridge remained to be crossed. They must secure recognition of their new state by the president of the most powerful country in the world, America.

President Harry S. Truman was a former farmer from the Midwest, a Baptist nurtured on the Bible and homely Christian precepts. As steeped in the world of the Jewish Old Testament as Lloyd George or Balfour, he needed no convincing that the few who remained of Abraham's descendants after the war must have a home, and that it must be in Palestine. The majority of Americans, millions of Christians like him as well as Jews, were deeply committed to the idea of helping to right the Holocaust's hideous wrong. Truman was also facing a re-election campaign in which the American Jewish vote in New York, Pennsylvania and Illinois might prove crucial; of course he supported the Zionists in their new state. However, the depth of his personal commitment was about to be tested.

When, in late 1947, Zionist American Jews bombarded the Oval Office with 100,000 letters and telegrams begging him to give his personal backing to a Jewish state, Truman simply 'struck a match' to a stack of them. 'The action of some of our US Zionists will eventually prejudice everyone against what they are trying to get done,' he complained to Eleanor Roosevelt.[xli] His State Department also caused him to waver. Headed by the war hero General George Marshall, it was deeply opposed to the idea of partition for some very sound reasons. First, the creation of a Jewish state in Palestine would inflame the Arab world on which western Europe relied for 80 per cent of its oil. Second, with Stalin's takeover of Czechoslovakia another war in Europe was looking imminent. America could not possibly afford to have a large part of her armed forces tied down in Palestine defending a tiny new Jewish state. General Marshall suggested the Jews might find a safer homeland in either Eritrea or Rhodesia (now Zimbabwe).

So weary of Palestine was Truman by early 1948 that he refused to meet Dr Chaim Weizmann, whom he liked and respected and who had sailed all the way across the Atlantic at the age of seventy-four to see him. At last, in March that year, a bare two months before the British mandate was due to end, Truman relented. Weizmann seems to have appealed to his Christian conscience by dangling before him the opportunity to make at least one political decision for purely moral reasons.* Weizmann got the pledge of support he had come for and departed happy, but there remained another hurdle to clear. Truman failed to inform his State Department of the informal promise of recognition for the new Jewish state he had just made to Weizmann. Oblivious, the State Department, backed by the CIA, informed the United Nations assembly that America was not quite ready to back partition and an independent Israel, that a safer option would be a transition period of United Nations rule in Palestine. Truman was deeply mortified by the mix-up: 'I'm now in the position of a liar and a double crosser. I never felt so in my life,' he wrote in his diary, 'Weizmann must think I'm a shitass.'[xlii]

* In his memoir *Trial and Error* (London, 1949, p. 579) Weizmann claims he told Truman, 'History and Providence have placed this issue in your hands, and I am confident that you will yet decide it in the spirit of the moral law.'

But it was mid-April before he made a final and definite decision to keep his word to Weizmann. By then Jerusalem was a battlefield. Partition was happening on the ground willy-nilly, without the help of either the British or the United Nations, 'through intimidation, through open or surreptitious fighting, and sometimes by sensible exchange of houses'[xliii] as one British journalist reported. Although barely an hour passed without the sound of gunfire in the city and no one in the city left home unless they had to, a young Armenian Christian later recalled venturing out to attend the Easter Saturday Holy Fire ceremony and bringing his fire safely home during a lull in hostilities. That evening a gigantic blast shook his house to its foundations and cut off the electricity. 'The only light we had was that of the candle, the *Nur*,* Holy Fire – which miraculously had not been extinguished,' he wrote, clutching at a grain of hope.[xliv] But there was none; no one doubted that the creation of a Jewish state, with or without American recognition, would mean not just war with the Palestinian Arabs but with all Palestine's Arab neighbours.

Two days before the end of the British mandate, Truman was still trying to win over his secretary of state with a quotation from the Book of Deuteronomy: 'Behold I have set the land before you: go in and possess the land which the Lord swears unto your father, Abraham, Isaac and Jacob, to give unto them and to their seed after them.' General Marshall was unimpressed and Truman rattled; he risked losing the most credible and popular member of his administration. There was deadlock for twenty-four hours and then, on the very day the British mandate ended and within a few hours of the Zionists in Jerusalem announcing the birth of an independent Israel, Marshall telephoned Truman to assure him he would not publicly oppose him over Palestine. That was enough for the president. Israel was born at midnight Jerusalem time and eleven minutes later America recognized the bawling infant, *de facto*.

Early the next morning the seventh and last British high commissioner, already an anachronism, departed from the old Kaiserin

---

* *Sabt-el-Nur* is Arabic for Holy Fire.

Augusta Victoria Stiftung on the Mount of Olives in a bullet-proof Rolls-Royce. Byzantine Christian rule over the Holy Land had lasted more than four times as long, and Crusader rule over twice as long, as this third Christian era. Israel would be an independent state for Jews with America taking up as the sponsoring power where Britain was leaving off. Truman set a standard of American care for Israel that no subsequent American president – Republican or Democrat – has been able to forget.

~

'To Passover, and Catholic and Orthodox Easter!'

Nasra, her only Jewish friend Ruth and I are toasting our three religious festivals in a Cabernet Sauvignon from the Golan Heights. We are outside the Old City, in modern West Jerusalem, but the little restaurant's red flock-papered walls hung with faded photographs of Jewish immigrants of the mandate era, its velvet-upholstered chairs, dim lighting and thick white table linen, all belong in the central Europe of the 1920s and 1930s.

Supping off anchovies on toast and goulash doused in sour cream, we are laughing together and trying not to mention the unmentionable, but there is no avoiding the subject. Ruth reveals that her granddaughter is following her own example by studying Arabic but is no longer as receptive as she used to be to her grandmother's view that there are good people on both sides of the conflict. Next she confides that her eldest son, a lawyer who serves two months a year in the Israeli army, has told her he would be displeased if she joined a peace movement.

Nasra is careful not to embarrass her friend by asking her if she will ignore her son's displeasure. Instead, she smiles too brightly and proposes we order a second bottle of wine. I sadly recall the three of us enjoying a candlelit meal on the terrace of Ruth's beautiful stone villa at Ein Kerem one hot evening last summer. Relieved to be breathing fresh air, relaxed, Nasra and I had admired the glow-worms in our hostess's flower beds, smoked a narghile and watched the stars while discussing the relative merits of London and Paris. Now, half a year later, almost 1,000 deaths later, even a friendship as close and courteous as Nasra and Ruth's is under serious strain.

'Nasra,' Ruth begins gently, 'my Jewish friends are wondering why the Palestinians don't just rise up and overthrow Arafat. They know how corrupt he is, don't they?'

'And the humiliation for us, Ruth?' Nasra retaliates sharply. 'Anyway, the other side is even worse than Arafat!' She has not said 'the Jews' or even 'the Israelis', only 'the other side'. This is a discussion, not a fight.

After a brief pause, Ruth bravely resumes: 'But people vote for Sharon out of fear, Nasra. You know that. Arafat is doing a terrible thing by supporting the suicide bombers and I just can't see why . . .' The nonchalant way she is playing with the remains of her goulash is unconvincing. Her need to understand the Palestinian point of view is sincere and urgent.

'Ruth!' says Nasra, louder now, leaning across the table towards her friend. 'What about Sharon's "terrible things"? Bad, bad, *bad*! We don't see what is happening in Hebron and Nablus and Gaza because we don't go there, but you don't even watch the Arab television news like we do. Bulldozers and tanks and weeping women, and dead children and closed shops – that's what we see. The numbers of dead show clearly that we are suffering more than Israelis. Ruth, I promise you, it's *terrible*!'

Ruth is nodding slowly, still playing with her food, but Nasra has not finished.

'The other night I was watching a film about Hitler and what he did to the Jews, and I felt the Jews' pain like a pain in my own flesh. Here!' And she beats the centre of her chest with her fist. 'You say *you* cannot understand something, but *I* cannot understand something! Why are the Jews who suffered so much at that time doing to the Arabs exactly what Hitler did to them? They know what we are feeling; they've felt it themselves! How can they do this to us?'

'That's too much, Nasra,' says Ruth quietly, putting down her spoon, 'Sharon is not Hitler.'

A high concrete wall of silence divides them now.

They are waiting for me to speak but I am suddenly over-whelmed by the thought of Arabs and Jews dying in their hundreds and thousands on account of mistakes made and crimes committed by a succession of Christian powers over hundreds of years.

The poison of anti-Semitism can be traced back seventeen centuries to the Byzantine Church's charge that the Jews had failed to recognize their messiah and had killed him. Throughout their diaspora there has rarely been a safe time for Jews in Christian Europe. When the continent's wars of religion abated and its peoples espoused nation states and nationalism, Jewish suffering only intensified. As Herzl learned in the 1890s in France, and so many German Jews discovered to their cost in 1930s Germany, they would always be aliens however much they strove to assimilate. The creation of a Jewish nation state was the only compassionate and realistic solution in those circumstances. What was perhaps not so realistic about the project was the decision that it had to be in Palestine at a time when the Arabs of the Middle East, tutored like the Jews by Christian Europe, were also aspiring to nation states. Almost equally risky was the sponsored establishment of a non-Arab people in a region both Europe and America would be relying on for a steady supply of oil.

I suspect that if the Earl of Shaftesbury, Arthur Balfour, Lloyd George and President Truman had not been so versed in the Old Testament and therefore so susceptible to Jewish emotionalism about a God-given homeland, so willing to dream the Jewish dream, an Israel would eventually have come into being, especially given the Nazi Holocaust, but it would not have been here.

I begin to say something about the history of Christian power-playing in the region, but Ruth stops me.

'History is no help, Victoria,' she says. 'The past is the past and we have this present to deal with. Israel is here to stay and the Palestinians want their land. That's all. It is for us – Israelis and Palestinians – to save ourselves. No one else can help us now.'

'And who will win the fight?' says Nasra quietly, swivelling in her chair to face me while Ruth signals for the bill. 'With America on their side, the Israelis of course!'

Nasra has a point.

For the first few critical months after Israel declared her independence in May 1948 it seemed that Soviet rather than American influence would prevail in the new state. Where Washington had been prepared to recognize Israel *de facto*, Moscow had been willing to go a step further and recognize her *de jure* and, a step further still, to break a United Nations arms embargo by arming her with enough Soviet weaponry to enable her to put to flight the armies of five neighbouring Arab states that year. Stalin's support for Israel, apparently based like President Truman's on an acknowledgement that the Jews deserved their own homeland as restitution for their appalling suffering, was short-lived however. It had evaporated by the mid-1960s, when Israel and the Soviet Union broke off relations. In the Six Day War of 1967, the Soviets supplied weaponry to Israel's Arab enemies while Israel defended herself with anti-aircraft batteries sold her by President John F. Kennedy and succeeded in doubling her territory.

America's support for Israel as an outpost of Western democracy and values in the Middle East, as another nation of pioneers who have made their deserts bloom, as a righteous little David confronting the Arab Goliath, has grown since the end of the Cold War. American grants and loans to Israel amounting to almost three billion dollars a year are useful but nowhere near as valuable as the power of the American veto in the Security Council of the United Nations which, alongside America's tolerance of Israel's unannounced nuclear arsenal, amounts to a firm guarantee of Israel's survival.

While on a visit to Israel in 1994 President Bill Clinton addressed the Knesset; he was proud to remind his audience that every American president since Harry Truman had 'understood the importance of Israel', but it was not until he reached the end of his speech and switched to a tone of personal reminiscence that the old emotive reasoning behind America's support for Israel revealed itself. Admitting that his only previous visit to Israel had been thirteen years earlier in the company of his wife and a Protestant pastor, he told a wondrous tale: 'I relived the history of the Bible, of your Scriptures and mine. And I formed a bond with my pastor. Later, when he became desperately ill, he said he thought I might one day become President, and he said . . . "If you abandon Israel, God will never forgive you." He said it was God's will that Israel, the Biblical home of the people of Israel, continue for ever and ever.' The ecstatically gratified members of the Israeli parliament were on their feet applauding before Clinton even reached his conclusion: 'Your journey is our journey, and America will stand with you, now and always . . . God bless you.'[xlv] He and Hillary proceeded to visit the Wailing Wall, not the Church of the Holy Sepulchre.

For tens of millions of Americans like Clinton's moribund pastor, Israel is more than just a brave little country. In its fifty-odd years of life it has shown itself to be no less than a visible, tangible proof that the Bible is literally true. Israel's capture of the West Bank, the Gaza Strip and Golan Heights and Jerusalem itself in the Six Day War of 1967 confirmed that belief. Far more influential in the Holy Land today than the Greek or Russian Orthodox, the Franciscans, the Armenians, the Lutherans or the Anglicans, are America's Bible-believing Christians, particularly the Christian Zionists.

Autumn 2003

'We can't just sit on the sidelines and let Islam lead the Jewish people into another Holocaust! This war is about the restoration to Zion that God promised! This conflict is prophesied!'

– David Parsons, International Christian Embassy in Jerusalem

Dangling low over the Dead Sea is a pale yellow moon. Desert dust swirls in gusts of warm wind, coating our picnic food, mussing our hair, blurring our sight.

'YOU FEEL THAT WIND?' booms the gigantically amplified voice of the preacher. 'IT'S THE HOLY SPIRIT MOVING AMONG US!'

Thousands cheer, a joyous thunder ricocheting off the bare hillsides. The distant black speck on the floodlit stage roars again: 'LIFT UP YOUR EYES TO THE MOUNTAINS OF THE LORD! STAND UP IN AWE AND MAJESTY!'

Thousands obediently stand, backs to the Dead Sea, eyes on the hills, their arms raised, palms outstretched to the heavens. A white stage light scans a scene that might be video footage of a World Cup football final, a rock concert or a political rally.

'HUG THE NECK OF THE PERSON NEXT TO YOU AND SAY "THE LORD IS GOOOOD!"'

The shout goes up, blasting across the river to the mountains of neighbouring Jordan beyond.

'IT IS VERY ACCEPTABLE IN THE SIGHT OF GOD TO VISIT ISRAEL AND BLESS THE ISRAELITES! CAN YOU BELIEVE YOU'RE HERE IN THE DESERT WHERE THE ANCIENT ISRAELITES WANDERED FOR FORTY YEARS GUIDED BY A COLUMN OF FIRE BY NIGHT?'

Much harder to believe is that at the start of a fourth year of intifada, when few but diplomats and humanitarian aid workers dare to visit this land and Israel's handling of the Palestinians has rarely excited more criticism, 3,500 Christians from all over the world have travelled here to demonstrate their love for Israel. That they should then have boarded coaches to this dust bowl by the Dead Sea to remember the ancient Israelites and praise their Lord for seven hours seems just short of miraculous.

I am surrounded by the modern equivalent of the Byzantine-era Armenian pilgrims who roamed Palestine in search of holy places to kiss, and of the herds of pre-First World War Russian peasants who trudged over the Mount of Olives to bathe and rinse their burial shrouds in the River Jordan. These are people who have seized the bold vision of Shaftesbury and preachers at nineteenth-century religious revival meetings and are still running with it. These Christian Zionists are players in the latest, and many of them ardently believe final, act in the long history of the Christian world's involvement with Palestine and its peoples.

As alert to miracles – which they, like Shaftesbury, would call God's Providence – as any believers in Holy Fire, they are as mightily secure in their literal reading of the Bible as Pastor Neil Cohen with his Palm Pilot, and as confident as he is that the end times are now upon us. History is hurtling to a climax. The re-creation of an independent Jewish homeland after more than 2,000 years in 1948 is one proud proof of the literal truth of Old Testament prophecies. The Israelis' capture of Jerusalem in the Six Day War of 1967 is another. And now they know, because this too is prophesied, that the Haram al-Sharif – the thirty-five-acre expanse of the Old City on which the Muslims' Dome of the Rock and the Al-Aqsa mosques stand – will be cleared to make way for a rebuilt Jewish Temple on its ancient site.

The sights of these Christian Zionists are set way beyond media headlines about Israeli incursions, targeted killings and curfews in the West Bank, beyond suicide bombings by groups loyal to Yasser Arafat, and the Israelis' security fence biting deep into the West Bank. They have discerned a divine purpose in this madness; the escalating horror is only an ordained prelude to the great Battle of Armageddon that will herald the end of the world as it is, Christ's reappearance on the Mount of Olives and the start of his glorious thousand-year reign of peace. Why rest their hopes on any man-made solution to the conflict? In their view, the current 'road map' peace plan, with its provision of a homeland for the Palestinians, is a snare and a delusion.* God promised Abraham and his descendants the ancient Israelites – whom the Christian Zionists unhesitatingly identify as modern Israelis – a homeland stretching from the 'great river of Egypt' to the Euphrates in modern Iraq. He never mentioned any Arab state.

The Christian Zionists I speak to here are sorry and puzzled to learn that I have not been 'saved' and that I cannot claim to 'have a heart for Israel'. When I ask a middle-aged man in a dusty baseball cap emblazoned with a blue star of David if he would describe himself as a Christian Zionist, he says he certainly would and adds, 'I guess I must really love Israel because right now I could be out of this heat, home in North Carolina, catching twenty speckled trout!' A middle-aged Englishwoman from Devon believes God is currently communicating his disapproval of the road map peace plan by pummelling America's east coast with hurricanes. A smiling young grandmother from Richmond, Virginia tells me that if a Palestinian state were ever to take shape, 'it could only be temporary because it's definitely not in God's plan'. A mother and daughter from the heart of America's Bible Belt – Augusta, Georgia – share her view. Pointing across the river towards Jordan, they say, 'That's the Palestinians' homeland. They got plenty of room over there.'

Land, land, land . . . Over and over again in the long history of Christian involvement with this region, the old territorial imperative appears, the same fixation with the land and its rightful owners. First came Constantine's demolition of the temple to Aphrodite and the Christians' eradication of Jerusalem's past as first a Jewish

* Launched in May 2003, it was sponsored by the United Nations, the United States, the European Union and Russia and set out steps aimed at the creation of a Palestinian state in 2005.

capital and then a pagan Roman town. The recapture of their Lord's homeland from the infidel was what motivated the Crusades. Centuries of inter-Christian battling and argument over every inch of space in the Church of the Holy Sepulchre and other holy places followed and were reproduced on a grand scale when, scenting the collapse of the Ottoman empire, all Christian Europe competed for position and prestige here in the late nineteenth century. That contest culminated in the British conquest of Palestine in 1917, and more land to paint empire red on the maps. The Christian Zionists' territorial imperative has a marvellous pedigree.

Righteous confidence and a genuine excitement at the speedy unfolding of the divine plan are fuelling the joy here tonight and helping to conceal any nervousness about the small army of grim-faced Israeli security men patrolling the rim of the dust bowl. If the festival organizers know that this crowd of devoutly pro-Israel foreigners is a possible target for Palestinian terrorism, the majority of those gathered here believe that, since God has brought them all here to 'bless' Israel, there is nothing to fear.

The hillsides rising steep behind the stage turn red, purple, green and white in the powerful lights and a catchy hymn blasts out in multiple megawatts, a mighty reminder of the Almighty himself: 'THESE ARE THE DAYS OF EZEKIEL! YOU ARE THE ARMY OF THE LORD! PREPARING THE WAY OF THE LORD! THERE IS NO GOD BUT JEHOVAH!' Behind me an American woman is dancing freestyle, her face tilted heavenward in ecstasy. In front of me rows of elderly Scandinavians sway stiffly to and fro in the swirling dust. Young Brazilians clap and stamp, kicking up more dust. Now everyone is singing a Hebrew hymn, following the strange words on a giant screen.

A young Norwegian beside me, here researching Christian Zionism for a university dissertation, quietly observes, 'The only god here is Israel.' After five hours squatting on our haunches in the dirt, we are both ready to leave. The blast of another hymn, 'SHOW ME YOUR FACE, LORD! YOUR POWER AND GRACE! IF I COULD JUST SEE YOUR FACE . . .' assaults the desert night as we trudge back to the coach park to negotiate a ride back to Jerusalem on a tour bus labelled PROPHECY WATCH TV.

On board is a crowd of cheerful American Christians who have dropped by the desert spectacular at the end of a fortnight's tour of the places mentioned in the Old Testament. Their leader is Phillip Goodman, veteran of the Vietnam War, vice-president of Thy Kingdom Come Inc. based in Tulsa, Oklahoma, and presenter of a weekly satellite television show devoted to examining biblical prophecies in the light of current world events. He makes us welcome and soon summons me to his seat at the front of the bus. He needs me to know how he knows that the end of the world and Christ's second coming are imminent.

'In the past fifty-odd years since the creation of Israel we have seen a truly remarkable speeding up of events that have been prophesied. There's no doubt in my mind, none whatsoever, that we are getting close to the end.'

'Could you put a date on it?' I ask.

'No, I'm not about to do that, but the signs are that it's very close now.'

The bus swings along beside the darkened River Jordan, illuminating only the winding road in front in the long narrow beam of its headlights. 'If you read your Bible you'll soon see that Israel is the hub of all the prophecies about the second coming of the messiah. Everything else is just like the spokes of a wheel. Israel is at the centre of everything so we're here to support Israel and love the Jews as God loves them.'

I suggest that it might be dangerous to champion one side over another simply on the basis of what many biblical scholars have described as a collection of myths, Jewish tribal history and ancient propaganda. With Nasra and Rahme in mind I ask him if he can imagine how Palestinian Christians feel when they discover that the only Christians exerting influence over affairs in the region today believe that they too should be deprived of an independent homeland.

Goodman pauses. I cannot see his expression under the visor of his baseball cap. 'I have nothing against any Palestinians, Muslims or Christians,' he replies steadily, 'but I know what the Bible says. This land, including Judaea and Samaria,* was promised to Abraham for his people, not to any Arabs. It belongs to the Jews.'

On arriving back in Jerusalem Goodman's young wife Mary, who has been listening to our conversation, waits until her husband has disappeared inside the hotel to introduce herself. She looks anxious, close to tears, and with good reason.

'I want you to know that I am a Palestinian,' she begins, 'so I do not agree with everything that my husband has been saying to you. In fact, we are having a lot of disagreements just now. But I have even more problems with the Israeli tour guide because he gives us only Israeli propaganda.'

It seems that, a Christian from Bethlehem, she met and married her husband in the United States but has failed to comprehend the full political implications of his beliefs and life's work until now.

'I have insisted that we go to Bethlehem to meet Palestinians, my family and friends, and talk to people who are decent and educated. These people here have the impression that all Palestinians are suicide bombers.'

Phillip Goodman reappears to suggest we remain in email contact.

~

Frowning over their morning coffees, Rahme and Nasra are objecting to my spending an entire week with Israel's Christian Zionist friends. Masking their distrust of my new companions with practical concern for my security, they tell me I must be mad to think of travelling to West Jerusalem every day when I am 'three hundred – five hundred – eight hundred per cent' safer in the Old City.

I explain that I have no choice in the matter, since neither the Old City nor any of the traditional Christian holy places plays any

---

* The West Bank, where most of a Palestinian state would be located.

part in this contemporary phase of the Christian world's engagement with the Holy Land. Christian Zionists want nothing whatsoever to do with any of the older forms of Christianity, with history and continuity and worship at holy places. They like deserts and rivers and feel more comfortable with Jews in West Jerusalem than with Arab Christians, or Armenians or Greeks—

Rahme interrupts. Narrowing her eyes and aiming a knitting needle at me, she says, 'Listen, I know everything about those people. They think that they will be able to watch Christ's second coming on television! Can you believe that? So they are crazies, not Christians. So you don't have to write about them. Finish!'

Nasra has a better grasp of realpolitik. 'Why should the Israelis care if they're crazy, Rahme? They can use the Americans especially to make good propaganda for Israel—What is that?' She is pointing at the red plastic band I am wearing on my wrist. I explain that security at the conference I will be attending every morning this week is tight, that all festival participants are obliged to wear one.

'No,' she says, snatching the cup of coffee from my hand. 'Take it off now! Go there, be with those people if you have to for your work, but never wear that bracelet in the Old City. It could be dangerous for all of us if people around here think that you are one of them. Don't you understand that if you're with those people you're on the other side?'

Removing the offending article I try to assuage their immediate fears; I will not be travelling to West Jerusalem until this evening, to attend the festival's opening ceremony and hear Prime Minister Sharon welcome the Christian Zionists to town. With hours to kill before then, I decide to wander across the busy Muslim Quarter, past the squatting coriander and grape sellers and the bread stall Rahme favours, up to Damascus Gate and out into the breezy autumn sunshine, along the Nablus Road to St George's Anglican cathedral.

I arrive just in time for the Sunday service. Warm morning sunshine streams in through Victorian Gothic windows, falling on rows of hassocks tapestried with the names of English cathedral towns.

The baptismal font that Queen Victoria donated and Kaiser Wilhelm II so admired is behind me and to my left are some wall plaques commemorating British policemen who lost their lives defending Britain's indefensible mandate.

The young Palestinian priest in the starched lace surplice steps aside, and an older, Episcopalian clergyman takes his place.* To my surprise, he launches straight into a fierce denunciation of Christian Zionism. Using the parable of the rich man asking Jesus what he must do to win eternal life as the starting point of his sermon, he speaks about the folly of hankering after heaven when it is life here and now that counts. A small leap of logic leads him straight on, to point out how little there is to choose between a Muslim suicide bomber and a Christian Zionist; the first dreams of the sensual services of seventy-two virgins while committing murder, the second of the end of the world and Christ's second coming while – he leaves this unsaid but clearly understood – championing a state which is destroying another people.

The late nineteenth-century American couple who founded an evangelical Christian commune in a pasha's palace a few steps up the road from the cathedral read their Bibles literally and ardently believed in the imminence of the second coming, but they were not fundamentalists by that Episcopalian's definition.

The pasha's palace is now the American Colony Hotel, the loveliest in Israeli-occupied East Jerusalem, a favourite haunt of the city's foreign press corps, and the perfect place for coffee this morning. I remember a warm evening on this terrace last summer with George and his friend Valentine Vester, an elegantly patrician Englishwoman in her nineties. Valentine's late husband was the grandson of Horatio and Anna Spafford, a couple who sailed from America to begin a new life here in Jerusalem in what they believed to be the end times of the early 1880s. Horatio had been an eminent Chicago lawyer and businessman before a series of appalling personal misfortunes – the loss of his livelihood in the great Chicago

* Episcopalians are the American equivalent of High-Church Anglicans.

fire of 1871, the loss of four of his children in a shipwreck in 1873 and of another in 1879 – awakened in him a burning desire to 'learn how to live, suffer, and especially to conquer' in the place where his 'Lord lived, suffered and conquered'.[i]

Valentine did not relish my suggestion that her grandparents-in-law had been proto-Christian Zionists. True, she conceded, Anna Spafford had applauded the restoration of the Jews to their Promised Land and once explained that part of the commune's motivation in transplanting themselves to the Holy Land had been their wish 'to be there when God brought the Jews back'. The Spaffords' daughter Bertha had also cited the tenfold increase in the Jewish population of Jerusalem between 1885 and 1895 as delightful proof that God was 'fulfilling his work'.[ii] But Valentine was quite certain that by the time Israel was born in 1948 her mother-in-law was firmly opposed to the creation of a Jewish state in Palestine. 'It is indeed curious,' Bertha had written with biting sarcasm, 'that liberals the world over who are loud in their condemnation of racist theories have lent their support to as unreal a racism as any yet propounded; or alternatively, that people who urge the radical separation of Church and State should give their approval to a new state baldly created on the basis of actual or ancestral loyalty to a particular creed.'[iii]

~

Cheers, wolf whistles, hooting blasts on Jewish shofars, clapping, stamping and flag-waving . . .

Prime Minister Ariel Sharon has only said 'Welcome!' but he is a superstar here tonight, heralded with as much razzmatazz as a new King David, a distant dark figure against the gigantic and lavish backdrop of an imagined new Jerusalem. 'Welcome to Jerusalem, the capital of the Jewish people for the last three thousand years and FOR EVER!' The completion of his greeting with its allusion to Jerusalem as the capital of Israel, a stumbling block so great that international peace negotiators have shelved it for later resolution, is provoking more delirious joy.

Support for the elderly farmer turned general and politician is at its lowest ever among his own people* but tonight the thousands of Christian Zionists crammed into Jerusalem's largest conference hall are showering him with adulation. His next words, 'Terror will achieve NOTHING!' and 'Israel will NEVER surrender!' are a cue for more ecstatic cheers. But it is not until he amends his 'We are willing to make painful compromises' to 'Israel is not ready to make any compromises . . .' that the hoorays and joyful amens threaten to raise the roof. The last part of his sentence, '. . . with the safety of her people', is barely audible. Emboldened, he continues to read in his laboured guttural English: 'We are fulfilling the biblical prophecy of the ingathering of the Jews to their ancestral homeland (more cheers and shofar blasts) and we will absorb many more! Your friendship will help us realize our dreams . . .'

Sharon's practised portrayal of brave democratic little Israel, besieged by enemies both inside and out, fighting for its very existence but struggling to do God's will by fulfilling her biblical mission, plays perfectly here. 'I have to see you more often! I would like to spend the evening with you!' he concludes.

Handshaking and bear-hugging, he quits the stage and for a moment I find myself asking why begrudge him a little respite from the cares of his traumatized state? What does it really matter if a few thousand Christians from all over the world see fit to marry their residual guilt over the Holocaust with respect for Israel and a literal reading of the Bible? Why? Because, for all the Scandinavian pensioners, burly Brazilians, happy Indonesians and dancing Fijians gathered here this week, this festival is really about Israel and the world's sole superpower.

All American presidents since Harry S. Truman have dealt kindly with Israel, but the tight bond between a significant section of America's 'Christian right' and Israel's right-wing Likud party was created a quarter of a century ago. The first Likud prime minister of

* A survey in *Ma'ariv* newspaper quoted in the *Jerusalem Post* of 15 October 2003, gave him an approval rating of 36 per cent. Of those surveyed 55 per cent said Sharon's government did not know how to fight Palestinian terror.

Israel, Menachem Begin, was the first to recognize in the late 1970s that a significant number of American Christians shared Likud's dream of a Greater Israel. An evangelical Christian and a Democrat, US President Jimmy Carter was typically evangelical in his belief that the existence of Israel was the 'very essence' of the fulfilment of biblical prophecy, but asserted that 'Palestinians deserve a right to their homeland.'[iv] Right-wing evangelicals from all over America wasted no time in letting Carter know that they viewed 'with grave concern any effort to carve out of the Jewish homeland another nation or political entity'.[v]

On taking office in 1977 Prime Minister Begin invited the renowned American televangelist the Reverend Jerry Falwell to Israel for the first of many visits. Convinced that only the 'intervention of God Almighty' could have explained Israel's speedy victory in the Six Day War of 1967, Falwell went home to begin popularizing the Christian Zionist position in terms the Likud party found thrillingly reassuring: 'To stand against Israel is to stand against God. We believe that history and scripture prove that God deals with nations in relation to how they deal with Israel.'[vi] An estimated four out of every ten American households were tuning in to Falwell's television shows at the time; Falwell was a powerful ally and a marvellous catch for Israel; Begin thanked him for his loyalty with the gift of a cut-price Lear Jet.

By 1980 Falwell was heading the Moral Majority, a powerful lobby group dedicated to boosting the Christian credentials of the Republican Party and securing the election of Ronald Reagan to the White House. Once installed in Carter's place, Reagan did not disappoint his Christian backers. He was Israel's friend, a natural Christian Zionist who once unguardedly mused to a Jewish political lobbyist, 'You know, I turn back to your ancient prophets and the signs foretelling Armageddon, and I find myself wondering if we're the generation that's going to see that come about.'[vii] Reagan had no trouble recognizing the prophesied end times in the Cold War confrontation between the 'evil empire' of the Soviet Union and the forces of the 'free world'.

That same year, two of Israel's most energetic Christian champions, white South Africans whose homeland's apartheid regime had close links to Israel and whose Dutch Calvinist Protestantism predisposed them to Christian Zionism, made a momentous decision. When thirteen foreign embassies relocated to Tel Aviv in protest at Israel's unilateral declaration of Jerusalem as her capital, they filled the vacuum by establishing their own, Christian, embassy*. The first home of the International Christian Embassy in Jerusalem (ICEJ), the former Chilean embassy, was a grateful gift from Prime Minister Begin. The new organization set to work fulfilling the commands of the prophet Isaiah to 'comfort, comfort' Israel and 'speak tenderly to Jerusalem' but the widening scope of its operations would soon betray its markedly political agenda. Reagan's administration was 'privatizing' American foreign policy at the time, hoping to halt the spread of communism, especially in Central America, by channelling covert support to right-wing groups through charities and aid organizations. Branches of the ICEJ opened in Guatemala and Honduras and ICEJ personnel became involved in distributing aid to Nicaraguan contras.†

Menachem Begin was an honoured guest at the embassy's first Feast of Tabernacles festival in 1981 and in the quarter century of ICEJ's existence only Israel's Labour Prime Minister Ehud Barak has ever turned down an invitation to address the festival's opening ceremony.‡ But no Likud leader has shown himself as adept as Barak's predecessor, the US-educated Binyamin Netanyahu, at whipping up support for Israel among American Christians.

On becoming prime minister in 1996 Netanyahu created the Israel Christian Advocacy Council to add muscle to the relationship and had seventeen evangelical pastors sign a pledge that 'America will never, never desert Israel'.[viii] Prayer breakfasts, full-

* Jan Willem van der Hoeven and Johann Luckhoff. Van der Hoeven subsequently left the ICEJ to set up the International Christian Zionist Centre in Jerusalem.
† The Bill Moyer TV show *God and Politics* (1987) showed boxes of aid stamped 'ICEJ' being unloaded from a Honduran military truck.
‡ Ehud Barak was Israel's prime minister from May 1999 to March 2001.

page news-paper advertisements, fund-raising gala banquets and sponsored trips to the Holy Land for groups of evangelical pastors were Netanyahu's favourite means of ensuring that the relationship between Likud and the American Christian right flourished in the mid-1990s. And Christian Zionist Americans, who never approved of the plan for an independent Palestinian state contained in the Oslo Accords of 1993,* met Netanyahu more than halfway. When he visited the United States in 1998 he first attended a pro-Israel rally addressed by Jerry Falwell, then met the Reverend Falwell privately, and only afterwards saw his host President Clinton.

For decades now the Christian Zionist message has been rammed home from American pulpits, over thousands of Christian radio and television stations, at rallies, on roadside billboards and over the Internet.† But the Christian right, the Christian Zionists' political home, only blossomed into the organized force it is today during the 2000 elections. Falwell's Moral Majority and the Christian Coalition – a successor organization led by one-time presidential candidate and televangelist Pat Robertson – had served their lobbying purpose so well that the first had withered away and the second was shrinking fast. The Christian right's new stronghold was the Republican Party itself and, in the person of George W. Bush, Republican evangelicals had a candidate more to their liking even than Reagan, one who confessed to having wallowed in sin as an alcoholic before being 'born again', one who believed himself appointed by God to his post, one who displayed no interest whatsoever in strong-arming the Israelis into surrendering some of the land God had given to their forefather Abraham.

Less than a year into Bush's presidency 11 September 2001 succeeded better than any prayer breakfast, sponsored trip, television show, website, renewed intifada or collapsed Oslo Accords ever

---

* Yasser Arafat and Yitzhak Rabin agreed on an Israeli withdrawal from the Gaza Strip and West Bank and the setting up of a Palestinian Authority.

† Co-founder of the Moral Majority Ed McAteer has erected 114 billboards across the Bible Belt. One quotes Genesis 'And the Lord said to Jacob "Unto thy offspring will I give this land"' and asks passing motorists to call the White House with that message.

could in confirming what evangelicals call the 'inerrancy' of the Bible. The signs of the end times which Ronald Reagan had mistakenly read as heralding a showdown between the Soviet Union and NATO in the 1980s were now revealing themselves far more certainly as a pre-apocalyptic clash between the Muslim and Western civilizations, between the Judaeo-Christian world on the one hand and Islam on the other, between the peoples of the Bible and those of the Koran. Here was the world as televangelists like Falwell had always known it to be: 'a war-zone where the forces of God do battle with the forces of evil'.[ix] The attacks on the World Trade Center and the Pentagon served as a Christian call to arms.

President Bush's declaration of a 'crusade' against terror, his identification of an 'axis of evil' stated in January 2002 and his serving notice on all other nations that 'You're either with us or you're with the terrorists' fits perfectly with fundamentalist Christians' notion of a battle-zone world divided between the saved and the damned. It gladdened many Israeli hearts too. Prime Minister Sharon was quick to point out that the sense of insecurity and fear Americans were feeling was one Israelis had been living with for the past half-century. Sharon's clear message was that Israel, a veteran in the free and democratic world's war on terror, was proud to be holding the front line. He seemed to imply that there was no qualitative difference between Al-Qaeda's attacks on Manhattan and Washington, and the Palestinians' long struggle for their land and independence.

In furious response to a campaign of almost daily suicide bombings culminating in a slaughter of elderly Israelis celebrating Passover in 2002, Sharon dispatched his tanks to the West Bank to put down the intifada in such a sudden and overwhelming show of force that the world, the United States included, felt constrained to protest. 'Withdraw! Withdraw your troops immediately!' President Bush demanded.[x] But Jerry Falwell, still a strident mouthpiece of American Christian Zionism, mobilized his Christian Republicans whom he claimed were ready to swing into action 'whenever we begin to detect our government becoming a little anti-Israel' to bombard the White House with 100,000 protest emails.[xi] Bush did not protest again and the tanks stayed. An open letter signed by forty-three American Church leaders who begged to remind their president that not all evangelicals were Christian Zionists, that there were many who 'reject the way some have distorted biblical passages as their rationale for uncritical support for every policy and action of the Israeli government instead of judging all actions – of both Israelis and Palestinians – on the basis of biblical standards of justice' made no difference.[xii] Combined pressure from the Christian right and American Jews resulted in President Bush describing Ariel Sharon as a 'man of peace'. Both houses of Congress passed motions recognizing Israel as an equal comrade in arms in America's new war against terror.

In the autumn of 2002 Falwell confidently told America's 60 *Minutes* current affairs TV show that 'Mohammad was a terrorist;' that where Moses and Jesus had set an example of love, 'Mohammad set an opposite example'.[xiii] Eight people died in Hindu–Muslim rioting in India; there were more protests in Kashmir and outside CBS in New York. Falwell's fellow Christian Zionist Pat Robertson compounded the grievous injury with, 'Adolf Hitler was bad but what the Moslems want to do to the Jews is worse.'[xiv] Franklin Graham, Billy Graham's son and the man chosen to give the sermon at Bush's inaugural address, weighed in too, labelling Islam 'a very evil and wicked religion'.[xv] These were embarrassing setbacks in President Bush's belated campaign to curb all references to a clash of civilizations and oblige his allies in Europe by keeping religion out of the conflict.

It is too late now to undo the damage. Christian fundamentalists, especially Christian Zionists, are in full cry. If, as one respected American academic who has been studying Christian fundamentalism and its impact on American politics for the past twenty years says, around a quarter of President George W. Bush's fifty-million-strong vote in the elections of 2000 belonged to Christian Zionists, to 'people who think it is contrary to God's will to put pressure on the Israeli government',[xvi] that number has undoubtedly grown since 11 September 2001.*

Right-wing Israelis draw strength from this situation. In the autumn of 2003 Israel's minister of tourism, an Orthodox rabbi named Benny Elon,† toured the heartland of American evangelicalism, the Bible Belt which extends from Virginia and the Carolinas in the east all the way across to Texas. While cultivating the niche market in Bible tourism to the Holy Land and assuring Christian Zionists of their value to Israel, he also seized the chance to lobby for Jewish settlements. 'I am here to ask for the support of Bible-believing Christians. No one else has the power to help save the settlers and the settlements,' he claimed.[xvii]

There is another source of comfort for Likud. The long intifada and a Europe-wide surge in attacks on synagogues, Jewish cemeteries and Jews have been ringing old alarm bells, concentrating diaspora minds on supporting their hard-won homeland in the Middle East whatever their doubts about Ariel Sharon. Distaste for the emotive religiosity of Israel's evangelical Christian friends counts for little when measured against what many American Jews perceive to be an urgent existential threat to the only safe haven they have in the world. A pro-Israel Lobby – a formidable new alliance between the Christian right and the American Jewish community – has been gaining muscle. When the most powerful Christian Zionist in Congress, the Texan House Majority Leader Tom DeLay, addressed a meeting of the American–Israeli Public Affairs Committee (AIPAC) in 2002, he won five standing ovations from American Jews for declaring, 'We should reject the idea that the United States should serve in the Middle East as a disinterested negotiator.'[xviii]

While the Jewish half of the new lobby partnership, AIPAC, excels in the arts of campaigning and fund-raising, Christian

---

* Bush's evangelical vote is estimated at 29–30 million, the Christian Zionist vote between 10 and 15 million.
† Sharon sacked Elon in June 2004 for opposing the dismantling of the Gaza settlements.

Zionists can muster millions more votes. Israelis have not been slow to recognize the powerful new weapon at their disposal. Writing in the *Jerusalem Post* in May 2003, the commentator Michael Freund issued a bald threat: 'Only by putting the president [George W. Bush] on notice that in the 2004 campaign American Christians and Jews will forge a direct linkage between how they vote and how he acts in the Middle East, can we hope to thwart this devious [road map peace] plan.'[xix]

Pat Robertson backed that with a threat of his own. Bush needed to know that the prophet Joel had spoken very fiercely about 'those who would divide my land', so he should 'walk very, very softly'.[xx]*

~

The Arab taxi driver is cross. We have been kerb-crawling up and down this leafy avenue in West Jerusalem's fashionable German Colony district for a good ten minutes, searching for house number twenty.

'The Christian Embassy! Why didn't you just say the name?'

'I thought you wouldn't know it . . .' Nasra's worries about my plastic bracelet meant I had deliberately avoided mentioning it.

'Of course I know the Christian Embassy! Who do they support?' he asks, sounding me out, suspicious.

'The Israelis.'

'Right. But they are Christians so why aren't they supporting me and all the other Palestinian Christians here?'

There is no short answer to that question. We have arrived in front of a blue metal gate in a high stone wall, and I am already ten minutes late for my meeting with David Parsons, one of the festival organizers and chief of the Christian Embassy's publicity department.

I speak into a shiny intercom system. The great gate slides

* In early 2004, Israel's Ministry of Tourism decorated Pat Robertson for bringing 400,000 Christian pilgrims to Israel. Robertson was scheduled to address the ICEJ's twenty-fifth Festival of Tabernacles in October 2004.

noiselessly open to reveal a spacious courtyard shaded by date palms and a limestone palace with a decorative balcony and two graceful flights of steps flanking its front entrance. This is not the former Chilean embassy; this is the third and largest of the premises the Christian Embassy has occupied since its foundation in 1980. At the top of one of the stairways I speak into another intercom and am admitted to a reception area furnished with modern armchairs, a water cooler and a scatter of Christian Embassy literature.

A big man in a jacket and tie, David Parsons is an American lawyer from North Carolina, in his early forties, I guess. This week of the festival is the busiest time of the year for the ICEJ. His mobile starts ringing as we pass through a room hung with large photographs of Israeli prime ministers. Only the Labour party's Ehud Barak is predictably missing.

'Barak? He was invited to speak at the festival two years running but he didn't come. I don't know why,' says Parsons disingenuously, after concluding his phone call with a 'God bless you.'

Once we are both comfortably seated on a large leather sofa in a small sitting room, Parsons proudly tells me that if it were officially accredited as a diplomatic mission ICEJ, with its sixty staff, would be the largest embassy in Israel after that of the United States in Tel Aviv. When I ask him to explain what he and all his staff do he begins, 'We're here to be a comfort to Israel. "Comfort ye, comfort ye my people, saith your God." That's Isaiah forty, verse one. We have to love her when others have abandoned her and left her all alone! We're here, looking at Israel today and asking what we can do to help her get to her promised destiny. Psalm 102, verses thirteen to sixteen, says a wondrous thing: "Thou shalt arise and have mercy upon Zion" – that's another name for Israel – "for the time to favour her; yea the set time is come." That time's here and now. Don't ask me when the end of the world will come, but the signs are certainly stacking up! "When the Lord shall build up Zion . . ."'

His familiarity with the Scriptures surpasses even Pastor Cohen's. I interrupt him to ask what the Christian Embassy is doing in Israel in a practical sense and learn that the annual Feast of

Tabernacles festival, timed to coincide with the eponymous Jewish celebration rather than with Christian Easter or Christmas, is only the most visible of its projects.

The Christian Embassy serves as a first port of call in Israel for visiting evangelical Christian tour groups, directing them towards an experience of the Holy Land which will leave them in no doubt as to which side to support in the conflict. A non-profit-making charity, the organization raises funds for projects designed to fulfil biblical prophecies.* In the early 1990s it collected $15,000,000 to 'restore' fifty-one planeloads of Soviet Jews to the Promised Land, and assisted the housing of many of them in the perilously front-line West Bank settlements. Another 60,000 Soviet Jews had their travel costs paid by the Christian Embassy.

'Jeremiah prophesied that God would bring the "people of Israel out of the north country" – that's got to be Russia – "and out of all the countries where he had driven them." Sure, take a note. Jeremiah sixteen, verses fourteen and fifteen. We're seeing the proof of those words every day!' says Parsons.

Deserving causes in the West Bank settlements, which he, like many Israelis, refers to as 'the communities of Judaea and Samaria' – namely, bullet-proof school buses, ambulances and secure playgrounds for settler children, support for Israeli army conscripts cut off from their families and educational programmes for new immigrants – all occupy more staff time. Then there is Parsons' own publicity department with its email news service, magazines, cassettes and videos. Finally, by way of almost a hundred representations around the world, the Christian Embassy is now in a position to orchestrate not just its great annual 'gathering of the nations' here in Jerusalem but also the steady lobbying of national governments on Israel's behalf.

I tell him that I worry about the wisdom and justice of involving oneself in the Israel–Palestine conflict and giving unconditional

* In 1999 ICEJ had a budget of approximately $8 million, half from American donors. (*New York Times*, 29 September 1999) David Parsons describes ICEJ's income as 'in the millions' but will not be more precise.

support – practical, political, diplomatic and financial – to one side, with only the Bible for a guide. Parsons nods purposefully.

'OK. Listen here! If this present conflict between Islam and the Judaeo-Christian world was the Boer War, we could talk about it in terms of just and unjust wars – I'm a trained lawyer so I know about that – and the Church would have to be a moral voice. But the Bible clearly says that this particular conflict will consummate in the end of the world. We can't just sit on the sidelines and let Islam lead the Jewish people into another Holocaust! This war is about the restoration to Zion that God promised! This conflict is prophesied!'

I cannot begin to argue with the list of Bible chapters and verses he reels off to prove his point, as authoritatively as if they were legal precedents. I want to tell him that if parts of the Arab world are indeed dreaming of leading Jews into another Holocaust that is perhaps due to rage at the fact that the world's single superpower is, in all the ways that truly matter, Israel's staunch defender. But I know he will parry that attack with a Bible quote; the one about God promising Abraham he will bless those who bless Israel and curse those who curse her would serve his purpose. A clever Texan televangelist, Dr John Hagee, has dubbed it 'God's foreign policy statement'.[xxi]

When I say that other Christians might accuse him of ignoring Christ's universal and inclusive New Testament message in favour of the letter of Old Testament prophecies, Parsons shakes his head sadly, as if my dim understanding of the subject pains him more than he can say. 'Oh no, we're not getting away from Christianity; it's Christianity that's gotten away from its Jewish roots! Thank God for the Reformation! It reminded people of the Jews and their chosen status!'

That seismic northern European uprising against the Catholic Church's trade in indulgences, miracles and pilgrimages had slowed the traffic to the holy places in Palestine. It had also sent Protestants to new vernacular translations of the Bible where they discovered the central role of the Jews in the Old Testament, a find that contributed to the rise of English Puritanism. David Parsons' spiritual

antecedents were two English Puritans who in 1649 piously peti-
tioned Oliver Cromwell's Puritan government to 'be the first and
the readiest to transport Izraell's sons and daughters in their ships to
the Land promised to their forefathers'.[xxii]* Other spiritual
antecedents were probably among the persecuted Puritans who fled
across the Atlantic aboard the *Mayflower* more than twenty years
before England turned Puritan. Convinced that the end of the world
was nigh and Christ's second coming imminent, these New England
settlers clung to their strict Hebrew mores long after old England's
Puritans had restored the monarchy. American Puritanism did not
soften into evangelical Christianity until the end of the eighteenth
century, but evangelicalism retained the Puritan reverence for God's
Word, his chosen people and the idea of radical conversion – being
'saved' or 'born again'.

Evangelical Christianity was as much a British export to
America as Puritanism had been. The upheavals and innovations of
the French and American revolutions raised waves of millenarian
interest on both sides of the Atlantic. Following the example of
their British counterparts, American pastors had searched the Bible
for clues about what all the turmoil meant and where it was leading
and, just like their British counterparts, concluded that the end
times were upon them. But in the same way as Puritanism put down
hardier roots in America than it did in Britain, so evangelicalism
thrived better in the New World than the old.

America's industrialization during the early nineteenth century
was ruthlessly speedy. Disorientating and painful, it was a perfect
breeding ground for millenarian cults that warned the world was
approaching its end but once destroyed at Armageddon would be
remade from scratch as a heaven on earth for the righteous and
the saved. One of the most successful millenarian preachers, a
former priest of the Church of Ireland named John Nelson Darby,
soon outdid all his rivals with a doctrine known as 'pre-millennial

* In 1656, 400 years after King Edward expelled England's Jews, Cromwell decided that
he would readmit them. He hoped they would espouse the perfected Puritan form of
Christianity and spy for him in his war against the Netherlands.

dispensationalism'. The secret of Darby's success lay in the clever new feature he had added, a theological innovation designed to provide Christians who baulked at the idea of being consumed in the flames at Armageddon with the perfect get-out. An imaginative interpretation of two lines from the first letter of St Paul to the Thessalonians – 'and the dead in Christ will rise first; then we who are alive, who are left, shall be caught up together with them in clouds to meet the Lord in the air'[xxiii] – was all it took. Darby's premillennial dispensationalists believed that before the great battle began they – the safely saved – would be caught up together into the clouds, out of reach of the bloodbath, in a swift and painless process known as the 'Rapture'.

It is pre-millennial dispensationalism with its lucky loophole that has won Christian Zionism its place in mainstream American culture today. While its media dissemination by televangelists like Jerry Falwell and Pat Robertson has been important, the disaster-movie drama of the prophesied end times has also proved a gift to fiction and science fiction writers. *The Late Great Planet Earth* by pre-millennial dispensationalist Hal Lindsey was the publishing sensation of the 1970s, selling eighteen million copies in English alone. Since the early 1990s the *Left Behind* series by a former leading member of Falwell's Moral Majority and a ghostwriter of sports biographies* has broadcast the pre-millennial dispensationalist vision still more widely. With sales of around fifty million, the ten *Left Behind* books detail the adventures of a group of characters who have not been faithfully Christian enough to be 'raptured' in time to avoid the end of the world but are nevertheless determined to destroy Christ's enemies and join the ranks of the saved. Babylon is the seat of the Antichrist Nicolae Carpathia, whose cohorts wear blue berets like United Nations troops. Israel is centre stage but the only good Jews are those who accept Christ as the messiah.

At the start of the twenty-first century, in the most powerful and advanced country on earth, pre-millennial dispensationalism is

---

* Tim La Haye and Jerry B. Jenkins.

spreading. A poll for *Newsweek* magazine in late 1999 discovered that 71 per cent of America's evangelical Christians believed that the world would end in the Battle of Armageddon, while almost as many believed that Christ would come again in their lifetime. The Washington religious broadcaster Dale Crowley has called pre-millennial dispensationalism 'the fastest growing cult in America' and noted that its adherents are 'mainstream, middle and upper class Americans [who] give millions of dollars each week to the TV evangelists who expound the fundamentals of the cult [and] read Hal Lindsey and Tim La Haye.'[xxiv]

Pre-millennial dispensationalist is how American academics prefer to categorize the majority of those who unconditionally support Israel today on the basis of Old Testament prophecy. But David Parsons is proud to call himself a Christian Zionist.

'I like to keep it simple,' he says. 'I just look at the promise – the covenant that God made with Abraham about the land.'

Parsons, I discover, sees himself as not so much the latest link in a chain stretching back to the Puritans via evangelicalism and the millenarian cults of nineteenth-century America but as proud heir to the vision of Lloyd George, Balfour and Harry Truman. I ask him if he thinks President George W. Bush is a Christian Zionist.

'I don't think he has the full revelation, but I'm sure he's in our camp,' he replies confidently. 'He's shown favour to Israel over these last couple of years by allowing Israel to go into those West Bank and Gaza Strip terror havens to clean them out.' He wishes Bush would stop pretending that religion can be kept out of the 'war on terror', stop peddling the notion that Islam is a religion of peace because he, Parsons, knows that in the backs of their minds, 'all Muslims are fighting jihad'. He also worries that a widening split in Israeli opinion will fatally enfeeble the great crusade against Islam.

'Right now, there's a battle here in Israel between those Ortho-dox Jews who want to hang onto their biblical destiny and the secular ones who want to become a nation like any other in the world and are happy to cede some of this Holy Land.' I know which side he supports even before he adds, 'But we Christians can't compromise over this because of what the Scriptures say.'

It may be some time since he talked to anyone – Jew or Christian – who was not in his 'camp'. Our minds are not meeting, not for a moment. When at last he accepts this fact, his disappointment is almost touching.

'You're a creature made by and beloved of God! I can see you're not a bad person, so what's blocking here? I blame myself for not finding the right way to communicate. What could I have done differently? I have to pray about this.'

~

Nasra wants to drive me to Bethlehem again – 'to have a nice lunch, maybe a facial, enjoy ourselves for a change' – but I have my own West Bank plan for the day.

I have signed up with one of the Christian Zionist organizations running a stall in the conference centre for a 'solidarity visit' to a couple of West Bank settlements. The Christian Embassy does not advertise its support for the illegal expansion of Jewish settlements in the West Bank but nor does it dissociate itself from such communities. Christian Friends of Israeli Communities specializes in arrang-ing adoptions of illegal settlements by evangelical Christian groups in America and Europe. Around fifty such groups have signed up to date and, while the financial assistance is not as significant as that offered by wealthy American Jewish philanthropic bodies, their moral support and funding for playgrounds, school books and medi-cal equipment is much appreciated.

Up at the conference centre I find David Parsons, who complains to me that a Japanese film crew and an American radio journalist are booked on the same tour as I am. 'They're going to make it look as if the Christian Embassy is all about supporting the settlements.'

'But you do support the West Bank settlements, don't you?'

'Oh Victoria, you still don't understand, do you? How can I

make you see? Everyone gets caught up in the latest political issue but the heart of the Israeli people is what God is after!' he says, dashing off in the direction of the press centre.

At 1.30 sharp a bullet-proof school bus laden with elderly Scandinavians, a few Americans and French, the Japanese film crew, the radio journalist, me, my Norwegian student friend, Parsons and an American-Israeli tour guide named Danny pulls out of the conference centre car park.

'OK, folks!' says the cheerful Danny into his microphone. 'First I want to point out that me and Micky our bus driver today are not just American-born Jews now living in Israel but the incarnation of biblical prophecy about the promised restoration of us Jews to our land!' He knows his audience and pauses for the answering amens before continuing, 'Now, we're headed north into Samaria this afternoon, into the land of the tribe of Benjamin. Here's a question: why does most of the world refer to Judaea and Samaria as the West Bank? Sure, that was the name the area had for only nineteen years during the period of Jordanian rule. Strange isn't it, when it's been Judaea and Samaria for millennia? Think about that . . .'

Danny is a consummate professional. He never wastes a chance to pepper his commentary with right-wing Israeli propaganda. The school bus we are on is bullet-proof because 'Arab terrorists deliberately target schoolchildren.' As we speed past the Palestinian Authority's capital of Ramallah he wryly comments, 'That's not a place I urge you to visit.' Indicating the barren hills around, he says, 'Look, empty land! The Arabs only started wanting this land when Jews began building it up again. Don't you think that's weird? Think about it . . .'

The bus is hurtling along an empty road between dun-brown hills through a harsh and unearthly landscape. Danny's spiel is reminding me of the bus ride back from the Dead Sea and Phillip Goodman's distraught Palestinian wife. I am thinking of the Gaza Strip enclave of 140 square kilometres, a fifth of which is occupied by 7,000 Israeli settlers and the remainder by a million Arabs who have no hinterland to escape into. I am remembering the permanent refugee camp visible from the balcony of Nasra's flat in Bethlehem when Danny raises the subject of the Palestinian Christian communities of Bethlehem and Nazareth.

He attributes the dramatic shrinkage of those communities since 1948 to 'Muslim pressure' rather than the fact that the lives of all West Bank Palestinians – Christians and Muslims – are becoming more and more circumscribed and steadily poorer. He does not mention the fact that Christian Palestinians tend to be highly educated at Christian mission schools and therefore better suited to thriving in exile than many Muslims. Instead, he asks, 'Now why are the old Churches keeping quiet about that Muslim pressure on their Christians? It's very simple. The Roman Catholics and the Orthodox have billions of dollars' worth of property all over the Middle East. They don't want anything to happen to that, do they? It's all about money and power. I think that's kind of sad when you consider that we're talking about Churches . . .'

A Norwegian woman sitting in front of me is photographing the passing vacancy. My Norwegian student friend translates for me: 'She's saying that people back in Norway have to understand how much room there is for the settlements.'

We are climbing high into the Ephraim Hills. Our first stop, the settlement of Shilo, adopted by Christian Zionists in Oakland, California, is above us now, a hilltop fortress. A gigantic pillared structure, very like one of the concrete mausoleums favoured by leaders in the former eastern bloc, is a synagogue modelled on the Jews' first tabernacle. Still higher up, on a neighbouring hill, is a vast and bulbous white building like a spaceship – a new yeshiva.*

'I'm wondering if any of you realize just how miraculous this place is,' Danny begins in a voice as sonorous as a Midwestern preacher's. He pauses dramatically, one arm outstretched towards the view of the concrete synagogue through the bus windscreen. 'After the Jews fled from Egypt they came here, to Shilo, to establish the first capital in the Promised Land. In the eleventh and

* A Jewish religious academy.

twelfth centuries BC – let me repeat that, about a thousand years before Christ was born – the tabernacle was here at Shilo. And here it stayed for three hundred and sixty-nine years! Only after King David conquered the Jebusites in 1000 BC did he move the capital and the tabernacle to Jerusalem.'

An awed murmur of amens is his reply, and Danny reaches for his Bible.

'Listen here now to Joshua, chapter eighteen, verses one to three, it's about how the Jews came to Shilo and what they did here. "Then the whole congregation of the people of Israel assembled at Shilo, and set up a tent of meeting there; the land lay subdued before them. There remained among the people of Israel seven tribes whose inheritance had not yet been apportioned. So Joshua said to the people of Israel, How long will you be slack to go in and take possession of the land, which the LORD, the God of your fathers, has given you?" Don't you think Joshua'd be smiling now if he were here in Israel today? I think he would be . . .'

By the time the chorus of amens and the clapping has died down the bus has come to a halt on the edge of the settlement. We disembark and are herded into a large wooden shed to view a model of the ancient settlement and watch a video. Escaping back out into the sunshine before the show starts, I wander about the little hill-top settlement, marvelling at the neat suburban-style houses with their front gardens, the tidy community buildings and pristine paths. I could have believed I was somewhere in small-town America were it not for the high bare hills all around and, far below, a single ambulance racing along the black ribbon of new road, its lights flashing.

A pale young man flanked by two little girls is approaching me now. One of Shilo's thousand or so Orthodox Jewish inhabitants, he tells me that he is from Edgware in north-west London but moved here with his young family a year ago. Soon tiring of staring at a stranger, the girls break away from their father and run on down the road to turn a corner out of sight

'Could I let them do that in London?' he says with a proud

smile. 'Shilo's a good safe place to bring up kids – no crime, fresh air, nice community . . .'

'Safe? Really?'

'I mean Shilo itself is safe. I wouldn't go a quarter of a mile out-side without protection, but we feel safe in here.'

For how long? If Israel is to abide by the spirit of the road map peace plan, Shilo will have to be abandoned.*

As I wander back towards the tour group, I pass a plaque donated by Christian Friends of Israeli Communities. The inscrip-tion on the stone reads simply: MAY GOD'S SALVATION COME SPEEDI-LY AND IN OUR DAY.

David Parsons is corralling the Japanese film crew while keeping an eye on the whereabouts of the American radio journalist and ask-ing me where I have been. We have spent barely an hour here but already it is time to board the bus again and set off to Psagot, one of the ring of newer settlements surrounding Jerusalem. Psagot, Danny informs us, is a very strategic place which defends the holy city 'in the interests of the whole of the Western world'. It is also 'a place of true miracles' because it is 'constantly shot at from nearby Ramallah'.

We disembark in the centre of another hill-top suburban development, newer, more heavily guarded than Shilo and ringed by an electric fence. A middle-aged settler, an immigrant from California, receives us politely but is unable to conceal his dis-appointment that so few of us are American Christians. He wants those that are to be sure to vote for Bush in the elections of November 2004.

'He's our man!' he says.

To the south lies the whiteish tumbling mass of Jerusalem. The

---

* Shilo was first scheduled for abandonment in 1978 as part of a gesture of goodwill in exchange for peace with Egypt, then again in 1994 as part of the 1993 Oslo Accords. In April 2004 Ariel Sharon was sadly admitting to a journalist from *Ha'aretz* that, 'There will be a parting from places that are connected to the whole course of our history,'[xxv] and Shilo was one of them. But a month later he seemed to have changed his mind. The security fence scheduled for completion in late 2004 is now likely to take in a number of settlements, including Shilo.

afternoon light is still clear enough to make out the Mount of Olives and the Russian Tower on its far side.

Herded into a Succoth tent* outside the settlement's community hall and seated on white plastic garden chairs, we are invited to ask our settler host questions. Someone asks if he believes there will ever be an independent Palestinian state in the West Bank.

'No,' he says firmly, 'because the Palestinians are not ready to accept that there must be a Jewish state here.'

A cheerful woman from Ohio, whose husband has just informed me that that they are attending the Christian Embassy's festival this year because God told them to, raises her hand to speak. 'Excuse me, but isn't there already a Palestinian state, called Jordan?'

The group – minus the Norwegian student, the American radio journalist, the Japanese television crew and myself – laughs appreciatively and choruses a joyful amen.

~

Arms and legs tightly crossed, flat cap pulled down low over his eyes, my Armenian mentor is anxious not to advertise his presence here; George warned me long ago that he wanted nothing whatsoever to do with my investigation into Christian Zionism. But it was he who picked up the flyer advertising this evening lecture by a rabbi who has devoted twenty-five years of his life to nurturing links between Israel and America's Christian right.

'I only agreed to come because I didn't want you travelling around West Jerusalem by yourself at night,' he grumbles, swivelling towards me suddenly to avoid being seen by an acquaintance. The audience in the back garden of this house in Talpiot is mostly Israeli, but there are a few American Jews here and some American evangelical Christians.

---

* The Jewish Feast of Tabernacles. The tents recall the forty years wandering in the wilderness before God conducted his chosen people to their Promised Land.

Rabbi Yechiel Eckstein is Israel's ambassador to the evangelical Christian world – appointed to the informal post by Ariel Sharon himself. A sleek, fit man, he has an engagingly modest manner for someone American Jews have just voted the third most important Jew in America. With a self-deprecating shrug, he accounts for that accolade by telling us that his charity, the International Fellowship of Jews and Christians, has collected twenty million evangelical Christian dollars for Israel in the past year, most of it spent on helping Jews to move to the country and settle there.

Eckstein has friends in high places thanks to his Stand for Israel project, a lobbying organization closely allied to AIPAC. 'We are now in a strong enough position to organize meetings in the White House,' he declares, claiming President Bush, Attorney General of the United States John Ashcroft and House Majority Leader Tom DeLay as Christian friends of Israel. Rabbi Eckstein declares himself as convinced as any Christian Zionist that the world is living its end days. The restoration of the Jews of the diaspora to their ancient homeland, the establishment of Hebrew as a modern language and the creation of Israel leave him no room to doubt the approach of the Apocalypse. He speaks of a righteous Judaeo-Christian alliance ranged against a resurgent Islam. 'It's all very scary,' he admits. 'The more I've come to know what Israel has to be prepared for and the more I know of the other side, the scarier the situation looks.'

'But I don't understand,' interrupts an earnest member of the audience. 'Why are you scared when we are looking forward to the coming of the messiah?'

'OK,' Eckstein backtracks with a light laugh, 'I'm not really scared, but the price that's going to have to be paid is very high.'

Eckstein is a controversial figure here in Israel. Rabbis more Orthodox than he is warn that evangelical Christians proclaiming their love for Jews are merely neo-Crusaders planning to fulfil another prophecy by converting as many Jews as possible to Christianity in order to hasten the second coming of Jesus. These rabbis strongly object to Rabbi Eckstein demeaning himself and all

Jews by accepting money from the old enemy. None of them is here tonight but Eckstein defends himself anyway.

'Those rabbis are totally wrong,' he explains. 'You can't lump all Christians together like that. Evangelicals don't have all the background of the Inquisition and the Crusades; they're Protestants. They're not like the Roman Catholics and Orthodox, who think of Jews as the descendants of the people who killed Christ. Evangelicals think of us as God's chosen people not Christ-killers, so naturally they're going to feel closer to us Jews than they do to that kind of Christian.'

Eckstein knows the evangelicals' love for Jews is unconditional and sincere, although sometimes, he acknowledges, they go to absurd lengths to show that love. He remembers once seeing an elderly American Christian reverently approaching a Jewish woman to ask her, 'Tell me please, how does it feel to be one of God's chosen people?' 'I don't know, I never thought about it,' was the woman's pithy reply. Once the ripple of audience laughter has passed, Eckstein says with a little giggle, 'I have to say, there are times when we Jews do feel smothered by all this Christian love.'

An American woman in the front row has not been listening. Bursting into tears, she sobs, 'I just want everyone here to know we Christians love Israel, and that we *really* love the Jews!' Beside me, George is shaking with silent mirth. 'With friends like these, who needs enemies?' he whispers in my ear.

I spent yesterday evening with Gershom Gorenberg, an American-Israeli author and journalist, who told me that he has been under attack from the Israeli right for saying precisely the same thing on precisely the same subject.

Gorenberg has made himself an acknowledged authority on American Christian engagement with Israel by writing a book called *The End of Days*, an investigation into the alarming manner in which Jewish, Christian and Islamic fundamentalists all focus their millennial hopes on what is the Jews' Temple Mount and the Muslims' Haram al-Sharif. Both Jewish and Christian fundamentalists believe that before the messiah appears – the first time for Jews, the second time for Christians – a third Jewish Temple will have to be built where the Muslim Dome of the Rock and Al-Aqsa mosques now stand. Modern Muslim fundamentalists meanwhile are refurbishing Islam's millennarian texts by borrowing from the Christian tradition. One popular contemporary work claims that the Jews have plans to destroy the Al-Aqsa mosque and install a false messiah in a third Jewish Temple.*

Welcoming me into his home, Gorenberg led me away from the din of his four cheerful children and the television, through his kitchen and out onto a patio, to the shelter of a Succoth tent furnished with plastic table and chairs and festive paper chains. There he treated me to a swift and lucid critique of Christian Zionism from a liberal but religious Israeli point of view, beginning with a powerful complaint about the way fundamentalist Christian Zionists relate to Jews as if they were mythical creatures.

'We're part of a Western myth for them, the equivalent of dwarves or hobbits or elves, or characters in some kind of medieval mystery play,' he said, and proceeded to draw a startling comparison: 'Imagine you have some guy who falls in love with Emma Thompson after seeing her act the part of Eleanor Dashwood in *Sense and Sensibility*. He's going to start stalking her because he thinks she *is* that character but how does he know what Emma Thompson's really like? He doesn't! It's *total* fantasy. Fundamentalists are like that stalker. They have a fantasy about what Jews are, which means they can't treat us or this country like they would anyone or anywhere else.'

Gorenberg agreed that dislocation between Bible-based fantasy and mundane reality may account for the puzzling ambivalence of prominent nineteenth- and early-twentieth-century Christian Zionists. The Earl of Shaftesbury wept over Hebrew singing at the consecration of Bishop Alexander in 1841 but publicly reviled Jews as a 'dark-hearted stiff-necked people, sunk in moral degradation'.[xxvi]

* Ayyub's *Al-Masih al Dajjal*, Cairo, 1987.

Balfour could shed a tear over 2,000 years of Jewish exile from their beloved Jerusalem but also confess to wishing them out of Europe. Truman could bring himself to ignore the advice of his State and Defense Departments and endorse the new state of Israel in 1948, but he once quipped, 'Jesus Christ couldn't please them [Jews] when he was on earth, so how could anyone expect that I would have any luck?'[xxvii] and confided to his diary that when Jews 'have power, physical, financial or political, neither Hitler nor Stalin has anything on them for cruelty or mistreatment to the underdog'.[xxviii]

'How much do these Christian Jew-stalkers matter?' I asked Gorenberg.

'A lot, and on two separate counts. Firstly, because they interpret the prophet Zechariah as saying that some Jews will be converted before the messiah comes, but that the two thirds of Jews who haven't recognized Christ as the messiah by the time of the great Battle of Armageddon will be destroyed. Likud is not focusing on that forthcoming bloodbath. You can ask me, why should they when there are so many short-term advantages to this relationship? But what's the subtext of the destruction of two thirds of all Jews at Armageddon? It's clear. There won't be any Jews in a redeemed world so one of the things wrong with the world now is that there are still Jews.'

'Anti-Semitism by another name?'

'Right! The second danger these fundamentalists present is a straightforward political one. The American Christian right is currently losing the battle to get abortion outlawed and kids saying prayers at school and so on, so it's using the Israel issue to re-energize the troops. Right now this means proposing and supporting policies that are morally damaging and practically dangerous for Israel.'

'More anti-Semitism?'

'Right!'

Gorenberg explained to me that because the Palestinian birth rate is higher than that of the Israelis, Arabs are about to outnumber Jews in the land between the Jordan and the Mediterranean Sea.* This means that unless Israelis intend to jettison democratic norms and rule an implacably hostile Arab majority by force, there cannot be a Greater Israel incorporating most of the West Bank settlements such as Christian Zionists would like to see. This simple demographic imperative leaves Israelis who value their country's Jewish character and democratic values with no alternative but to accept the creation of a viable Palestinian homeland.

By the time I left that Succoth tent Gorenberg had convinced me that the current refusal of many right-wing religious Israelis and Christian Zionists to cede the West Bank is far more likely to speed the end of Israel than the end of the world.

---

* Professor Sergio Della Pergola of Jerusalem's Hebrew University estimates that in the whole area of Israel, the West Bank and Gaza Strip 'Arabs will command a demographic majority before 2010'. (*Jerusalem Reporter*, October 2003, 'Has the Demographic War Already Been Lost?') Other estimates set the crucial overtaking date between 2007 and 2013, or in 2035.

AFTERWORD

An international conference titled 'Challenging Christian Zionism: Theology, Politics and the Palestine-Israel Conflict' gave me an excuse to return to Jerusalem in the spring of 2004.

I arrived at the Arkhangelos flat on a swelteringly hot Easter Sunday afternoon to find Rahme chattering in Greek to twelve intrepid Cypriot pilgrims she had lodging with her. I was a day late for the Holy Fire ceremony, but her fancy candle was still lit and the Cypriots were able to report that the miracle had happened without any delay, and beautifully. The Israeli police had been out in force again but only a minor stampede, caused by a rumour of a bomb inside the edicule, had marred the occasion.

Bishop Theophanis received me with his customary energetic hospitality, feeding me chocolates and coloured boiled eggs. Though still under-employed he could not see how a conference about Christian Zionism might concern him. Father Athanasius whom I visited in his office in the empty Christian Information Centre was equally uninterested but wasted no time in warning me that the Church of the Holy Sepulchre was stinking badly on account of its drains backing up from all the Easter traffic. I reassured him that I had been putting off going there anyway because our mutual acquaintance, George Hintlian, had greeted me with news that I would find someone sadly missing. The church's one-man news agency, Artin, had died of a heart attack at the age of seventy-five. It was affectionately rumoured among the souvenir sellers along

Christian Quarter Road that the tiny guide had breathed his last while in flagrante delicto with an elderly French lady. I regretted not hearing the noisy band of the Arab Catholic Scouts escort him to his rest.

The conference was being held just outside the walls of the Old City, opposite New Gate, at the vast pilgrims' hostel the French built in the 1880s to challenge the barrack-hostels of the Russian Compound. While Nasra met and taught her students of Arabic in the cool of Notre Dame's veranda cafe, I and 500 theologians, academics and churchmen from all over the world, but principally the United States and northern Europe, sweltered in its conference centre for eight hours a day.

Only one of the speakers, a strident Northern Irish Catholic priest, academic and author named Father Michael Prior, came close to expressing what I was feeling having completed my survey of the Christian world's involvement with this land. Father Michael was the only speaker to suggest that before Christians of the more traditional churches set about attacking Christian Zionist ideology they would do well to examine their own record in this region. They might discover that Christian Zionists are merely the latest in a long line reaching all the way back to the Byzantines. They might also learn that there is nothing so surprising about the desire of many Christian Zionists to see all Palestinians deported to Jordan; Christian occupation of the Holy Land has usually entailed ridding it of its previous inhabitants in the brutal manner God recommended to Moses: 'If you do not drive out the inhabitants of the land before you, then those of them whom you let remain shall be as pricks in your eyes and thorns in your side and they shall trouble you in the land where you dwell.'[i]

The land's Byzantine rulers drove the Jews out of Jerusalem. The Crusaders incinerated Jews, massacred Muslims and evicted their fellow Christians of the eastern Churches from the Anastasis. The petty politicking of Christian consuls and Churches in the nineteenth century was merely a veneer over the European powers' mortal struggle to oust each other and the Turks from Jerusalem, a struggle that climaxed in the Crimean and First World Wars. It should have been easy to predict that Arthur Balfour's breezy dismissal of the 'desires and prejudices' of Palestine's Arab population would lead to another cruel ousting of the land's inhabitants.

Because the Arkhangelos flat was full to overflowing with Cypriots, I stayed at the Austrian Hospice for a couple of nights, enjoying the pristine tranquillity of the place. One pearl-pink very early morning I stood on my second-floor balcony gazing out over the Old City and saw a battlefield: rooftops cluttered with the small arms of satellite dishes and television aerials, the sharp sword of a church steeple, the spears of many minarets, two domes – one golden, one black – clad like tanks in riveted metal, and blue and white Israeli flags like battle standards.

Shutting my eyes – as everyone does before a violent accident – I forced myself to listen to the cheerful chirruping of hundreds of sparrows in the cypress trees.

CHRONOLOGY

AD 70	Destruction by Romans of the Jewish second Temple in Jerusalem
312	Emperor Constantine's victory at Milvian Bridge and conversion to Christianity
325	Constantine defines Orthodoxy at Council of Nicaea and orders excavations in Jerusalem
c.326	Empress Helena discovers Christ's cross at Anastasis
335	Anastasis completed
632	Death of Mohammad
638	Caliph Omar conquers Jerusalem
688	Building of Dome of the Rock starts
1009	Caliph al-Hakim's assault on Anastasis
1048	Smaller Anastasis rebuilt by Byzantine Emperor Constantine IX
1053	Formal schism between Rome and Constantinople
1099	First Crusaders' conquest of Jerusalem
1147	Second Crusade begins
1177	Pope Alexander solicits aid of 'Prester John' Richard the Lionheart's Third Crusade
1187	Saladin reconquers Jerusalem
1204	Sacking of Constantinople; collapse of Fourth Crusade
1219	Fifth Crusade led by Cardinal Pelagius St Francis meets Sultan al-Kamil
1227	Frederick II's Sixth Crusade sets sail
1229	Frederick II gains Jerusalem without fight

1244	Truce expires; Jerusalem reverts to Arab control
1291	Last Crusader stronghold falls to Egyptian Mamluks
1333	Franciscans installed in Church of the Holy Sepulchre
1517	Ottoman Sultan Selim the Grim takes Jerusalem
1528	Francis I of France awarded first Capitulation by Sultan Suleiman the Magnificent
1555	Holy Roman Emperor Charles V and son Philip II of Spain fund rebuilding of Renaissance edicule
1644–68	Georgian and Ethiopian possessions inside Church of the Holy Sepulchre lost
1757	Catholics predominant in holy places
1799–1801	Napoleon's failed Holy Land campaign
1808	Fire in Church of the Holy Sepulchre; edicule rebuilt in present Ottoman Baroque style
1809	London Society for Promoting Christianity Amongst the Jews founded
1839	First European consul in Jerusalem, Britain's William Young
1842	Anglican-Prussian Diocese of Jerusalem established; Bishop Solomon Alexander departs for Jerusalem
1847	Silver Star in Bethlehem's Church of the Nativity disappears
1852	Status Quo established
1854–6	Crimean War, Britain, France and Ottoman Turkey fight Russia
1898	Kaiser Wilhelm II and Augusta Victoria's pilgrimage to Holy Land
1914–18	First World War
1917	November: Balfour Declaration
	December: General Allenby's conquest of Jerusalem for Britain
1920	First Eastertide Arab riots
1922	British mandate for Palestine agreed by League of Nations
1936–8	Arab uprising against British and Jews
1939	Neville Chamberlain's White Paper, start of Zionist anti-British uprising
1939–45	Second World War
1941	Mufti al-Husseini seeks help of Hitler
1946	Zionists bomb King David Hotel

1947   Britain surrenders Palestinian Mandate to the new United Nations; UN votes for independent Jewish state

1948   Dr Chaim Weizmann secures personal backing of President Harry Truman; Israel declares independence; first Arab–Israeli war

1967   Six Day War: West Bank, Gaza Strip, Golan Heights and all Jerusalem under Israeli control

1977   Israel's first Likud government under Prime Minister Menachem Begin begins courting US Christian right

1980   Reagan wins US elections
International Christian Embassy in Jerusalem founded

2000   Al-Aqsa intifada begins with rioting after Ariel Sharon visits Haram al-Sharif
George W. Bush elected US President

2001   September 11, Al-Qaeda attacks on Manhattan and Pentagon

2002   April–May siege of Bethlehem's Church of the Nativity

NOTES

Easter 2002

   i Bouyer, Louis, *A History of Christian Spirituality*, Vol. I, London, Burns & Oates, 1968, p. 418

  ii Cameron, Averill and Hall, Stuart G. (eds.), *Eusebius:Life of Constantine*, Oxford, Clarendon Press, 1999, p. 123

 iii Walker, P.W.L., *Holy City, Holy Places: Attitudes to Jerusalem and the Holy Land in the 4th Century*, Oxford, Clarendon Press, 1990, p. 240

 iv Cameron and Hall, p. 133

  v Ibid. p. 136

 vi Ibid. p. 135

 vii Baer, Y.F., 'Israel, the Christian Church and the Roman Empire', *Scripta Hierosolymitana*, Vol. VII, Jerusalem, Magnes Press, 1961, p. 136

viii Ibid. p. 137

 ix Wilkinson, John, *Egeria's Travels to the Holy Land*, Jerusalem, Ariel Publishing House, 1981, p. 137

  x Ibid. pp. 127, 138

 xi Duff, Revd James, *The Letters of Saint Jerome*, Dublin, Browne & Nolan Ltd, 1942, p. 96

 xii Wilkinson, John, *Jerusalem Pilgrims before the Crusades*, Warminster, Aris and Philips Ltd, 1977, p. 81

xiii Ibid. p. 49

xiv Walker, p. 19

 xv Heer, Friedrich, *God's First Love: Christians and Jews over Two Thousand Years*, London, Orion Books Ltd, 1970, p. 37

xvi   Internet: http://www.fordham.edu/halsall/source/chrysostom-
      jews6.htm#HOMILY_1
xvii Internet: http://www.holylight.gr/agiofos/holyli.html
xviii Koran 29:46
xix   Williams, Revd George, *The Holy City*, London, John W. Parker,
      1845, p. 202
xx   Ibid. p. 203
xxi   Armstrong, Karen, *A History of Jerusalem: One City, Three Faiths*,
      London, Harper Collins, 1996, p. 231
xxii Goodrich-Freer, A., *Inner Jerusalem*, London, Archibald
      Constable & Co. Ltd, 1904, p. 139
xxiii Armstrong, p. 254
xxiv Wilkinson, p. 144
xxv   Gil, Moshe, *A History of Palestine 634–1099*, Cambridge,
      Cambridge University Press, 1992, p. 374
xxvi Couret, Alphonse, *Les Légendes du Saint Sépulcre*, Paris, Maison
      de la Baine, 1984, p. 76
xxvii Luke, Sir Harry Charles, *Ceremonies at the Holy Places*, London,
      The Faith Press Ltd, 1932, p. 30

Summer 2002

i   Ullendorf, Edward and Beckingham, C.F., *The Hebrew Letters of
      Prester John*, Oxford, Oxford University Press, 1982, p. 3
ii   Runciman, Steven, *A History of the Crusades*, Vol. 2, London,
      Penguin, 1990, p. 288
iii   Beckingham, Charles F. and Hamilton, Bernard (eds.), *Prester
      John: The Mongols and the Ten Lost Tribes*, Aldershot, Variorum,
      1996, p. 243
iv   Ibid.
v   Philippos, His Holiness Abuna, *Know Jerusalem*, Addis Ababa,
      Berhannena Salem Haile Selassie Printing Press, 1971, p. 53
vi   Levine, Robert (tr.), *The Deeds of God through the Franks: A
      Translation of Guibert de Nogent's Gesta Dei per francos*,
      Woodbridge, Boydell Press, p. 218
vii   Zander, Walter, *Israel and the Holy Places of Christendom*,
      London, Weidenfeld & Nicolson, 1971, p. 14
viii Ibid. p. 17

ix   Hamilton, Bernard, *The Latin Church and the Crusader States: The Secular Church*, London, Variorum Publications, 1980, p. 12

x   Asal, Kamil J. (ed.), *Jerusalem in History: 3000 BC to the Present Day*, London, Kegan Paul International, 1989, p. 144

xi   For what follows on Abbot Daniel's visit, see Wilkinson, John (ed.), *Jerusalem Pilgrimage 1099–1185*, London, Hakluyt Society, 1988, pp. 166–70

xii Ibid. p. 217

xiii Peters, F.E., *The Distant Shrine: The Islamic Centuries in Jerusalem*, New York, AMS Press, 1993, p. 96

xiv Fabri, Felix, *The Wanderings of Felix Fabri*, London, Palestine Pilgrims' Text Society, Vol. VII, 1897, p. 337

xv   Hitti, Philip K. (tr.), *An Arab-Syrian Gentleman and Warrior in the Period of the Crusade*, London, I.B. Tauris Co. Ltd, 1987, pp. 165–6

xvi Throop, Palmer A., *Criticism of the Crusades: A Study of Public Opinions and Crusade Propaganda*, Amsterdam, N.V. Swets & Zeitlinger, 1940, p. 98n

xvii Prawer, Joshua, *The World of the Crusaders*, London, Weidenfeld & Nicolson, 1972, p. 88

xviii Prawer, *The Latin Kingdom of Jerusalem*, p. 189

xix Ibid. pp. 188–9

xx   Moschopoulos, Nicephore, *La Terre Sainte*, Athens, 1956, p. 140

xxi Maalouf, Amin, *The Crusades Through Arab Eyes*, New York, Schocken Books, 1984, p. 1

xxii Hamilton, p. 362

xxiii Moschopoulos, op. cit., p. 142

xxiv Prawer, Joshua, *The History of the Jews in the Latin Kingdom of Jerusalem*, Oxford, Clarendon Press, 1988, pp. 75–6

xxv Read, Piers Paul, *The Templars*, London, Weidenfeld & Nicolson, 2001, p. 201

xxvi Masson, Georgina, *Frederick II Hohenstaufen: A Life*, London, Secker & Warburg, 1957, p. 136

xxvii Abulafia, David, *Frederick II: A Medieval Emperor*, London, Pimlico, 2002, p. 180

xxviii Van Cleve, Thomas Curtis, *The Emperor Frederick of Hohenstaufen*, Oxford, Clarendon Press, 1972, p. 219

xxix Ibid. p. 225

xxx Ibid.

xxxi Masson, p. 143

xxxii Van Cleve, p. 224

xxxiii O'Mahony, Anthony, 'Pilgrims, Politics and Holy Places: The Ethiopian Community in Jerusalem until ca.1650', Levine, Lee I. (ed.), *Jerusalem: Its Sanctity and Centrality to Judaism,Christianity and Islam*, New York, Continuum, 1999, p. 471

xxxiv Benoist-Mechin, Perrin, *Frédéric de Hohenstaufen ou le Rêve Excommunié*, Paris, Librairie Academique, 1980, p. 192

xxxv *Daily Telegraph*, 30 July 2002, by Alan Philps

AUTUMN 2002

i Roger, Eugène, *Terre Sainte*, Paris, Antoine Bertier, 1646, p. 340

ii Gabashvili, Timothy, *Pilgrimage to Mount Athos, Constantinople and Jerusalem, 1755–1759*, Richmond, Curzon Press, 2001, p. 144

iii Prescott, H.F.M., *Jerusalem Journey: Pilgrimage to the Holy Land in the Fifteenth Century*, London, Eyre & Spottiswoode, 1954, p. 118

iv Calahorra, Fr Ivan de, *Chronica de la Provincia de Syria y Tierra Santa de Gerusalén*, Book 3, Chapter 18, 1684, p. 208

v Ibid. Book 7, Chapter 5, pp. 601–2

vi Fabri, Felix, *The Wanderings of Felix Fabri*, London, Palestine Pilgrims' Text Society, Vol. II, Part I, 1897, pp. 249–54

vii Butler-Bowdon, W. (ed.), *The Book of Margery Kempe*, London, Johnathan Cape, 1936, p. 103

viii Ibid. p. 107–8

ix Ibid. p. 116

x Newett, Margery J., *Canon Pietro Casola's Pilgrimage to Jerusalem in the Year 1494*, Manchester, University of Manchester Press, 1907, p. 279

xi Prescott, p. 140

xii Ibid. p. 177

xiii Ibid. p. 187

xiv 'Palestine Pilgrims' Text Society, p. 268

xv Zander, Walter, *Israel and the Holy Places of Christendom*, London, Weidenfeld & Nicolson, 1971, p. 21

xvi Bremer, Frederika, *Travels in the Holy Land*, Vol. 1, London, Hurst & Blackett, 1867, p. 110

xvii Setton, Kenneth M., *Europe and the Levant in the Middle Ages and the Renaissance*, London, Variorum Reprints, 1974, p. 151

xviii Suriano, Fra Francesco, *Treatise on the Holy Land*, Jerusalem, Franciscan Press, 1949, pp. 84–91

xix Howard, Deborah, *Venice and the East: The Impact of the Islamic World on Venetian Architecture 1100–1520*, New Haven, Yale University Press, p. 190

xx de Khitrowo, Madame B., *Itinéraires Russes en Orient*, Geneva, Imprimerie Jules-Guillaume Fick, 1889, p. 210

xxi Quecedo, P. Francesco, *Cooperación Economica International al Sostenimento de los Santos Lugares*, Barcelona, Editorial Serafica, 1951, p. 31

xxii Ibid. p. 103

xxiii Ibid. p. 86

xxiv Ibid. p. 113

xxv Paxton, Revd J.D., *Letters from Palestine, 1836–8*, London, Charles Tilt, 1839, p. 121

xxvi Duckworth, Revd H.T.F., *The Church of the Holy Sepulchre*, London, Hodder & Stoughton, 1922, p. 284

xxvii Churchill, Col. Charles Henry, *Mount Lebanon: A Ten Years Residence from 1842 to 1852*, London, Sanders & Otley, 1853, p. 361

xxviii Neri, P. Damiano, *Custodia di Terra Santa 1342–1942*, Jerusalem, Tipografia dei Padri Francescani, 1951, p. 77

xxix Quecedo, p. 51

xxx Zander, p. 24

xxxi Calahorra, Book 7, p. 634

xxxii Asal, Kamil J. (ed.), *Jerusalem in History: 3000 BC to the Present Day*, London, Kegan Paul International, 1989, p. 209

xxxiii Zander, p. 24

xxxiv Sandys, George, *A Relation of a Journey Begun in AD 1610*, London, Ro. Allot, 1627, pp. 163–5

xxxv Ibid. p. 173

xxxvi Ibid. p. 159

xxxvii Timberlake, Henry, *A True and Strange Discourse of the Late Travailes of Two English Pilgrimes*, London, Thomas Archer, 1603, pp. 6–19

xxxviii Ibid.

xxxix Ibid.

xl   Golubovich, P. Girolamo, *Dell'Oriente Francescano*, Vol. 8, Firenze, Quarrachi Press, 1930, pp. 38–9

xli   Ibid. p. 122

xlii   Hintlian, Kevork, *History of the Armenians in the Holy Land*, Jerusalem, Armenian Patriarchate Printing Press, 1989, p. 5

xliii   Ibid. p. 35

xliv   Hintlian, George, 'Mapping a Pilgrimage', *Jerusalem Quarterly File*, Autumn 2001, pp. 39–43

xlv   Polarean, Archbishop Norayr, *Grand Catalogue of St James Manuscripts*, Vol. I, 2nd edn, Jerusalem, 1966, p. 109

xlvi   Ibid. p. 110

Christmas 2002

i   Schur, Nathan, *Napoleon in the Holy Land*, London, Greenhill Books, 1999, p. 167

ii   Ibid. p. 54

iii   Clarke, Edward Daniel, *Travels in Various Countries of Europe, Asia and Africa*, Part II, Vol. I, London, T. Cadell and W. Davies, 1812, p. 547

iv   Thackeray, William Makepeace, *Notes of a Journey from Cornhill to Grand Cairo etc.*, London, Elder & Co., 1865, pp. 148–9

v   Curzon, Robert, *Visits to the Monasteries in the Levant*, London, John Murray, 1849, p. 214

vi   Ibid. pp. 215–17

vii   Ibid. p. 224

viii   Bayford, John (ed.), *Missionary Journal and Memoir of the Rev. Joseph Wolff*, Vol. I, London, James Duncan, 1827, p. 314

ix   Ibid. p. 317

x   Ibid. Vol. II, p. 32

xi   Ibid. p. 4

xii   Gidney, Revd W.T., *The History of the London Society for Promoting Christianity Amongst the Jews 1809–1908*, London, 1908, p. 120

xiii   Shepherd, Naomi, *The Zealous Intruders: The Western Rediscovery of Palestine*, London, Collins, 1987, p. 246

xiv   Ibid. p. 251

xv   Bremer, Frederika, *Travels in the Holy Land*, London, Hurst & Blackett, 1862, p. 102

xvi Hodder, Edwin, *The Life and Work of the Seventh Earl of Shaftesbury KG*, London, Cassell & Co. Ltd, 1887, p. 521

xvii Ibid. p. 517

xvii Ibid. p. 123

xix Tuchman, Barbara, *The Bible and the Sword: England and Palestine from the Bronze Age to Balfour*, London, Phoenix Press, 1984, p. 190

xx Hodder, p. 125

xxi Ibid. p. 127

xxii Ibid. pp. 168–9

xxiii Eliav, Mordechai, *Britain and the Holy Land 1838–1914: selected documents from the British Consulate in Jerusalem*, Jerusalem, Yad Izhak ben-Zvi Press 1997, p. 28n

xxiv Tuchman, p. 176

xxv Hodder, p. 100

xxvi Ibid. p. 127

xxvii Ibid. p. 198

xxviii Ibid. p. 199

xxix O'Connell, Marvin, *The Oxford Conspirators: A History of the Oxford Movement 1833–1845*, Lanham, University Press of America, 1969, p. 352

xxx Crombie, Kelvin, *For the Love of Zion: Christian Witness and the Restoration of Israel*, London, Hodder & Stoughton, 1991, p. 39

xxxi Hodder, p. 375

xxxii Ibid. p. 202

xxxiii Ibid.

xxxiv Ewald, Revd F.C., *Journal of Missionary Labours in the City of Jerusalem 1842-3-4*, London, B. Westheim, 1846, p. 3

xxxv Tibawi, A.L., *British Interests in Palestine 1800–1901: A Study of Religious and Educational Enterprise*, Oxford, Oxford University Press, 1961, p. 56

xxxvi Crombie, p. 47

xxxvii Tibawi, p. 58n

xxxviii Ben-Arieh J. and Davis, Moshe, *Jerusalem in the Mind of the Western World 1800–1948*, Westport Conn., Praeger, 1997, p. 99

xxxix Ibid. p. 59

xl Hyamson, Albert M., *The British Consulate in Jerusalem 1838–1914*, Part I, London, Jewish Historical Society of England, 1939, p. 64

xli   Ibid. p. 65

xlii   Hodder, op. cit., p. 329

xliii   Finn, James, *Stirring Times*, London, Kegan Paul & Co., 1878, p. 81

xliv   Ibid. p. 30

xlv   Wasserstein, Bernard, *Divided Jerusalem: The Struggle for the Holy City*, London, Profile Books Ltd, 2001, p. 34

xlvi   Internet: http://65.107.211.206/Victorian/painting/whh/whhmission.html

xlvii   Rosen, Friedrich, *Oriental Memories*, London, Methuen and Co. Ltd, 1930, p. 8

xlviii   Eliav, p. 177

xlix   Finn, p. 266

l   Ibid. p. 156

li   Philippos, His Holiness Abuna, *Know Jerusalem*, Addis Ababa, Berhannena Salem Haile Selassie Printing Press, 1971, p. 97

lii   Bartlett, William H., *Jerusalem Revisited*, Jerusalem, Ariel Publishing House, 2000, p. 19

liii   Ibid. pp. 33–4

liv   Baldi, Fr Pascal, *The Question of the Holy Places*, Rome, Tipografia Pontifica 'Istituto Pio IX', 1919, p. 156

lv   Zander, Walter, *The Holy Places of Christendom*, London, Weidenfeld & Nicolson, 1971, p. 52

lvi   Thouvenel, L., *Nicolas 1er et Napoleon III d'après les papiers inédits de M. Thouvenel*, Paris, Calmann levy, 1891, p. 38

lvii   Finn, pp. 18–19

lviii   Bartlett, p. 102

lix   Mange, Alyce Edythe, *The Near Eastern Policy of Emperor Napoleon III*, Urbana, University of Illinois Press, 1940, p. 23

lx   Royle, Trevor, *Crimea: The Great Crimean War 1854–1856*, London, Abacus, 1999, p. 60

lxi   French-Blake, R.L.V., *Crimean War*, London, Sphere Books, 1973, p. 6

lxii   Baldi, p. 133

lxiii   *The Speech of the Earl of Shaftesbury in the House of Lords on Friday, March 10 on the Manifesto of the Emperor of Russia*, London, John Murray, 1854, p. 30

lxiv   Tuchman, p. 255

EASTER 2003

i Finn, James, *Stirring Times*, Vol. II, London, Kegan Paul & Co., 1878, p. 263

ii Loti, Pierre, *Jerusalem and the Holy Land*, London, Kegan Paul, 2002, p. 46

iii Hopwood, Derek, *The Russian Presence in Syria and Palestine: Church and Politics in the Near East*, Oxford, Clarendon Press, 1969, p. 121

iv Rasputin, Maria, *My Father*, London, Cassell & Co. Ltd, 1934, p. 151

v Ibid. p. 155

vi Graham, Stephen, *With the Russian Pilgrims to Jerusalem*, London, Macmillan & Co., 1916, p. 84

vii Ibid. p. 81

viii Ibid. p. 131

ix Ibid.

x Blyth, Estelle, *When We Lived in Jerusalem*, London, John Murray, 1927, p. 125

xi Fromkin, David, *A Peace to End All Peace: The Fall of the Ottoman Empire and the Creation of the Modern Middle East*, London, Phoenix Press, 2000, pp. 269–70

xii Ibid.

xiii Wasserstein, Bernard, *Divided Jerusalem: The Struggle for the Holy City*, London, Profile Books Ltd, 2001, p. 80

xiv Wavell, Sir Archibald, *Allenby: A Study in Greatness*, London, George Harrap & Co. Ltd, 1940, p. 231

xv Fromkin, p. 313

xvi Baldi, Fr Pascal, *The Question of the Holy Places*, Rome, Tipografia Pontifica 'Istituto Pio IX', 1919, p. 97

xvii Vester, Bertha Spafford, *Our Jerusalem: An American Family in the Holy City 1881–1949*, Beirut, Middle East Export Press Inc., 1950, p. 280

xviii Finley, John, *A Pilgrim in Palestine after its Deliverance*, London, Chapman & Hall, 1919, p. 29

xix Storrs, Ronald, *Orientations*, London, Nicholson & Watson, 1943, p. 273

xx Ibid. p. 307

xxi Ibid. p. 407

xxii Ibid.

xxiii Ibid. p. 281

xxiv Ibid. p. 294

xxv Ibid. p. 408

xxvi Fromkin, p. 287

xxvii Hamilton, Jill, *God, Guns and Israel*, Stroud, Sutton Books, 2004, p. xi

xxviii Tuchman, Barbara, *The Bible and the Sword: England and Palestine from the Bronze Age to Balfour*, London, Phoenix Press, 1984, p. 315

xxix Sharif, Regina, *Non-Jewish Zionism: Its Roots in Western History*, London, Zed Press, 1983, p. 77

xxx Ibid. p. 122

xxxi Internet: www.codoh.com/zionweb/ziondark/zionoppo2.html

xxxii Segev, Tom, *One Palestine, Complete: Jews and Arabs under the British Mandate*, London, Abacus, 2001, p. 45

xxxiii Fromkin, p. 297

xxxiv Archive of Susanna Emery, Middle East Centre, St. Antony's College, Oxford

xxxv Archive of Richard Adamson, Middle East Centre, St. Antony's College, Oxford

xxxvi Meinertzhagen, Col. Richard, *Middle East Diary 1917–1956*, London, The Cresset Press, 1959, p. 52

xxxvii Fabrizio, Daniela (ed.), *Fedinando Diotallevi: Diario di Terra Santa 1918–1924*, Milan, Editori Biblioteca Francescana, 2002, pp. 187–8

xxxviii Sherman, A.J., *Mandate Day: British Lives in Palestine 1918–1948*, London, Thames & Hudson, 1997, p. 96

xxxix Dayan, Moshe, *Story of My Life*, London, Weidenfeld & Nicolson, 1976, p. 30

xl Sherman, p. 176

xli McCullough, David, *Truman*, New York, Simon & Schuster, 1992, p. 598

xlii Ibid. p. 610

xliii Wasserstein, p. 142

xliv Melkon Rose, John H., *Armenians of Jerusalem: Memories of Life in Palestine*, London, The Radcliffe Press, 1993, p. 187

xlv Internet: http//:www.Israel.org/mfa/go.asp?MFAHObz2o

AUTUMN 2003

i Spafford Vester, Bertha, *Our Jerusalem: An American in the Holy City 1881–1949*, Beirut, Middle East Export Press Inc.,1950, p. 58

ii Dudman, Helga and Kark, Ruth, *The American Colony: Scenes from a Jerusalem Saga*, Jerusalem, Carta, 1998, pp. 15–16

iii Spafford Vester, p. 369

iv *Daily Star*, 10 September 2003, 'Bible and Sword' by Donald Wagner

v Ibid.

vi Internet: www.English.aljazeera.net/Article/News/Arabworld/features/Israel+and+Christian+Zionists.htm

vii Halsell, Grace, *Forcing God's Hand: Why Millions Pray for a Quick Rapture – and Destruction of Planet Earth*, Washington DC, Crossroads International Publishing, 1999, p. 17

viii *The Christian Century*, 4 November 1998, 'Evangelists and Israel', by Donald Wagner

ix Falwell, Jerry, *Strength for the Journey: An Autobiography*, New York, Simon & Schuster, 1987, p. 443

x President Bush, 2 April 2002 news conference

xi Internet: www.cbsnews.com/stories/2002/10/03/60minutes/main524268.shtml

xii *Cornerstone*, Issue 25, Summer 2002, p. 5

xiii Internet: www.cbsnews.com/stories/2002/10/11/60minutes/printable525316.shtml

xiv Internet: www.revise.com/general131/nazis.htm

xv Internet: www.beliefnet.com/story/124/story_12422.html

xvi Dr John Green of Akron University, Ohio, interviewed by Victoria Clark for 'Christian Zionists' in *Prospect*, July 2003

xvii Internet: www.forward.com/issues/2003/03.06.13/news7.html

xviii Internet: www.sweetliberty.org/issues.Israel/bbc_transcript_Zionists.htm

xix *Jerusalem Post*, 28 May 2003, by Michael Freund

xx Internet: www.jnewswire.com/news_archive/03/10/031003-bush.asp

xxi *New York Magazine*, 29 September 2003, 'Christian Soldiers' by Craig Horowitz

xxii Tuchman, Barbara, *The Bible and the Sword: England and Palestine*

from the Bronze Age to Balfour, London, Phoenix Press, 2001
(1984), p. 201

xxiii   1 Thessalonians 4: 17

xxiv   Crowley, Dale, *Errors and Deceptions of Dispensational Teaching*,
Washington, Capitol Hill Voice, 1996–7

xxv   *Ha'aretz*, 13 April 2003

xxvi   Sharif, Regina, *Non-Jewish Zionism: Its Roots in Western History*,
London, Zed Press, 1983, p. 42

xxvii   McCullough, David, *Truman*, New York, Simon & Schuster,
1992, p. 599

xxviii   *Daily Telegraph*, 12 July 2003, by Toby Harnden

Afterword

i   Numbers 33: 55

SELECT BIBLIOGRAPHY

GENERAL

Armstrong, Karen, A History of Jerusalem: One City, Three Faiths, London, HarperCollins, 1996

Biddle, Martin, The Church of the Holy Sepulchre, New York, Random House, 2000

Elon, Amos, Jerusalem: City of Mirrors, London, HarperCollins, 1996

Peters, F.E., Jerusalem: The Holy City through the Eyes of Chroniclers, Visitors, Pilgrims and Prophets from the Days of Abraham to the Beginnings of Modern Times, Princeton, 1985

Thubron, Colin, Jerusalem, London, Arrow Books, 1969

Wasserstein, Bernard, Divided Jerusalem: the Struggle for the Holy City, London, Profile Books Ltd, 2001

Wilken, Robert, The Land Called Holy: Palestine in Christian History and Thought, New Haven, Yale University Press, 1992

BYZANTINES AND ARABS 300–1099

Dalrymple, William, From the Holy Mountain: A Journey in the Shadow of Byzantium, London, HarperCollins, 1997

Gil, Moshe, A History of Palestine, 634–1099, Cambridge, Cambridge University Press, 1992

Peters, F.E., The Distant Shrine: The Islamic Centuries in Jerusalem, New York, AMS Press, 1993

Walker, P.W.L., Holy City, Holy Places, Christian Attitudes to Jerusalem and the Holy Land in the 4th century, Oxford, Clarendon Press, 1990

Zander, Walter, *Israel and the Holy Places of Christendom,* London, Weidenfeld & Nicolson, 1971

CRUSADERS 1099–1291

Abulafia, David, *Frederick II, A Medieval Emperor,* London, Pimlico, 2002
Hamilton, Bernard, *The Latin Church in the Crusader States: The Secular Church,* London, Variorum Publications, 1980
Maalouf, Amin, *The Crusades Through Arab Eyes,* New York, Schocken Books, 1984
Prawer, Joshua, *The Latin Kingdom of Jerusalem,* London, Weidenfeld & Nicolson, 1972
—— *The World of the Crusaders,* London, Weidenfeld & Nicolson, 1972
Riley-Smith, Jonathan (ed.), *The Oxford History of the Crusades,* Oxford, OUP, 1999

OTTOMANS 1291–1800

Frazee, Charles A., *Catholics and Sultans: The Church and the Ottoman Empire 1453–1923,* London, CUP, 1983
Hintlian, Kevork, *History of the Armenians in the Holy Land,* Jerusalem, Armenian Patriarchate Printing Press, 1989
Prescott, H.F.M., *Jerusalem Journey: Pilgrimage to the Holy Land in the Fifteenth Century,* London, Eyre & Spottiswoode, 1954

OTTOMANS AND BRITISH 1800–1853

ben Arieh, Yehoshua, *Jerusalem in the 19th Century,* Vols. I and II, New York, St Martin's Press, 1986
Crombie, Kelvin, *For the Love of Zion: Christian Witness and the Restoration of Israel,* London, Hodder & Stoughton, 1991
Sharif, Regina, *Non-Jewish Zionism: Its Roots in Western History,* London, Zed Press, 1983
Shepherd, Naomi, *The Zealous Intruders: The Western Rediscovery of Palestine,* London, Collins, 1987

Tibawi, A.L., *British Interests in Palestine 1800–1901: A Study of Religious and Educational Enterprise*, Oxford, OUP, 1961

Tuchman, Barbara, *The Bible and the Sword: England and Palestine from the Bronze Age to Balfour*, London, Phoenix Press, 1984

Wars, Mandate, War and Israel 1856–1948

Fromkin, David, *A Peace to End All Peace: The Fall of the Ottoman Empire and the Creation of the Modern Middle East*, London, Phoenix Press, 2000

Hamilton, Jill, *God, Guns and Israel: Britain, the First World War and the Jews in the Holy Land*, Stroud, Sutton Publishing, 2004

Hopwood, Derek, *The Russian Presence in Syria and Palestine: Church and Politics in the Near East*, Oxford, Clarendon Press, 1969

La Guardia, Anton, *Holy Land Unholy War: Israelis and Palestinians*, London, John Murray, 2001

Segev, Tom, *One Palestine Complete: Jews and Arabs under the British Mandate*, London, Abacus, 2001

Shepherd, Naomi, *Ploughing Sand: British Rule in Palestine 1917–1948*, London, John Murray, 1999

Israel and the United States 1948–2003

Armstrong, Karen, *The Battle for God: Fundamentalism in Judaism, Christianity and Islam*, London, HarperCollins, 2000

Gorenberg, Gershom, *The End of Days: Fundamentalism and the Struggle for the Temple Mount*, Oxford, OUP, 2000

Halsell, Grace, *Forcing God's Hand: Why Millions Pray for a Quick Rapture – and Destruction of Planet Earth*, Washington DC, Crossroads International Publishing, 1999

Hirst, David, *The Gun and the Olive Branch: The Roots of Violence in the Middle East*, London, Faber & Faber, 2003

Longley, Clifford, *Chosen People: The Big Idea that Shapes England and America*, London, Hodder & Stoughton, 2002

Wagner, Donald, *Anxious for Armageddon*, Scottdale, Penn., Herald Press, 1995

INDEX